Practicing Faith

"The task of integrating social-vocation practice and sound theology is always urgent and necessary, but also daunting. Through integration of practice and theology, we are all better placed to enable people to find healing and restoration of the whole person. This book is not daunting and offers both practitioners and theologians superb assistance with the integrative task."
 —Peter Carrell, Anglican Bishop, Christ Church, New Zealand

"There is much to chew on in this most helpful book that connects faith and social practice, and theology and therapy. The focus is on interpersonal relationships, incarnational ministry, transformation, and divine grace. God's comfort flows among human beings who, in their pain and mess, can recognize his presence and power and find healing and wholeness in community. Those in the helping professions, including pastors, would immensely benefit from this thoughtful book."
 —Robert Solomon, Bishop emeritus, The Methodist Church,
  Singapore

"This collected conversation is impressive in exploring song, grief, the theology of friendship, and the power of hospitality. Yet, it is more than an interdisciplinary dialogue. It is an integration of theology and social practice, each giving fresh meaning to the other, creating fascinating juxtapositions and challenges. It asks, Can I cultivate both courage and humility, risking vulnerability in being both host and guest, as you, God, and myself discover a purposed existence?"
 —Jill Shaw, University Chaplain and Public Theologian,
  Auckland, New Zealand

"Beautifully written, this collection of essays and responses embodies the integration of theology with social vocations. Returning again and again to the importance of relationships—within God, with God, and with one another—these scholars ground their integrative aspirations in these dynamisms. These essays are refreshingly personal, intellectually rich, and spaciously dialogical. *Practicing Faith* is a fabulous read for those wondering about the merits of integration as well as how to do this well."
 —Christa McKirland, Lecturer of Systematic Theology,
  Carey Baptist College

Practicing Faith

Theology and Social Vocation in Conversation

EDITED BY
Lisa Spriggens
and Tim Meadowcroft

FOREWORD BY
Marty Folsom

◆PICKWICK *Publications* · Eugene, Oregon

PRACTICING FAITH
Theology and Social Vocation in Conversation

Copyright © 2022 Wipf and Stock Publishers. All rights reserved. Except for brief quotations in critical publications or reviews, no part of this book may be reproduced in any manner without prior written permission from the publisher. Write: Permissions, Wipf and Stock Publishers, 199 W. 8th Ave., Suite 3, Eugene, OR 97401.

Pickwick Publications
An Imprint of Wipf and Stock Publishers
199 W. 8th Ave., Suite 3
Eugene, OR 97401

www.wipfandstock.com

PAPERBACK ISBN: 978-1-7252-7637-6
HARDCOVER ISBN: 978-1-7252-7636-9
EBOOK ISBN: 978-1-7252-7641-3

Cataloguing-in-Publication data:

Names: Spriggens, Lisa. | Meadowcroft, Tim. | Folsom, Marty, foreword.

Title: Practicing faith : theology and social vocation in conversation / by Lisa Spriggens and Tim Meadowcroft; foreword by Marty Folsom.

Description: Eugene, OR : Pickwick Publications, 2022 | **Includes bibliographical references and index.**

Identifiers: ISBN 978-1-7252-7637-6 (paperback) | ISBN 978-1-7252-7636-9 (hardcover) | ISBN 978-1-7252-7641-3 (ebook)

Subjects: LCSH: Vocation—Christianity.

Classification: BV4740 .P73 2022 (print) | BV4740 .P73 (ebook)

Contents

Contributors | ix
Foreword | *Marty Folsom* | xi
Introduction | *Lisa Spriggens* | xvii

PART I: WELLBEING

Chapter 1: Friendship, Social Vocations, and Communities of Practice | *Anne-Marie Ellithorpe* | 3
Chapter 2: A Song in the Night: A Reflection on Singing in Scripture and Social Vocation | *Ryan Lang* | 20
Chapter 3: Found by Love | *Lex S. McMillan* | 39
Response 1: Wellbeing: Formation through Friendship, Love, and Song | *Jonathan Rivett Robinson* | 50

PART II: FORMATION

Chapter 4: Towards a Christian Spirituality for Counselors | *Neil Pembroke* | 63
Chapter 5: Conversation Partners: Stories of Integration | *Lisa Spriggens* | 78
Response 2: Formation: Quests and Questions | *Sarah Penwarden* *(with found poetry by Yael Klangwisan)* | 91

PART III: HOSPITALITY

Chapter 6: Food, Table Fellowship, and Human Flourishing in Luke | *Theresa Lau* | 99
Chapter 7: Breaking Bread: The Power of Hospitality in the Gospel of Mark | *Jonathan Rivett Robinson* | 118

Response 3: Hospitality: Serving Sacred Food in Secular Spaces: The *Missio Dei* and Ordinary Christian Counseling | *Art Wouters* | 135

PART IV: THERAPY

Chapter 8: Sailing with the Wind: Counseling Support in the Solomon Islands | *Art Wouters* | 143

Chapter 9: Grief as the Sounding of Multiple Notes: Grief and Loss as Seen through the Movements of the Triduum | *Sarah Penwarden* | 162

Chapter 10: Person-Centered Care and the Love of Neighbor | *Mark G. Brett* | 178

Response 4: Therapy: Interdisciplinary Conversations as Expressions of Neighbor Love | *Anne-Marie Ellithorpe* | 192

PART V: THEOLOGY

Chapter 11: Social Trinitarianism and Christian Counseling: A Critical Discussion | *Cameron Coombe* | 201

Chapter 12: Verbalizing Hate in the Psalms | *Richard Neville* | 218

Chapter 13: Creation and Social Practice: Psalm 104 as Prequel to Theology and Social Practice | *Tim Meadowcroft* | 238

Response 5: Theology: Finding Middle Ground | *Lex S. McMillan* | 248

Afterword | *Lisa Spriggens and Tim Meadowcroft* | 253

Contributors

Mark G. Brett teaches Hebrew Bible and ethics at Whitley College in Melbourne, Australia, within the University of Divinity.

Cameron Coombe is a recent graduate from the doctoral programme in theology at the University of Otago, Dunedin, New Zealand. His research interests include Jürgen Moltmann and the doctrine of the Trinity.

Anne-Marie Ellithorpe is Research Associate at Vancouver School of Theology in Vancouver, Canada, and co-chair of the Religious Reflections on Friendship seminar unit of the American Academy of Religion. She is also the author of *Towards Friendship-Shaped Communities: A Practical Theology of Friendship* (2022).

Marty Folsom, PhD is Executive Director, Pacific Association for Theological Studies, Contingent Faculty, Seattle Pacific University, Seattle University, Northwest University, The Seattle School for Theology and Psychology, Trinity Lutheran, and Shiloh University. As well as an author and academic, Marty also works as a therapist.

Yael Klangwisan is Senior Lecturer in Education at Auckland University of Technology, New Zealand, and a poet. Her poetry and creative writing appear in a number of publications. She is also the author of *Jouissance* (2015), a poetic response to the Hebrew Song of Songs.

Ryan Lang is a doctoral candidate in theology at the University of Otago, New Zealand. He teaches in Christian spirituality at Laidlaw College, Auckland, New Zealand.

Theresa Lau is Dean of the Chinese Department at Melbourne School of Theology, Australia.

Lex McMillan is a professional teaching fellow in counseling at Laidlaw College in Christchurch, New Zealand, and relationship therapist in private practice at the Arahura Centre in Christchurch.

Tim Meadowcroft is Senior Research Fellow in Biblical Studies at Laidlaw College, Auckland, New Zealand, and editor of the *Journal of Theological Interpretation*. He is also a priest assistant in the Anglican parish of Henderson/Swanson in West Auckland.

Richard Neville is Senior Lecturer in Biblical Studies on the Christchurch campus of Laidlaw College, New Zealand.

Neil Pembroke is Associate Professor of Christian Studies in the School of Historical and Philosophical Inquiry, the University of Queensland, Brisbane, Australia. He is a Minister of the Word in the Uniting Church in Australia.

Sarah Penwarden is a senior lecturer in the counseling programme at Laidlaw College, Auckland, New Zealand. She is also a therapist and supervisor in her private practice, with an interest in how creativity can enhance therapy. Sarah is also an ordained Anglican priest in the Local Shared Ministry context of the Auckland diocese.

Jonathan Rivett Robinson is the Pastor of Musselburgh Baptist Church, Dunedin, New Zealand, and Researcher with the Centre for Theology and Public Issues at the University of Otago. He recently completed a PhD on Scripture interpretation in the Gospel of Mark.

Lisa Spriggens is a counselor and Head of Counseling at Laidlaw College in Auckland, New Zealand. She is also undertaking a PhD at University of Melbourne researching trauma counselors and their stories of self-care.

Art Wouters is a practicing psychologist in Melbourne, and head of the School of Counseling at Stirling Theological College, Melbourne, Australia.

Foreword

PRACTICING FAITH CALLS US to envision serving the Living Word of God who is expressed in, and stands implicitly behind, all faithful Christian forms of practicing therapy and healing. Because this Word is a person, all our healing practices must be understood *personally* in compliance with his mode of engaging in therapeutic relationships.

Like Jesus' Jubilee commitment in his first sermon (Luke 4:14–21), this text echoes forth a diversity of restorative practices. All of Jesus' acts of restoration embody God's grace. He is the face of his Father meeting the estranged, deranged, sick, and disillusioned along the way. In these modes of activity, he firstly restores relationship with the God who is the source of all love. From this restoration comes specific acts to overcome fear, shame, blame, and guilt, and to holistically embrace the broken. He deals with the plagues of human dysfunction that disorder the emotional and physical world that the triune God loves.

Jesus came as a friend. He broke down the walls to friendship between ethnic groups, genders, economic groups, age difference, and a myriad of other prejudicial fracturing practices. He opened the way for transformation. He set minds free from all forms of imprisonment to cultural and religious systems that cracked the foundations of connection. In his deeds, the love of God was expressed. The person of Jesus opened the way for reasonable and redemptive engagement within human communities and their participants.

Jesus modeled a therapeutic life. We cannot import modern therapeutic practice back onto him, but in contemporary expressions we can align and intuitively attune to his intentions. As Jesus walked, he met "ordinary" people mostly unaware of needing his help. He talked with those he met. He touched them. He ate with them. He lived deeds that had healing intent. His love and personal manner were not fixed in a formula. They took on unique contextual expressions with each situation he encountered. This is how the Spirit leads.

Jesus offered friendship to sinners and tax collectors. He struggled with those who were self-righteous and judgmental of others. Jesus was invested in "othering," centering his concern on the well-being of the marginalized of society. Friendship was his medicine, not drugs. He exposed injustice and healed those who needed other cures.

Jesus stood against authoritative powers that crippled others with their control. The power of his Spirit opened new frontiers. Future generations could personally indwell his mission of reconciliation and healing of the nations. With the power of humility and service, he still invites us to care for others from a love birthed in the Father's heart.

The endeavors of Christian therapeutic practice echo this Living Word. He speaks and acts through churches, but also through therapists and social workers who come alongside as contextual specialists to restore loving, sustaining relations. Therapeutic theology transforms the breakdowns in thought, feelings, behavior, and the ultimate failure in relating. We set our work in the appropriate context of the God of all relating. Jesus' word and deed still bring orderliness to the disorders that refract into human failure. His revelation of God's love has expansive implications for every detail of human interaction.

This book echoes the practices of Jesus in contemporary embodiments of word becoming deed. Like Jesus, it critiques the inadequacies of modern philosophies and modalities that miss the good of God's intent. The age of the individual is still strong. It still informs the urge of humans to seek "health" in isolation from the deep ills that contaminate relationships. This book assumes the priority of personal relating as the context for the conversation about wholeness. This ordering grants dignity to each person and the hope of healing through friendships, hospitality, and therapy not merely attentive to the individual, but the whole system of personal relating—including with God, the author and sustainer of personal life.

In pursuing wellness, the first three essays recognize the disintegration of relationships in our contemporary context, both human and divine. This is foundational for the whole of the book in seeking an integration of theology and the social sciences. What was created whole by God has suffered disconnection, alienation, and individualization, and deflated into performance-based cultures. In empathetic response, we need the connection of friendship, to share the story of Jesus as an invitation to love, and to find the harmony of incarnational alongsidedness. We need to reformat our understanding of the relational constitution of humanity as created by God for God and human fellowship. This leads to a whole lot of human playfulness and participation, an indwelt presence filled with wonder, gratitude, and transformation. Wellness is holistic in that it is the outworking of love in the practices of intertwining lives. Faith is not a leap in the dark in this section. It is faithful and risky vulnerability to express Jesus' reign among us in practiced engagement committed to hearing the Word and being compelled by his love to deeds that restore and nurture.

Formation follows wellness in the practice of holistic, personal development. As counselors extend the love of the Trinity in creating dialogical space, the flourishing of relationships is made possible. Jesus came vulnerably, compassionately, and was available to all. In him, we still live truth in the form of faithfulness to the freeing love of God, one encounter at a time. In these encounters, we pilgrimage as we share in the stories of those who call us travel companions, moving toward wholeness. We are called to conform to no ideal; rather, we learn to improvise as conversation partners, voicing the trauma and yearning in hope. We seek faithful practices in relating and in maintaining overtly safe spaces adequate for the complexity of every relationship. Formation is a dance that constantly transforms. We mutually yield as partners who care more about relationships than performance. We are formed in the process of *withness*.

Hospitality follows in this sequence as a human expression of God's self-giving and invitation to community. Jesus comes down the road of the New Testament as hospitality in action. He affirms and heals as he travels. Consequently, the therapeutic life of Christian care resonates with this practice of inviting, befriending, and connecting body and soul. The hospitality of God in the flesh becomes a "field hospital" for persons. He has no excluding doorways. He creates a place of security and attachment. In him, we find the One who is the meal of peace. He envisions the flourishing of persons as friends-in-community. Hospitality is therapeutic in its openness to the other. It is the way Jesus defuses power structures to fulfil his vocation of salvation in this reconciling act at a lively table.

Therapy can be seen as a fix-it program of know-it-alls meeting with those needing-to-know. However, in this therapy section, the patterns of relating are played in a new key. Relinquishing power positions makes way for mutual participation in the healing process. In coming alongside as a listener, helping those dealing with various forms of suffering, we may empathetically attune to the issues in their particularity. This opens the way for dialogue in a safe space—led by the Spirit who comes like a wind to empower and blow away our power-constrictions and create the waiting sail of "not knowing" that can then be filled with attentive listening. This orients us as lovers of neighbors who have specific needs. Therapy responds as a theological re-narration, not asking what Jesus did, but what we do because he is with us. We live in the story as those gifted with bringing a peaceable process. In the context of the triune commitment to restore human dignity and well-being, we may co-create patterns of renewal in collaboration with our fellow humans.

Theology culminates the discussion of *Practicing Faith*, but it has been humming in the background all along. The section explores how well we orient ourselves to our therapeutic foundation. It reflects on the tools of theology and biblical studies we may use to serve the purposes of God and not insert human agendas. For example, Social Trinitarianism may have much to offer and clarify. We need conversation to critique and construct ways forward. Are there variations of theology on relational themes requiring investigation? We need a robust theology that both affirms the value of persons and relationships, and maintains the priority and uniqueness of God. We cannot work with a God reduced to our desires and structures, built from a human starting-point to fulfill human agendas. The Bible, especially in the Psalms, provides therapeutic insight in dealing with human challenges and possibilities. It understands our context within God's creation as the setting for inquiring into the meaning of therapeutic activity that engages human emotions, thinking, and behavior. Theology for therapy cannot be abstract, merely talking about God out there. Theology must teach us to hear God's heart. We must learn to participate in God's continuing redemptive work, and to facilitate human flourishing. Our work occurs in the context of the ongoing mission of God who is available. God is not a distant theorist to be studied. Nor is God an occasionally visiting therapist to be called in for difficult situations. God is extravagantly loving and working to this very day. He invites us to share in the work of restoring and sustaining divine love that acts for all of God's creation.

Within that context, we find this book as a gathering around a campfire. We hear the stories that reveal creative imagination and action where the Word has been transposed into deed in diverse contexts. As a theologian who practices therapy, I am grateful for the safe and creative space opened in this book. This work goes with Jesus into the wilderness as well as the gathering places of the authors to explore and inspire.

Practicing Faith is an explorer's map into the wilderness of human struggle and opportunity, a journey taken with courageous guides. It traces where the adventurous learners have been. It sketches out the "still to be explored" in the theological science of the personal. The particular voices in this gathering form a community which seeks to listen to the living God known in Jesus. Each in their own way seeks to shape knowledge and practices that fit the realities encountered. Respect for the uniqueness of each place and person resonates with the compassion of Jesus. This tension needs to guide our conversations when we do the work of theology and therapy, listening to the Word and echoing the deeds born in the gracious and compassionate heart of God.

Marty Folsom
Good Shepherd Sunday, 2021

Introduction

Lisa Spriggens

In 2017, Tim Meadowcroft was invited to speak at the launch of the book *Stories of Therapy, Stories of Faith*, a collaboration which emerged from the counseling faculty in the School of Social Practice at Laidlaw College.¹ This collection of essays was a conversation among counselors around their integration of theological understandings with their counseling practice. During his response to this collection of essays, Tim recognized the emerging integrative conversation and issued a challenge: the next step needed to be an extension of the integrative conversation to include the theological disciplines. The result was a conference designed to enable counselors and other practitioners of "social vocations" (on more of which see below) and theologians to think together about the integrative task.

Whakawhiti Kōrero: Conversations between Theology and Social Vocation was convened in October 2018.² This current volume of essays and responses arises out of that conference.

We have intentionally used the term "social vocation" in the title of this book, rather than "social practice" or other similar terms. Social vocation reflects the myriad different expressions of care for and alongside people during their lifetimes. In the use of the word vocation, we recognize that often the jobs or roles which represent these expressions

---

1. McMillan et al., *Stories of Therapy, Stories of Faith*.

2. *Whakawhiti* is a Maori term carrying the sense of "crossing over," "exchange," or "negotiation." *Kōrero* is about speaking together. Thus *whakawhiti kōrero* anticipates a "speaking together" that enables a crossing over to the other, an exchange, a negotiation.

of care carry a depth of meaning and shape identity in ways that are more substantive than mere tasks that are done, or jobs that pay bills. Some may even consider these roles a calling from God. Some authors in this collection use the term social practice as virtually synonymous with social vocation, while at the same time other terms, and even specific practices, are identified in the various essays. Yet, whatever the terminology deployed in particular essays, we invite you to hold this concept of *vocation* with you as you read, and to notice how your own sense of vocation might be evoked in response. In our original conception of the project, we had hoped to welcome a broad range of such vocations into the conversation. In the event, the two social vocations that emerge most strongly in this book are counseling and pastoral ministry in its various forms. We hope that the unfinished conversation might encourage others in the integrative task.

Steven Sandage and Jeannine Brown suggest that, to the extent that such conversations are characterized by open listening and respect for the Other and the knowledge that the Other brings, participants in integrative conversations experience an opportunity to create new understandings and collaborations. At the same time, they need to be humble in their engagement, and prepared for experiences of anxiety and tension.[3] Humility, openness, and the resulting vulnerability are not common positions attributed to scholarship. It takes some courage to offer carefully tended work to people who will approach it from very different fields of knowledge. However, we believe a willingness to take the risk is a key starting site from which the integration of theology and social vocation can emerge.

The structure of this book is akin to how the original conference was set up, as a space for conversation between different areas of scholarship, professions, and practices. Within the limits of a static text, this book reflects a slice of that conversation. The essays are divided into sections, each reflecting a particular theme. There are a range of disciplines or sub-disciplines represented by contributors towards each theme, as well as a response from somebody who brings a different disciplinary and/or experiential perspective. All of the respondents have also contributed their own substantive essay.

The theme of *wellbeing* is addressed by Anne-Marie Ellithorpe in her exploration of friendship and the integral role she sees it playing in

---

3. Sandage and Brown, *Relational Integration of Psychology and Christian Theology*.

social vocation, within communities of practice. Ryan Lang reflects on the role singing holds in Scripture and what it can offer those engaged in social vocation. Finally, Lex McMillan offers a particular vision of relating drawing on the story of Jesus' meeting with Zacchaeus. Jonathan Robinson responds to these essays at the end of the section.

The next series of essays speak to the theme of *formation*. Neil Pembroke considers qualities he regards as critical for counselors engaged in personal and spiritual growth. Lisa Spriggens reflects on her own integration journey and those of counseling students. Sarah Penwarden offers her response to these essays, and in the process incorporates found poetry based on the Pembroke and Spriggens chapters written by Yael Klangwisan.

The third section centers around the theme of *hospitality*. Theresa Lau invites us to sit with Luke and explore how images of food and eating together might have something to say about human flourishing. Jonathan Robinson extends an invitation for the reader to notice how hospitality is experienced in the Gospel of Mark and how this might inform social practitioners. Art Wouters reflects on these two essays in light of his own therapeutic practice.

In the fourth section, our contributors have spoken to different aspects of *therapy* and its integration with theology. Art Wouters reflects on the intersection of faith and practice as he navigates the dynamics of colonial and indigenous power in the context of working in the Solomon Islands. Sarah Penwarden offers a way of engaging with the dynamics of grief through the liturgy of the Triduum. Mark Brett explores the complexity of personhood in the aged care context to highlight key conceptions which should underpin spiritual care. Anne-Marie Ellithorpe offers a response to these essays.

In the final section, with a focus on *theology*, Cameron Coombe challenges the uncritical use of social Trinitarianism as a theological anthropology commonly drawn on in social vocation. Richard Neville unpacks the verbalizing of hate in the Psalms drawing on biblical studies, psychology, and philosophy. Tim Meadowcroft also invites us into the Psalms—Psalm 104, in particular—to propose a theology of creation as a place to start in the integration of theology and social vocation. Lex McMillan responds to these contributions.

The result is inevitably open-ended. It has never been our aim to arrive at firm conclusions and defined modes of action. Rather, it is our hope that this slice of a long and ongoing interaction may provide some more conversational hooks and stimulate further investigation and interaction. Each iteration of dialogue holds the potential for new connections and understandings of self and other, expanding the ways in which deeply held faith and belief can be lived out in the daily practice of life and work. We hope you experience this invitation in the collection of essays.

About the Editors

As a counselor-educator in this context, Lisa Spriggens has an interest in drawing on different disciplines to enrich, inform, and deepen the counseling work she does and teaches. As a relatively new profession, counseling has drawn on multiple disciplines as it has developed theory and practice. Some examples of these include psychology, anthropology, sociology, and neuroscience. Theology has also informed many counseling theories. Reaching across disciplines expands opportunity for new ways of working with people.

Tim Meadowcroft is an academic specialist in Old Testament studies, and from that starting point has also long been interested in and written on the interface between the Bible and other academic disciplines and life experiences. His earlier roles as a high school teacher and his ongoing pastoral context further inform his sense of the importance of this particular engagement between the theological disciplines and what we are calling social vocation. When the reading of Scripture and theological reflection are brought into contact with other professions and modes of thought, both are changed. We learn to be better readers of Scripture when we encounter the lived experience of social vocation, and we are deepened in our exercise of vocation as our understanding of Scripture and our intimacy with God are deepened. Hence the importance of dialogue or conversation.[4]

Acknowledgments

We would like to acknowledge the support of Laidlaw College and their contribution to the publication of this book, the contributors and their

---

4. See Marshall, *All Things Reconciled*, xx, in the context of a dialogical encounter between restorative justice and Scripture.

enthusiasm for this project, and finally to Marty Folsom, who contributed the foreword.

Bibliography

Marshall, Christopher D. *All Things Reconciled: Essays on Restorative Justice, Religious Violence, and the Interpretation of Scripture*. Eugene, OR: Cascade, 2018.

McMillan, Lex, Sarah Penwarden, and Siobhan Hunt, eds. *Stories of Therapy, Stories of Faith*. Eugene, OR: Wipf & Stock, 2017.

Sandage, Steven J., and Jeannine K. Brown. *Relational Integration of Psychology and Christian Theology: Theory, Research, and Practice*. New York: Routledge, Taylor & Francis Group, 2018.

Part I

WELLBEING

Chapter 1

Friendship, Social Vocations, and Communities of Practice

Anne-Marie Ellithorpe

WHAT PLACE DOES FRIENDSHIP have within contemporary communities, and of what relevance is friendship to the outworking of social vocations? Some regard friendship as simply a recreational relationship, and of little relevance to community, while others consider the preferential love of friendship to be detrimental to community. However, I have become convinced that friendship, broadly construed, is not only relevant but integral to the faithful outworking of social vocations within communities of practice.[1]

I use the term *social vocation* broadly, as inclusive of all callings that include the encouragement and nurturing of relationships. Thus, parenting, teaching, and pastoring may all be described as social vocations that are outworked within communities of practice. *Communities of practice* may be broadly defined as "groups of people who share a concern

---

1. This essay is adapted from a section of the strategic chapter of my doctoral dissertation, within which I seek to develop a practical theology of friendship. Within earlier stages of the research, I consider the current status of friendship within the West, explore what a variety of normative texts have to say about friendship, and seek to develop core ideals in relation to the importance and formative potential of friendship. Within the strategic phase, I identify implications of these ideals for the more fully informed *practice* of this relationship. See Ellithorpe, "Towards a Practical Theology of Friendship." See also Ellithorpe, *Towards Friendship-Shaped Communities*.

or a passion for something they do and learn how to do it better as they interact regularly."[2] Such communities are an integral part of daily life, and may be found within homes, schools, workplaces, and congregations.[3]

Within this paper I advocate for an ideal of friendship that recognizes the intertwining of various loves, along with the public non-exclusive dimensions of friendship, and consider specific ways in which this ideal of friendship may be nurtured within various vocations and communities. Consideration is given most specifically to families and faith communities, and to parenting and pastoral vocations.

Friendship is of course a challenging word to pin down, with the meanings attributed to friendship varying within different contexts. Friendships are consistently identified as voluntary relationships, characterized by affection for the other. Yet while friendships may also be described as private exclusive relationships characterized by reciprocity, they are not entirely so.

Alasdair MacIntyre asserts that the modern notion of friendship is essentially private: "friendship has been relegated to private life and thereby weakened in relation to what it once was."[4] Yet public dimensions are evident within contemporary friendships. Within the context of their various vocations (social and otherwise), many inter-related networks of small groups of friends share together in the common project of nurturing and sustaining in various ways the life of their city, town, or village.[5]

Friendships are typically described as relationships of reciprocity and mutuality. Reciprocity is generally evident in affection, in willing good for the other, and in action on behalf of the other.[6] Yet friendships, particularly in their early stages, are not always consciously mutual. Moreover, while civic friendship ideally includes mutual awareness of, good will towards, and action on behalf of fellow citizens, such friendship may not be fully reciprocated.[7] Within civic friendship, the willing and doing good for the other inherent to personal friendship is extended to

---

2. Wenger-Trayner, "Introduction to Communities of Practice," 1.

3. Communities of practice are a crucial locus of learning and integral to all social vocations. See Wenger, *Communities of Practice*, 8.

4. MacIntyre, *After Virtue*, 156.

5. I hope within this chapter to encourage these public dimensions further.

6. Ellithorpe, "Towards a Practical Theology of Friendship," 56. See also Aristotle's *Rhetoric*, 1381a2; and Schwarzenbach, *On Civic Friendship*, 44–45.

7. Civic friendship, for Aristotle, is the concern of fellow citizens for one another's "good character" (*Politics*, 1295b23).

the broader community. Whether considered at a local, national, or global level, there is certainly inconsistency in awareness of and action on behalf of others. (Yet, as became evident with early responses to the COVID-19 pandemic, crisis has the potential to provoke a greater commitment to civic friendship).

Some philosophers and theologians have focused on the perceived exclusivity of friendship, comparing it negatively with a universal ethical love. Søren Kierkegaard and Anders Nygren, for example, have argued against friendship, identifying it as a preferential love. Kierkegaard and Nygren fail to recognize the potential for friendship to be a school of love and a gift through which a broader love is nurtured. They do not recognize that "within the context of the Christian narrative, *agapē* describes a love so generous that friendship with all is desired."[8] Yet others recognize that there is something universal about friendship. Philosopher Simone Weil describes friendship as consisting of "loving a human being as we should like to be able to love each soul in particular . . ."[9] She continues: "As a geometrician looks at a particular figure in order to deduce the universal properties of the triangle, so he who knows how to love directs upon a particular human being a love which is universal."[10] Weil identifies all our loves as implicitly love for God.[11] Similarly, Christian ethicist Paul Wadell notes that within the context of love for God, friendship does not oppose Christian love. Rather than *agapē* being a love beyond or opposed to friendship, friendship is the relationship within which such love is learned. *Agapē* then is "friendship's perfection."[12]

An Ideal of Friendship

Friendship that contributes to the faithful outworking of social vocations intertwines public and private dimensions as it overflows into a broader love expressed through civic friendship and reform. The public-private character of such friendship links personal intimacy with a shared

---

8. Ellithorpe, "Towards a Practical Theology of Friendship," 130.
9. Weil, "Friendship," 135–36.
10. Weil, "Friendship," 135–36.
11. Weil developed an acute sense of God's universal presence not only animating human love, but indeed "making all love possible" (Carmichael, *Friendship*, 169).
12. Wadell, *Friendship and the Moral Life*, 119. Wadell finds confirmation of this assertion within the work of Augustine, Aelred of Rievaulx, and Karl Barth.

recognition of and concern for the greater good. Public-private friendships are not vague, exclusive, or sentimental; nor are the civic friendships, solidarity, and communal responsibility that they foster.

Civic friendship retains integral aspects of personal friendship, while extending both "willing good" and "doing good" to the broader community.[13] Within Deut 10:18–19 we find indications that such civic friendship is to be theologically grounded. In response to God's befriending, God's friends are to befriend the stranger. God is identified as upholding the cause of the fatherless and the widow, and befriending the stranger. The entire community is likewise to image God in pursuing justice for the marginalized, and befriending the Other.[14]

Thus, communities of friends working together towards reform within various contexts may be seen as expressions of civic friendship in alignment with the *shalom*, justice, and mutuality that reflect God's character, and characterize the fullness of God's reign. Further, friends can work together towards approximations to this reign as they seek to foster civic friendship, and to embody (and where appropriate, institutionalize) social justice.

Theological perspectives grounded in and inspired by God's friendship must be both local and global in orientation. Positive regard for friendship, and for the value of each and every person, must ultimately foster the flourishing of civic friendship not only nationally, but also internationally, as well as between people groups and between treaty partners. Local, national, and global dimensions of civic friendship may be expressed through learning about how people live in other parts of one's country and beyond, and by learning about the faith traditions of others. These dimensions of civic friendship may also be expressed in seeking to understand the impact of histories of oppression, whether through colonization or slavery. Actively challenging various forms of injustice, including unjust laws and social customs, may well be a necessary outworking of civic friendship, along with a willingness to help others in

---

13. As I have acknowledged elsewhere, some contemporary writers focus predominantly on politics within the context of government when they speak of civic friendship, while others use it more broadly. See Ellithorpe, "Towards a Practical Theology of Friendship," 5–6.

14. While the Hebrew word 'āhāb within this text is more typically translated as love, 'āhāb implies affection expressed in action, and is thus an appropriate translation. See Tigay, *Deuteronomy*, 77, 108. It is worth noting that within the context of the ethics of Deuteronomy, the stranger is a liminal figure; befriended and integrated within the community, he or she is no longer a stranger. See Glanville, *Adopting the Stranger*, 124.

times of crisis, and to not begrudge others basic assistance with essential needs.[15]

The ideals of friendship that I have articulated clearly have relevance for thinking about relationality, friendship, and human flourishing both within and beyond the context of communities of faith.[16] Yet I acknowledge that while ideals have the potential to guide human flourishing, they can also be crushing. Thankfully, as practical theologian Don Browning notes, the tension between our positive visions on the one hand, and our human frailty on the other, is sustained by grace.[17] As friendships contribute to and emerge from the experience of grace, it is highly likely that persons sharing in these friendships will not consistently live up to the ideals articulated here. Nevertheless, these ideals are offered with the hope that they promote the flourishing of holistic friendships within communities, along with the overcoming of obstacles to—and distractions from—such friendships.[18]

Current trends within contemporary Western culture that must be navigated in living out these ideals include the devaluing, sidelining, and trivialization of friendship, indifference or hostility towards those who are *other*, the neglect or narrowing of the concept of civic friendship, and perceptions of friendship as a private concern, disconnected from community. Further, technology and globalization contribute to rising

---

15. I identify the challenging of injustice as an aspect of civic friendship in a yet to be published paper exploring friendship and non-violent resistance to oppression, with reference to both the Parihaka prophets in Taranaki, Aotearoa, in the later nineteenth century, and to Martin Luther King, Jr. and the more recent civil rights movement within the United States.

16. I further advocate for an ideal of multidimensional friendship, including friendship with others, God, earth, and self. The experience of God as friend overflows into concern for the advancement of well-being and justice for all. Having been claimed by God as friends, this friendship impacts other dimensions of life as it spills over into concern for and friendship with others, earth, and self. This multidimensionality is in keeping with ancient Hebrew understandings (inherent, for example, within the second creation story in Genesis), feminist insights, indigenous perspectives, and with an engaged and porous stance towards the universe (to use Charles Taylor's terminology within *A Secular Age*). See further Ellithorpe, "Towards a Practical Theology of Friendship," 155. These themes are also evident within Elisabeth Moltmann-Wendell, *Rediscovering Friendship*.

17. Browning, *From Culture Wars to Common Ground*, 272.

18. On the one hand, then, friendships are not to be rejected because they fall short of cultural ideals of "BFF's" or "besties." On the other hand, friendships should not be rejected for failing to live up to the ideals articulated in this paper. Rather, openness to receiving and expressing the gift of friendship within various forms is encouraged.

inequality, which in turn damages the sense of shared purpose necessary for the pursuit, let alone the realization, of the common good. The elevating of instrumentalist, materialist values over relational values, and the detaching of individual freedom from communal responsibility, continues to have a negative impact on relationality in general, and on friendship in particular.[19]

Nurturing Ideals through Communities of Practice

Given current realities, where then are we to begin in nurturing these ideals of friendship? I suggest we begin with Etienne Wenger's concept of communities of practice. Communities of practice are found in homes, schools, workplaces, community centers, and congregations. Communities may foster or discourage friendship; they may reproduce justice or injustice.[20]

What attitudes and actions contribute towards communities of practice promoting these ideals of friendship? I begin by making several general recommendations. Within all contexts, friendship should be recognized as a basic human need and therefore a pre-moral good, as integral to life as food, clothing, housing, and rest.[21] Further, authentic friendship should be recognized as a school of love, hospitality, wisdom, and compassion, advancing a moral good and ultimately civic friendship, as it fosters love founded on equal regard.[22] Within faith contexts, friendship can be recognized as consistent with visional dimensions. This includes the *imago Dei* motif, as it contributes to an overarching theological narrative of friendship, along with the ideals of covenant community. Imaging God includes befriending the stranger and being concerned for the basic needs of all.

---

19. As such themes infiltrate communities and friendships, they are deterrents to the development of friendships that are characterized by trust, that resist accounting. See May, *Friendship in an Age of Economics*, 108, 13.

20. Wenger, *Communities of Practice*, 132.

21. The concept of the pre-moral good is widely used in modern moral philosophy and is recognized within Catholic natural law (Browning, *Fundamental Practical Theology*, 161).

22. Friendships are morally formative as, even through seasons of pain, friends seek justice, pursue freedom, and foster healing. They are fundamental to a full human life.

Within families I suggest friendship be recognized as foundational to both marriage and parenting. Friendship provides a paradigm for marital relationships, encouraging spouses to nurture relationships with one another characterized by mutuality and equal regard. Such mutuality may require the further development of relational skills, and the challenging and adapting of cultural ideals or of patterns of behavior acquired from our family of origin. Here it may also be helpful to consider ways in which the birth of children radically changes the rhythms of friendship, and the impact of the presence and age of children on ways mutuality is outworked within spousal friendship.[23]

Parenting and Friendship

Turning now to the social vocation of parenting, parents are uniquely positioned to nurture multidimensional friendships within the immediate family, the extended family, and beyond. Parents exhibit characteristics of friendship as (to paraphrase Aristotle's *Nicomachean Ethics*, 1159a 27–32) they live together with their children, enjoying one another's company, sharing in discussion, wishing their child well for the child's sake, and doing an endless amount of things for them.[24] Home life provides an important context for the nurturing of friendship with self, others, God, and creation, as well as an introduction to civic friendship through the encouragement of learning about and caring for others.

I advocate for parents to consider friendship, with its personal and civic dimensions, as a telos for parenting. Such a telos is in alignment with what political philosopher Sibyl Schwarzenbach describes as "ethical reproductive praxis," that is, "all those reasoned and conscious activities which go towards reproducing flourishing human relations for their own sake."[25] I concur with Schwarzenbach that in the ideal case this implies relationships of friendship.[26]

Friendship as a telos for parenting does not imply a "soft" approach to parenting. Nor does it imply a strictly egalitarian relationship, parents abdicating their leadership and mentorship roles, or parents treating

---

23. See Browning, *From Culture Wars to Common Ground*, 292.

24. See also Schwarzenbach, *On Civic Friendship*, 46.

25. Schwarzenbach, "Fraternity, Solidarity, and Civic Friendship," 4.

26. Schwarzenbach, *On Civic Friendship*, 11; "Fraternity, Solidarity, and Civic Friendship," 4.

children as confidants. Rather, friendship as a telos for parenting implies seeking to raise children in such a way that they become adults with the capacity for relationships with others in the wider community that exhibit the characteristics and practices of friendship. It further implies the nurture of civic friendship within the family. Parents are uniquely positioned to foster civic friendship, as they model and encourage care and compassion for, and the befriending of, those who are other. While racial bias can be instilled at a young age, so can compassion, empathy, and care for those who are other, whether in ethnicity, ability, family status, or health.

Schwarzenbach identifies a reciprocal moral equality as being a "critical ideal or goal in the best parent-child relationships."[27] But it is a commitment from parents to mutuality over time, rather than equality, that is inherent to friendship as telos. Expressions of mutuality must of course be age-appropriate. Ultimately, however, mutual give and take between parents and children takes place over the course of a complete life, as youthful dependency on parents is eventually reciprocated in some shape or form by the care that adult children extend to their parents as elders.

Friendship as a telos for parenting is congruent with the valuing of multidimensional relationality and right-relatedness expressed in ancient biblical texts and in indigenous cultural contexts, and with the mutuality inherent within Christian theology. A truly Christian doctrine of creation calls for relationships of mutuality, care, and friendship, in the midst of diversity.[28] Friendship as a telos for parenting would also seem to be in keeping with attachment theories of development, with their focus on relational repair, and the recognition that children internalize parental responsiveness toward them in the form of "internal working models of the self."[29] These models in turn influence the quality of children's relationships with others.[30]

Admittedly, there are numerous challenges to such a telos. These include narrow cultural stereotypes of friendship, along with one or both parents lacking important relational skills, and cultural ideals regarding

---

27. Schwarzenbach, *On Civic Friendship*, 47.

28. Ellithorpe, "Towards a Practical Theology of Friendship," 107.

29. Way and Silverman, "Quality of Friendships During Adolescence," 93.

30. Children who experience relationships of warmth and trust with their parents are more likely to experience similar qualities in their relationships with peers (Way and Silverman, "Quality of Friendships During Adolescence," 93).

hierarchy and submission between generations that may seem to be at odds with a telos of mutuality. Nevertheless, there is potential for such challenges to be overcome, as relational skills are learned, and cultural ideals reconsidered.

Parental practices that support and foster friendship-like relationships within and beyond the home include "the soothing of fears, the nurturing of talents, the fortifying of hopes" as well as conversations with, and practical action on behalf of, the other.[31] Yet the fostering of relationships through practices such as these takes time, time that within many contemporary Western families is constrained by the pressure of work commitments. As Browning notes, and many of us have experienced, the tension between family needs and the demands of paid work can be a major source of strain.[32]

Thus, families need to consider ways in which they can make time and create space for relational practices. To this end, parents may need to curb their use of technology in order to be more fully present to one another and to their children. For both adults and youth, technology can offer "the illusion of companionship without the demands of friendship and… the illusion of friendship without the demands of intimacy."[33] Regular rhythms of Sabbath and sabbatical also have potential to contribute towards the fostering of covenantal friendships within the family and beyond.[34]

Further, parents may want to explore the possibility of shorter working hours, in order to free up time to nurture friendship between themselves, their children, and the communities in which they participate. For example, a combined work week of no more than sixty hours, shared between the marriage partners, can serve to challenge the tyranny of the market, and provide increased opportunities for relationality and friendship.[35]

31. Schwarzenbach, "Fraternity, Solidarity, and Civic Friendship," 7.
32. Browning, *From Culture Wars to Common Ground*, 316.
33. Turkle, *Reclaiming Conversation*, 7.
34. The Sabbath is "a sanctuary which we build, a sanctuary in time" (Heschel, *Sabbath*, 29). It is a time for fellowship, friendship, and togetherness.
35. This suggestion is also articulated by Browning and his co-researchers within their development of a practical theology of families. See Browning, *From Culture Wars to Common Ground*, 316–18. I acknowledge, however, that not all parents are able to restrict their working hours. The relative inability of some adults to work less, without financial penalties or jeopardizing their jobs, is a situation which civic friendship needs to address. One way to do so is through advocacy for a living wage.

Friendship and Pastoral Relationships

From families and parents, I turn now to consider communities of faith, and specifically pastors. Communities of faith will benefit from giving attention to the images of God cultivated through their shared life and considering ways in which the concept and possibility of friendship with God can be explored and encouraged. Moreover, communities of faith will benefit from considering their identity as an open community of friends, modeling the open welcome and hospitality of God. For faith communities to recognize their fundamental identity as a community of friends is not to downplay issues of order or organization, but rather to situate them appropriately, and provide an important perspective for considering the fruitfulness of organizations and ministries.[36]

Acknowledging there is a certain fragility to both friendships and communities, faith communities must be prepared to navigate the ups and downs of potentially difficult friendships, including conflict, hurt, and rejection. They must be encouraged and equipped to overcome the principle of likeness, to extend friendship to those who are other, and to foster civic friendship.

Faith communities can advocate for economic, legal, and health care practices that promote justice and friendship. They can support local economies and community initiatives that seek to resist dominant ways of doing business and to "create new ways of surviving and thriving."[37] Where mental health services have focused on the independence of clients rather than on relational needs, faith communities may advocate for adequate attention to be given to relationality and opportunities for friendship.

Further, faith communities are encouraged to consider whether there is a particular group that they are called to collaboratively befriend, whether shut-in elders, isolated immigrants, those with mental health challenges, or another marginalized group. Faith communities need to be supported in the struggle to live lives of friendship and grace within the broader community, including finding ways to connect with the marginalized. As they do so, there is potential for liberation from fears and false assumptions of those who are different, and for the liberation of others through friendship. Yet, while some will accept the offer of friendship, there is also the possibility that friendship may be rejected.

36. See John of Taizé, *Friends in Christ*, 119–20.
37. Bargh, "Small Issue of Sovereignty," 144.

Once again, the value of learning to navigate conflict, hurt, and rejection is evident.

What then of pastoring? Embracing a rich practical theology of friendship requires pastors to revisit the ways in which they characterize their relationship with God, self, congregants, and community. It is imperative for pastors to consider the nature of the vision that informs their work and relationships, and to challenge cultural norms when it comes to friendship. As I have asserted elsewhere, "the vision of Christian theology, inherent within many of the biblical texts, is of communities that are characterized by a culture of positive reciprocity, based on recognition of the dignity of all, and on positive regard for each person within the community."[38] Such a vision is essentially one of friendship.

God's reign will ultimately be characterized by friendship. As Aelred of Rievaulx asserts, when God's reign comes in all its fullness, the friendship to which we now admit but few "will pour out over all and flow back to God from all, for God will be all in all" (*De spiritali amicitia* 3:134). Given their role and responsibilities, pastors are uniquely situated to nurture and encourage communities that are shaped by mutuality and open friendship, as they seek to live into this eschatological reality. Further, pastors are well placed to explore and encourage the concept of friendship with God within their congregations. The theological imagination has an impact on theological experience; the images people have of God impact their relationship with God. The image of friendship with God is powerful and transformative, with implications for spirituality, ecclesiology, and ethics. This image of friendship implies that God is for us; it is suggestive of intimacy, trust, generosity, and closeness. Yet detachment, respect for otherness, and for the mystery of strangeness are also inherent within this image.[39] While there is danger in depicting God as friend, due to the contemporary sentimentalizing of friendship, there are also dangers associated with the more traditional focus on father images of God, including dependency, and "a perpetual childhood" without growth in responsibility, maturity, and self-determination.[40] I suggest that images of God as friend need not replace those of parenthood, but rather complement them.

---

38. Ellithorpe, "Towards a Practical Theology of Friendship," 148.
39. Moltmann-Wendel, *Rediscovering Friendship*, 6.
40. Moltmann-Wendel, "Friendship," 36.

Pastors are also well placed to encourage practices that foster friendship with God, self, and others. They can encourage talking with God as with a friend, and the fostering of discernment strategies for learning to listen in response. Friendship with self can be encouraged through modeling and teaching the importance of healthy self-love and self-care. Friendship itself can be recognized and encouraged as a spiritual discipline.[41] Further, the purpose of all spiritual disciplines can be recognized as relational, and as fostering love for and friendship with both God and neighbor.

As pastors seek to nurture communities of friendship, they need to wrestle with ways in which they can most appropriately attend to their own need for friendship. Friendship contributes to both personal and pastoral resiliency. Yet for those in formal pastoral roles within the church, there is evidence of friendship being a deeply felt yet largely unmet need.[42] While early career clergy typically *intend* to develop collegial and congregational friendships, this intention is often superseded by the perceived need to develop ministry, with typical approaches to doing so resulting in diminishing close social ties. Clergy tend to focus on church relationships and neglect other friendships. Many engage in this emotionally and relationally demanding role with a minimal core support network that ultimately negatively impacts the effectiveness of their ministry.[43] Opportunities to maintain friendships outside of their workplace may be limited by work hours, and by the timing demands of church programs.

Clearly pastors will benefit from close mutual friendships with others in similar roles who struggle with similar issues, as well as from *anam cara* (soul friend) or spiritual direction type friendships, which may not be fully mutual. As those who carry responsibility within communities, they may also carry a load of frustration that needs to be safely poured out to another. Such a person may be referred to as a "dustbin" friend; that is, a person who has the wisdom to collect the outpoured words and emotions without judging, getting worked up, or taking on an inappropriate problem-solving role.[44] Such a person is most appropriately found outside one's congregation. Having close friends as confidantes and as

---

41. See Phillips, *Cultivated Life*, 180–82.

42. See Sison, "Clergy Struggling." Many clergy expressed desire for friendship within an Australian study. See also Beaumont, "Pastor, Counsellor and Friend."

43. See Barrett, "Does Your Pastor Need a Friend?"

44. Vanier, *Community and Growth*, 184.

sources of encouragement outside one's church community provides grounding and balance, given the power dynamics that may need to be navigated within pastoral friendships.[45]

Opportunities to maintain friendships within the church community may be limited by pastors' own perceptions of their role, as well as by parishioners' perceptions of pastoral roles. Further, pastoral mentors and supervisors have tended to discourage long-term friendships with parishioners, expressing concern that such relationships would "compromise healthy boundaries."[46] Pastors who seek formal counseling training are warned to be wary of friendship, as compounding dual/multiple role issues. Literature on boundary violations asserts that social relationships such as friendship have no place in what may be termed *professional models of care*. Rather, it is thought that allowing movement towards more social forms of relationships will likely lead the pastoral practitioner down a slippery ethical slope.[47]

Pastors need to wrestle with whatever warnings they may have received against becoming too familiar with their congregation as they explore ways in which friendship is of pastoral and ethical value, and relevant to their role. Some pastors do identify friendship as central to their understanding of ministry relationships. For these pastors, friendship may serve as an image or model of care, as well as being used to describe particular relationships.[48] Yet for others, restricted cultural concepts about friendship may result in it being understood too narrowly, and being rejected. For example, Tim Brown's *Reluctant Xtian* blogpost portrays friendship as an enmeshed co-dependent relationship, where there is no tolerance for distance, whether physical or emotional.[49]

---

45. On a practical note, Jason Byassee suggests pastors spend a weekend annually with several people they hold dear. By making this an annual tradition, one can avoid accidentally letting a whole year go by without rekindling supportive and sustaining friendships. See Proeschold-Bell and Byassee, *Faithful and Fractured*, 52, 74.

46. Proeschold-Bell and Byassee both acknowledge and critique this discouragement of pastor-parishioner friendship (*Faithful and Fractured*, 69).

47. According to an online resource by Ruth Kibbie, "Pastoral Relationships v. Friendships," pastors are to "avoid the slip" from the one-directional public pastoral role to the mutuality of the private relationship of friendship.

48. Beaumont, "Pastor, Counsellor and Friend," 184. Further, in this Australian study, the majority of sample clergy considered that the existence of a prior friendship had the potential to add traction to the pastoral encounter ("Pastor, Counsellor and Friend," 210, 217).

49. Brown, "Why Your Pastor Is Actually Not Your Friend."

Cultural ambivalence and imbalance when it comes to friendship is rarely challenged by a theology of friendship. Contemporary understandings of friendship are seldom brought into conversation with classical and theological ideals of friendship within community.[50] Yet rather than avoiding friendships with congregants altogether, friendship needs to be understood more broadly and more multidimensionally. Friendship needs to be reclaimed as an ethical relationship, integral to the Christian life, to pastoral life, to civic life, and to reform. Towards this end, pastors may find the concept of civic friendship, with its focus on willing and doing good for the broader community, to be a challenging yet more straightforward starting point for exploring friendship within their church community than personal friendship.

For the pastor, as for others, personal friendship both contributes to and requires discernment. Even with a commitment to open friendship, the pastor cannot maintain close friendships with all. Rather, she must love specific human beings in ways that she would ultimately desire to be able to love each and every person.[51] Nevertheless, as love characterized by mutuality and equal regard guides the inner disposition of the pastor, and her actions toward others, her desire will be to promote friendship and justice for all.[52] Further, through her preaching, teaching, and pastoral care, she has the opportunity to encourage open multi-dimensional friendships that serve as schools of love, hospitality, freedom, wisdom, and compassion, and that foster civic friendship.

Summary

Current social norms within many Western contexts disconnect friendship and community, and reflect sentimentalized, trivialized perspectives on friendship. Yet friendship (broadly construed) is integral to the faithful outworking of social vocations within communities of practice. The ideal that I have advocated for throughout this paper is one of public-private friendship that overflows into communal responsibility, reform, and civic friendship. Within consumerist, individualistic

---

50. See Pembroke, *Renewing Pastoral Practice*, 52.

51. See Weil, "Friendship," 135–36.

52. See Janssens, "Norms and Priorities in a Love Ethics," 229. This is more nuanced than simply seeking "the greatest good for the largest number" (Browning, *Fundamental Practical Theology*, 162–63).

contexts, public dimensions of friendship are not widely encouraged, and holistic friendships may be difficult to sustain. Nevertheless, these ideals have the potential to promote the flourishing of holistic friendships within communities, along with the overcoming of obstacles to—and distractions from—such friendships.

Communities of practice have been identified as an appropriate context for nurturing holistic multidimensional friendships. Attitudes and actions that contribute towards communities of practice promoting holistic friendships have been explored. These include recognizing friendship as a basic human need *and* as a school of love.

I have recognized friendship as foundational to families and faith communities, and as integral to the social vocation of parenting and pastoring. Friendship has been recognized as a telos for parenting, requiring a commitment on the part of parents to mutuality, over time. Pastors have been encouraged to consider the relevance of friendship to the vision that informs their work and relationships, to wrestle with ways in which they can most appropriately attend to their own need for friendship, to challenge restrictive cultural concepts about friendship, and to recognize friendship as an ethical relationship, with personal and civic dimensions.

While I have given specific focus to Christian communities of faith, such shaping is ultimately on behalf of all, and various insights will be relevant to other communities. All are encouraged to foster a pervasive, transformative culture of friendship, shaped and empowered by the Spirit, and to celebrate and nurture those forms of friendship that are integral to life within communities.

Bibliography

Bargh, Maria. "A Small Issue of Sovereignty." In *Resistance: An Indigenous Response to Neoliberalism*, edited by Maria Bargh, 133–46. Wellington: Huia, 2007.

Barrett, Justin. "Does Your Pastor Need a Friend?" *Christianity Today*, September 20, 2017. https://www.christianitytoday.com/ct/2017/october/does-your-pastor-need-friend.html.

Beaumont, Stephen Murray. "Pastor, Counsellor and Friend: Exploring Multiple Role Relationships in Pastoral Work." PhD diss., University of Queensland, Brisbane, Australia, 2012.

Brown, Tim. "Why Your Pastor Is Actually Not Your Friend." *Reluctant Xtian*, September 25, 2017. https://reluctantxtian.com/2017/09/18/why-your-pastor-is-actually-not-your-friend/.

Browning, Don S. *From Culture Wars to Common Ground: Religion and the American Family Debate*. 2nd ed. Louisville: Westminster John Knox, 2000.

———. *A Fundamental Practical Theology*. Minneapolis: Fortress, 1996.

Carmichael, Liz. *Friendship: Interpreting Christian Love*. London: T&T Clark, 2004.

Ellithorpe, Anne-Marie. "Towards a Practical Theology of Friendship." PhD diss. University of Queensland, Brisbane, Australia, 2018.

———. *Towards Friendship-Shaped Communities: A Practical Theology of Friendship*. Oxford: Wiley Blackwell, 2022.

Glanville, Mark R. *Adopting the Stranger as Kindred in Deuteronomy*. Atlanta: Society of Biblical Literature, 2018.

Heschel, Abraham Joshua. *The Sabbath: Its Meaning for Modern Man*. New York: Farrar, Straus and Giroux, 1975.

Janssens, Louis. "Norms and Priorities in a Love Ethics." *Louvain Studies* 6 (1977) 207–38.

John of Taizé. *Friends in Christ: Paths to a New Understanding of Church*. Maryknoll: Orbis, 2012.

Kibbie, Ruth. "Pastoral Relationships v. Friendships." *Kyros*, 2012. http://kyros.org/resources/pastoral-boundaries/.

MacIntyre, Alasdair. *After Virtue*. 3rd ed. Notre Dame: University of Notre Dame Press, 2007.

May, Todd. *Friendship in an Age of Economics: Resisting the Forces of Neoliberalism*. Lanham: Lexington, 2012.

Moltmann-Wendel, Elisabeth. "Friendship—the Forgotten Category for Faith and Christian Community: A Perspective for the Twenty-First Century." In *Passion for God: Theology in Two Voices*, 25–43. Louisville: Westminster John Knox, 2003.

———. *Rediscovering Friendship: Awakening to the Power and Promise of Women's Friendships*. Translated by John Bowden. Minneapolis: Fortress, 2001.

Pembroke, Neil. *Renewing Pastoral Practice: Trinitarian Perspectives on Pastoral Care and Counselling*. Aldershot: Ashgate, 2006.

Phillips, Susan S. *The Cultivated Life: From Ceaseless Striving to Receiving Joy*. Downers Grove: InterVarsity, 2015.

Proeschold-Bell, Rae Jean, and Jason Byassee. *Faithful and Fractured: Responding to the Clergy Health Crisis*. Grand Rapids: Baker Academic, 2018.

Schwarzenbach, Sibyl A. "Fraternity, Solidarity, and Civic Friendship." *AMITY* 3, no. 1 (2015) 3–18.

———. *On Civic Friendship: Including Women in the State*. New York: Columbia University Press, 2009.

Sison, Marites N. "Clergy Struggling with Identity and Feelings of Loneliness, Exhaustion." *Anglican Journal*, December 1, 2006. https://www.anglicanjournal.com/clergy-struggling-with-identity-and-feelings-of-loneliness-exhaustion-6979/.

Taylor, Charles. *A Secular Age*. Cambridge: Harvard University Press, 2007.

Tigay, Jeffrey H. *Deuteronomy: The Traditional Hebrew Text with the New JPS Translation*. The JPS Torah Commentary. Philadelphia: Jewish Publication Society, 1996.

Turkle, Sherry. *Reclaiming Conversation: The Power of Talk in a Digital Age*. New York: Penguin, 2015.

Vanier, Jean. *Community and Growth*. New York: Paulist, 1989.

Wadell, Paul J. *Friendship and the Moral Life*. Notre Dame: University of Notre Dame Press, 1989.

Way, Niobe, and Lisa R. Silverman. "The Quality of Friendships During Adolescence: Patterns across Context, Culture, and Age." In *Adolescence and Beyond: Family Processes and Development*, edited by Patricia K. Kerig, Marc S. Schulz, and Stuart T. Hauser, 91–112. Oxford: Oxford University Press, 2011.

Weil, Simone. "Friendship." Translated by Emma Craufurd. In *Waiting for God*, 131–42. New York: HarperCollins, 1951.

Wenger, Etienne. *Communities of Practice: Learning, Meaning, and Identity*. Cambridge: Cambridge University Press, 1998.

Wenger-Trayner, Etienne, and Beverly Wenger-Trayner. "Introduction to Communities of Practice: A Brief Overview of the Concept and Its Uses." *Wenger-Trayner* blog, April 7, 2015. https://wenger-trayner.com/introduction-to-communities-of-practice/.

Chapter 2

A Song in the Night:
A Reflection on Singing in Scripture and Social Vocation

Ryan Lang

One night in my early twenties, I found myself ten thousand metres above one of the world's largest cities, my face pressed against the airplane window as we began a slow descent. I had finished at university the year before and had been given an opportunity to intern with an anti-slavery organisation here, for twelve months. It was after midnight. As we floated toward a flickering carpet of lights, I felt something for the first time—something that is still hard to articulate. It was a heaviness of spirit, not concentrated in any person or event, but larger than that: the length and breadth of an entire city.

The feeling would fade. Within hours, I was exploring my new home in the daylight, taking in the playful calls of vendors and the laughter of children, the splashes of bright color and the mouth-watering spices. Within weeks, I had found a new normal. I grew to love this place. But there is one moment in those first few days that I will never forget. One evening, I picked up my guitar and sang an old hymn—and for the first time in my life, I felt as if my guitar was a weapon in my hands, and as if I was singing *through* something.

I believe Scripture gives meaning to this experience, and that is what this chapter considers through a figural interpretation of three images of singing: at the Red Sea, at the Last Supper, and beside a sea of glass and fire. We will explore these biblical images, reflect on how they may be connected, and contemplate two of my own experiences, from a season in social vocation, in light of what surfaces in our reading.

But first, let us set out a definition. Song, as a *form of expression*, has not been a major focus of Christian theology, and theologians lack much of an intentional language about it—even if the biblical vocabulary for the form is textured and profound.[1] To frame our discussion, we use Aaron Ridley's broad understanding of song as "a distinct musical form that contains words or some other kind of vocal component."[2] We will follow John Arthur Smith in using *music* as "a term of convenience for all vocal and instrumental delivery at fixed pitches, ranging from semi-melodic chant to melodic song, from trumpet calls to plucked-string heterophony."[3]

The Red Sea

> Sing to the LORD, for he has triumphed gloriously;
> horse and rider he has thrown into the sea. (Exod 15:21)[4]

And there the song ends. Or begins—for as Miriam lifts her face to the one who has given her life, her words become the song of a people. Miriam's song is one of the oldest texts in the Bible.[5] It is the earliest articulation of Israel's freedom from slavery, providing the foundation for the more expansive song of Moses (Exod 15:1–18).[6] It is the climax of the Exodus narrative, in which Israel's emergence from the Red Sea is the emergence

---

1. For a preliminary discussion see Foley, *Foundations*, 40; Dowley, *Christian Music*, 21. See John Arthur Smith on common mistranslations of Hebrew words as "song." Isaiah 12:6a, for example, is often translated "and sing for joy," but is better read "and rejoice" or "and shout for joy" (Smith, *Music in Ancient Judaism and Early Christianity*, 29–31).

2. This is Jeanette Bicknell's paraphrase. See Jeannette Bicknell, *Philosophy of Song and Singing*, 20.

3. Smith, *Music in Ancient Judaism and Early Christianity*, xvii.

4. All quotations from the Bible are taken from the NRSV.

5. Friedmann, *Music in Biblical Life*, 31.

6. Friedmann, *Music in Biblical Life*, 31.

of a people into new life.[7] At Passover, God provided a lamb for a people in darkness and set in motion their passage out of Egypt and onto this new shore. In freedom, they breathe their first word, in response to his.

Israel's address to God, and about him to creation, opens here—not in plain speech, but in the melody of the human singing voice, bursting forth in collective recognition of life divinely given. Their heart pours out in wonder, gratitude, and joy. They sing as one, from shared experience and emotion. They sing of YHWH's glory and saving presence. They enthrone him above all other gods.[8] Their song proclaims their peoplehood, soon to be confirmed at Sinai.[9] YHWH is God. He has redeemed Israel. Now he is *their* God, and they are his people. It is a sound that will reverberate through the life of Israel, and into the life of the church.

> O Lord, open my lips,
> and my mouth will declare your praise. (Ps 51:15)

Israel is born in song—and from this moment on, they will be a singing people. In the biblical witness, Israel sings in all of life, in times of sorrow as well as joy: in lament and petition, thanksgiving and praise, at banquets, at work, in love, in battle, to bless, and to curse. The Old Testament (OT) overflows with song, usually in response to experiences that evoke high emotion and call for marking with special recognition. It also says something significant about song as a form. The following notes are drawn from a survey of songs, and texts *about* song, in the OT, which focused on a tapestry of Hebrew terms that belong within our definition.[10] I include them here to help us interpret our three images.

Song, in Israel's theological witness, is a characteristically *human* form of expression. Other terms are used for non-human expression, with one exception: a reference to the singing of God in Zeph 3:17, "he will exult over you with loud singing."

Song is *musical*, by definition. It is worth noting three aspects of music that might help us to understand our images. Music has psychological power in its ability to affect the emotions.[11] It carries

---

7. Friedmann, *Music in Biblical Life*, 31.
8. Friedmann, *Music in Biblical Life*, 42.
9. Friedmann, *Music in Biblical Life*, 46.
10. The survey mentioned is part of my doctoral research and will be made available in due course.
11. Begbie, *Music in God's Purposes*, 2–3. This is not a new idea for Christian theology. See Stainer, *Music of the Bible*, 4.

specific meaning.[12] And because music is dynamic, experienced only in time, it always involves a "journey" of sorts.[13] Music has power, in other words, to move a hearer into an emotional state imbued with specific meaning.

To song's musicality we can add the *poetic* character of Israel's songs. All songs in the OT use poetic language; in fact, it appears all poetry in the world of the OT writers was *sung*.[14] Poetry is elevated, involving language that grasps at what is really beyond words. As R. B. Y. Scott notes, biblical poets select and order words to "touch our imagination, awaken memory, and arouse our feelings"—to help hearers see what they see and feel what they feel.[15]

The wedding of music and poetry in song is often experienced as *beautiful*. The OT as well as rabbinical writings speak of the "sweetness" of song.[16] This is important. Beauty ignites desire, calling us to "seek our flourishing in something beyond the present experience."[17] Augustine, Bonaventure, and many others in the Christian tradition have believed the desire that beauty stirs is, ultimately, a longing for and movement toward God.[18]

Taken together, song's musical, poetic, beautiful nature can draw us into an emotional, imaginatively invested kind of "beholding" analogous to that which, for Kevin J. Vanhoozer, takes place in a theatre.[19] Songs move our deepest selves into sung realities that can only, finally, be experienced. Perhaps we can begin to see why Israel presents song as so *self-involving*. The psalmists summon the whole self, the essence of the

---

12. Begbie, *Music in God's Purposes*, 4–7.

13. Colin Gunton describes music as "that which perhaps most expresses the life in movement of the creation, while other art forms are more directly linked to human feeling" (cited in Begbie, *Voicing Creation's Praise*, 245).

14. Smith, *Music in Ancient Judaism and Early Christianity*, 184.

15. Scott, *Psalms as Christian Praise*, 13.

16. 2 Sam 23:1 gives David the title "sweet [*na'iym*] psalmist of Israel." On the artistry of the Psalms, see Sendrey, *Music in Ancient Israel*, 162, 72–79. For a discussion of relevant rabbinical references, see Sendrey, *Music in Ancient Israel*, 212, 17–18.

17. Dyrness, *Poetic Theology*, 27.

18. For a recent and helpful discussion of biblical reflections on positive and negative aspects of desire and how they have been viewed in Christian theology, see Dyrness, *Poetic Theology*, 57–63.

19. See Vanhoozer, *Drama of Doctrine*, 16.

human person (*nephesh, kabod*), to sing:[20] "Bless the LORD, O my soul" (Ps 103:1), "Awake, my soul!" (Ps 108:1).

It is worth noting two more aspects of Israel's songs. First, they tend to use particular kinds of *performative language*. In John Austin's classic framing of performative speech, we could say the majority of language in OT songs is "assertive," that is, it narrates a state of affairs in the singer's experience.[21] Importantly, songs also use a good deal of "commissive" and "directive" language, which respectively commit the singer and call the hearer to action: "For this I will extol you, O LORD, among the nations" (Ps 18:49); "Come, let us return to the LORD" (Hos 6:1). Second, songs in the OT are very intentionally *relational*, always sung to an "other," even if that other is the self: "Why are you cast down, O my soul?" (Ps 42:5). Songs open spaces of meeting. They facilitate a dialogical communion between singer and hearer.

In summary, we have touched on the musical and poetic aspects of song in Israel's witness, its beauty and involvement of the self, the types of performative language it uses, and its high relationality. It seems fair to say that, in Scripture, humans sing to enter a significant, affecting state of affairs (or "reality") with their deepest being, and to draw others into the same reality, with an intention to commune within and live from it together, and often to bring about a concrete response. The sung reality, commonplace or not, will carry meaning that is not easily expressed in plain speech. It must be experienced. Songs tell stories. They are sung to inhabit and to share worlds. The governing story behind all of Israel's songs, in grief and in hope, is the reality of God, the covenantal relationship, and a covenanted world. In their songs, the people of Israel commune in this story—with themselves, with one another, and ultimately with God.

The power of song as a form is reflected in the high-stakes responses to it in the OT. We have said that singing can involve a person's innermost self in a movement toward and into a sung reality. No wonder, then, we find suspicion as well as appreciation when it comes to song. Prophets rail against singing in oracles of judgment. "Take away from me the noise of your songs . . . But let justice roll down like waters" (Amos 5:23–24). Here is a clash between a "happy" song and a grievous reality; singing

---

20. *Nephesh* is used in relation to song in Pss 35:9; 42:4–5, 11; 43:5; 71:23; 84:2; 103:1–2, 22; 104:1, 35; 119:175; 139:14; 142:7; 146:1. *Kabod* is used in Pss 30:12 and 108:1.

21. Austin, *Philosophical Papers*.

has been involved in a self-deception. Yet, in the prophets, singing is also a paradigmatic sign of hope during, or of life following, a time of desolation (See, e.g., Isa 30:29; 42:10; 51:3; Jer 20:13). Rabbinical writings, too, perceive both this danger and unique potential for good. The contrast is articulated in the Talmud: "Profane songs of love and lust are sufficient cause to destroy the world, but Israel's religious song saves it."[22] Such a profound valuing of song is seen in the rabbinical prohibition of sung worship after the sacking of the Temple in 70 CE—an expression of overwhelming national grief and, perhaps, an inability to imagine a new dawn.[23]

The Last Supper

We have sketched a picture of song in the OT, the theological witness of a singing people. I would like now to explore two images of song in the New Testament (NT).

There are many scenes in the Gospel narratives in which Jesus or those with him may have sung. Jesus probably sang pilgrim songs, for instance, on his way to Jerusalem for the Passover festival when he was a boy (Luke 2:41–42). Songs of celebration were likely heard at the wedding in Cana (John 2:1–12). Jesus would have read the scroll in a Nazarene synagogue in a semi-melodic chant (Luke 4:16–20).[24]

Yet there is only one event, found in two Gospels, in which our attention is drawn to the act of singing using a musical term. This is the Last Supper, in the accounts of Mark and Matthew. The song comes at a critical moment in both stories. Most interpreters agree this meal, and Jesus' words of institution, are the center-point of the passion narrative in these Gospels.[25] Each year at Passover, Israel remembered the Exodus from Egypt and looked toward a "new" exodus: when God would forgive

---

22. Cited in Sendrey, *Music in Ancient Israel*, 223.

23. Sendrey, *Music in Ancient Israel*, 227.

24. On the use of melodic forms in synagogal prayer and Scripture reading at this time, see Foley, *Foundations*, 51–57; Hurtado, *At the Origins*, 31–32.

25. See Wright, *Jesus and the Victory of God*, 554–631; also Hays, *Echoes of Scripture in the Gospels*, 15–190; Watts, *Isaiah's New Exodus*. Whether this was a real Passover meal will not concern us here. The authors portray it as such, and Jesus clearly intends to draw Passover symbolism to himself. On the relevant debates see Cole, *Gospel According to Mark*, 291; Keener, *Gospel of Matthew*, 622; Witherington, *Gospel of Mark*, 371–72.

his people's sins, return to redeem them, and bring about a final victory over evil.[26] On his way to Jerusalem, in Mark and Matthew, Jesus enacts YHWH's return to judge and to save, the replacement of Temple and sacrificial system with himself, and a new exodus, drawing onto himself a central tradition of Jewish hope.[27] The two writers emphasize different aspects of this story, but in both, the plotline around the meal is the same, and in the pivotal interpretive moment, Jesus evokes the same symbolic world.

In Mark 14 and Matthew 26, in an upper room, Jesus takes the symbols of the Passover meal to frame his mission for the disciples.[28] He interprets the bread as his body. Their eating becomes a participation in his being and in the benefits of his death.[29] He interprets the cup as his "blood of the covenant . . . poured out for many" (Matthew adds "for the forgiveness of sins"), defining his death in sacrificial terms, within an Exodus-covenant narrative, and their drinking as a participation in its effects.[30] His vow, "I will never again drink of the fruit of the vine until that day when I drink it new in the kingdom of God" (Matt 26:29 adds "with you"), anticipates his vindication and casts a vision of renewed fellowship at the messianic banquet.[31] For Leon Morris, the saying is a farewell and a moment of divide; Jesus' death will inaugurate a new world.[32] The last detail of the meal is the same in each account: "When they had sung the hymn [*hymneō*], they went out to the Mount of Olives." (Mark 14:26; Matt 26:30)

The song is usually overlooked in readings of these texts.[33] This is understandable, given its proximity to the weighty matter of the words

---

26. For Wright, this was the controlling story in Jesus' ministry. See Wright, *Jesus and the Victory of God*, 576.

27. Wright, *Jesus and the Victory of God*, 558.

28. Wright, *Jesus and the Victory of God*, 554–631; see further Hays, *Echoes of Scripture*, 15–190; Watts, *Isaiah's New Exodus*.

29. Edwards, *Gospel According to Mark*, 425.

30. Here Jesus engages in a creative fusion of the ideas of the paschal lamb, the blood of the covenant (Exod 24:8), and potentially the sin offering, infused with a prophetic new covenant motif (Zech 9:11; Jer 31:34; cf. Ezek 37:36). See Cole, *Gospel According to Mark*, 293.

31. Lane, *Gospel According to Mark*, 508.

32. Morris, *Gospel According to Matthew*, 662.

33. Most scholars simply mention Israel's *Hallēl* was sung. William L. Lane is an exception, commenting Jesus "took the words of these psalms as his own prayer of thanksgiving and praise . . . When Jesus rose to go to Gethsemane, Psalm 118 was

of institution. Yet that very nearness, and the fact this is the only explicit reference to singing in the Gospels, should make us pay attention. The Gospels are compressed biographical narratives. Mark and Matthew tend to avoid superfluous details in their stories.[34] The writers have framed the supper as a Passover liturgy, yet in their telling of the story, they omit almost all the elements that were likely present in this meal in the first century, including other songs, in their focus on what is most significant about Jesus' actions and words. What is the role of this song, then, at the focal point of a new exodus narrative?

Maybe the first question to ask is: what song do Jesus and his friends sing? The "hymn" Mark and Matthew cite is most likely Pss 115–18, the last portion of Israel's *Hallēl*.[35] The *Hallēl* psalms are among the most significant in Jewish tradition. By the first century, they probably had a stable place in Temple liturgy, including at Passover, when Levitical singers would have sung them as families made their paschal sacrifices.[36] Families likely sang them again near the beginning (Pss 113–14) and end (Pss 115–18) of the meal in the home.[37] In time, the *Hallēl* became so closely associated with Passover that the Palestinian Targum inserts it at Exod 15:18, the last verse of the song of Moses.[38] This hymn holds the heart of Israel's song at the Red Sea.

Psalms 115–18, the verses likely sung near the end of the meal, open with a blessing that had defined Israel's worship for centuries; the psalmist glorifies God for his steadfast love and faithfulness (Ps 115:1). As the psalms unfold, he calls for God's universal praise as creator and protector.

---

upon his lips. It provided an appropriate description of how God would guide his Messiah through distress and suffering to glory" (Lane, *Gospel According to Mark*, 509).

34. Mark's Gospel is especially terse. See Burridge, *Four Gospels*, 36–41. On the Gospels and their similarities to Greco-Roman biographies, see Burridge, *What Are the Gospels?*

35. On this discussion see Morris, *Gospel According to Matthew*, 662; Chosen People Ministries, "Messianic," 273; France, *Gospel According to Matthew*, 370; Davies and Allison Jr., *Gospel According to Saint Matthew*, 483–84; Cole, *Gospel According to Mark*, 293; Witherington, *Gospel of Mark*, 376; Edwards, *Gospel According to Mark*, 423; Lane, *Gospel According to Mark*, 509; France, *Gospel of Mark*, 188. Some students of Passover hold that the Passover seder ended with a fifth cup, of Elijah, being poured into the sink and the family singing the song "Next Year in Jerusalem." See Feldman, "Gospel," 207.

36. Silva, "*Hymnos; Hymneō*."

37. One member of the family likely led the song, with the others answering each half verse with "Hallelujah!" See Lane, *Gospel According to Mark*, 509.

38. Beale, *Book of Revelation*, 793.

God has conquered the forces of death that encompassed the psalmist. In response the psalmist sings of the victory, lifts the cup of salvation, and offers his life to God with thanksgiving, in the presence of God's people.

The final psalm, Psalm 118, grows immediate, and urgent. The psalmist *will not die*, but live, and recount the deeds of the Lord (118:17). He calls for the gates of righteousness to open so he may give thanks. He praises God for saving his life, using messianic language for the act. The verses are infused with language of new creation.

> I thank you that you have answered me
> and have become my salvation.
> The stone that the builders rejected
> has become the chief cornerstone.
> This is the Lord's doing;
> it is marvelous in our eyes.
> This is the day that the Lord has made;
> let us rejoice and be glad in it.
> Save us, we beseech you, O Lord! . . .
> Blessed is the one who comes in the name of the Lord . . .
> The Lord is God,
> and he has given us light.
> Bind the festal procession with branches,
> up to the horns of the altar.
> You are my God, and I will give thanks to you;
> you are my God, I will extol you.
> O give thanks to the Lord, for he is good,
> for his steadfast love endures forever. (Ps 118:21–29)

The *Hallēl* is Israel's paradigmatic response to God's paradigmatic saving act. In the last lines, we hear, again, an echo of the song of Moses:

> In your steadfast love you led the people whom you redeemed;
> you guided them by your strength to your holy abode.
> (Exod 15:13)

There is much we could explore about this song. I want to focus on just one aspect of it here: its connection to the song at the sea.

We see something old and something new in the song at the Last Supper. In one sense, Jesus and his disciples participate in an ancient tradition. Every year at Passover, Jews relived the story of God's saving act in the Exodus, through sacrifice, prayer, storytelling, food, drink, and conversation. At the end of the meal, they enacted the story in a final way. They stood and sang Israel's response at the sea. Jesus and his friends sing the wonder, gratitude, and joy of a people in the moment they were given life, joining all of Israel throughout history in declaring the reality of God's love and their salvation. In song's musical, poetic speech, they not only tell of God's victory; they *experience* it; they *feel* it anew; they remember what it means. They answer as Israel, offering their heart in response to the gift of life, communing with God and one another in the reality of his steadfast love for his people. They stand, again, on the shore.

Yet, for Mark and Matthew, this is also a moment of re-interpretation. Jesus sings the song of the sea as Israel, and he also sings a new song, as the Lamb. He has just identified himself as the sacrifice effecting a new covenant, drawing together the image of the paschal lamb with an allusion to Moses' offering at Sinai (cf. Exod 24:8).[39] Moses, the first redeemer, sacrificed a surrogate for the people. Now, the second redeemer offers himself, in order to effect a new exodus and to mark a new covenant.[40] As Jesus the Messiah sings, he stands in a new victory of God.

The disciples join him. They have participated in Jesus by imbibing his body and blood. Now they sing Israel's song, and they join a new song: a song of thanksgiving to God, with Jesus, *in* and *through* him, though they do not yet understand what it means. This, I believe, is our first glimpse of the song of the church. As they sing, Jesus' followers commune with him in a new covenantal story, a new *reality*, "as the foundation of the redeemed community."[41]

"When they had sung the hymn, they went out to the Mount of Olives." Mark 14:26 and Matt 26:30 tie the hymn directly to a movement "out" to the Mount, and this is important. The song is a hinge in our texts, and in the passion narrative of which the meal is the center. It closes a moment of interpretation and opens a sequence of action leading to the cross. The writers see a group step into darkness.[42] It is late, likely near midnight. More critical than the physical darkness of the hour, though, is a gathering relational darkness in the narrative. The fellowship of the

39. Hebrews 9:21–22 refers to this same blood as being for the forgiveness of sins. See Davies and Allison Jr., *Gospel According to Saint Matthew*, 475. Several images come together to interpret Jesus' "ultimate, sacrificial act of redemption," in which he draws the symbols of Passover into a new story about his death and its effects (Cole, *Gospel According to Mark*, 293; Witherington, *Gospel of Mark*, 374).

40. Davies and Allison Jr., *Gospel According to Saint Matthew*, 473.

41. Torrance, *Theology in Reconciliation*, 106.

42. See France, *Gospel According to Matthew*, 370; Morris, *Gospel According to Matthew*, 662; Cole, *Gospel According to Mark*, 294; France, *Gospel of Mark*, 188; Lane, *Gospel According to Mark*, 509.

meal is set between two betrayals.[43] After Judas leaves, the friends observe a new covenant, share a vision of unending fellowship, sing together, and then enter the night, the prediction of Peter's denial, the dissolution of fellowship, and the forsakenness of Golgotha. The song is their final act of communion. The language shifts from "he," as Jesus leads the ritual of institution, to "they," as the friends sing as one. As the writers pivot from the song to the Mount, where the next three scenes of the passion unfold, we hear an echo of 2 Sam 15:30. David ascended this same hill, weeping over a betrayal and praying for deliverance.[44] The scenes grow increasingly dark, from Jesus' words with Peter, to his closest friends' inability to pray with him, to his desertion by them all.[45]

The emphases on darkness and light point to something else that will become a theme in the NT: the song in the night. Jesus and his friends sing the covenantal story within a gathering darkness. They stand at the sea, in song, and indwell the victory of a loving God. Then they step from the light of communion into the deepest of all nights, with the song on their lips and in their heart.[46]

A Sea of Glass and Fire

There is another song beside a sea in the NT. The last explicit reference to singing in Scripture is in Revelation 15. Earlier in his vision, John sees a church in a time of earthly struggle (Rev 1–3). Then, in Revelation 4, he is taken into heaven in the spirit and glimpses reality in a new perspective.

Three times in his heavenly vision, John perceives the whole of redeemed humanity, of all history, in song. They sing in response to God's victory won through the Lamb, in the soaring language of new exodus, covenant, and people. In Rev 5:8–10 the elders, representatives of the redeemed, sing a "new song" *to* the Lamb before the throne of God. In 14:2–3, the redeemed sing a "new song" *with* the Lamb, gathered to him on Mount Zion.

---

43. Edwards, *Gospel According to Mark*, 421. This sandwich pattern is found often in Mark. See Burridge, *Four Gospels*, 36–41.

44. Davies and Allison Jr., *Gospel According to Saint Matthew*, 484.

45. Witherington, *Gospel of Mark*, 376.

46. Christopher H. J. Wright is one of the few commentators to notice the fact Jesus sung this song hours before his crucifixion and wonder whether the words went with him to "the agony of Gethsemane." See Wright, *To the Cross*, 30–32.

Finally, in Rev 15:1, the redeemed stand on a shore. John has just witnessed God's judgment of the beast, who deceived the earth and brought violence to all who resisted it (Rev 14:6–20). Now he sees something like a sea of glass and fire.[47] The clear allusion in this image, in light of the following song, plagues, and tabernacle, is to the Red Sea, in conjunction with a new exodus.[48] The waters represent evil, and the fire signifies judgment.[49] The sea of glass and fire is a figure of God's ultimate, cosmic judgment upon evil. He has calmed the beast's chaotic abode through the work of the Lamb.[50] He has made the sea still. This is the consummation of history: God is shown to be God—his victory final, his kingdom everlasting.

Standing on the shore, with "harps of God in their hands," the people lift their voice. In Revelation 5 and 14, their song to and with the Lamb was described as a "new song." Now, they sing (*adō*) "the song [*ōdē*] of Moses, the servant of God, and the song [*ōdē*] of the Lamb."[51]

> Great and amazing are your deeds,
>> Lord God the Almighty!
> Just and true are your ways,
>> King of the nations!
> Lord, who will not fear
>> and glorify your name?
> For you alone are holy.
>> All nations will come
>> and worship before you,
> for your judgments have been revealed." (Rev 15:3–4)

The people sing to the one on the throne. Israel praised this loving God for his victory over Egypt. These praise him for his victory over evil.[52] They sing in wonder and joy at his acts of judgement and at his ways.[53]

---

47. The image of the sea of glass most immediately echoes sea seen in the throne room in 4:6. It is also reminiscent of Jewish tradition that described the Red Sea as appearing congealed after it closed over the Egyptians (this is the basis of Exod 15:8) (Beale, *Book of Revelation*, 792). For Aune, this is a heavenly representation of God's punitive action on earth (Aune, *Revelation 6–16*, 869–72).

48. G. B. Caird, cited in Beale, *Book of Revelation*, 789; see the longer discussion in Beale, *Book of Revelation*, 789–92.

49. Beale, *Book of Revelation*, 789; Aune, *Revelation 6–16*, 871.

50. Beale, *Book of Revelation*, 789–90.

51. This is generally thought to be a single song given two titles (Beale, *Book of Revelation*, 792; see further Aune, *Revelation 6–16*, 873; Osborne, *Revelation*, 564).

52. Beale, *Book of Revelation*, 792.

53. "Ways" here signifies that the acts of God are "not demonstrations of raw power

"Who will not fear and glorify your name?" echoes Israel's song at the sea (Exod 15:11).[54] "For you alone are holy" completes Moses' thought in that song. They sing of the day of judgment and the gathering of all nations into the presence of God, the fullness of history in Israel's prophetic hope—a day of new creation, which has finally come.[55] Like the *Hallēl*, the song John hears is full of allusions to the Exodus narrative developed through the OT.[56] It ends with an echo of Psalm 98, which remembers the Red Sea and calls Israel to take harps and sing a new song, for God comes to judge the earth (cf. Ps 98:9).[57]

The singers of Revelation 15 are those who have "conquered the beast and its image and the number of its name." They are the whole people of God, the same ones who in 14:4 "follow the Lamb wherever he goes."[58] In 14:4–5, John perceives that they not only are with the Lamb; they are *like* him. They are "conquerors" in their identification with the one who wins the victory by his self-gift.[59] Their voice is like the "sound of many waters" (14:2), words used of Christ's voice in 1:15,[60] and their song takes his name: "the song of Moses and the song of the *Lamb*."

The meaning of this last phrase is debated. Because the Greek genitive is ambiguous, some interpreters, leaning on other textual parallels (references to a Lamb, victory, harps, and so on), believe the song in Rev

---

but moral expressions of his just character." For Beale, in the light of the judgment narrative in Revelation and the events recounted in ch.14, the sense of the song is that "[r]edemption through Christ has brought to supreme expression how he demonstrates justice" (Beale, *Book of Revelation*, 794–95).

54. This formula is used to evoke the Exodus later in the OT (Beale, *Book of Revelation*, 798).

55. Beale, *Book of Revelation*, 799.

56. Beale, *Book of Revelation*.

57. Beale, *Book of Revelation*, 798–99.

58. For Beale, this is the same group as totality of redeemed pictured in 14:1–5, since they also hold harps in their hands, in contrast to others who picture them only as Christian martyrs (Beale, *Book of Revelation*, 791). Aune argues the sense of "conquering" is restricted to their victory over the beast (Aune, *Revelation 6–16*, 871).

59. Thus they participate in the Lamb's victory through identification (Beale, *Book of Revelation*, 790). In a secondary sense, they have conquered by enduring in their identification with the Lamb and offering of self to God. Beale suggests "standing" may include the idea of resurrection, since the passage appears linked with 4:6 and 5:5–9 (*Book of Revelation*, 791). Even if this is the case, the focus of these passages would seem to be conquering by self-offering.

60. On this connection, see Thomas and Macchia, *Revelation*, 253; Morris, *Book of Revelation*, 170.

15:3–4 must refer to the "new song" of 5:8–10, effectively rendering the phrase: "the song sung *by* Moses, that is, the song *about* the Lamb."[61]

But there may be a stronger reading. We can hear this as a song sung *by* the Lamb, paralleling the song sung *by* Moses in Exodus 15. David Aune suggests this could be how to read the phrase, but he dismisses the possibility due to a lack of precedent for a singing Lamb in John's vision.[62] Yet, he may dismiss it too easily. The song in Revelation 15 is directed to God. The judgements it cites, unlocked by the *work* of the Lamb, are brought about by the hand of God. Moses, the first redeemer, brought Israel out of Egypt and lifted a song of praise to God. He and Christ are paralleled in other ways in the NT, including, as we have seen, in their sacrifice to seal a covenant. Like Moses, Jesus praises God throughout the Gospels, not least when he sings the *Hallēl* at the Last Supper, immediately after revealing himself as the new Lamb.

I want to suggest that the singers in Revelation 15 are singing the Lamb's own song.[63] They are identified with him, in life and word, throughout John's vision. Their voice is like his. Their song is to God. Their harps are "of" (belonging to) God.[64] With heavenly sight, John beholds a people standing beside a sea, in view of God's ultimate victory. He hears their voice rise. It is the voice of the church, gathered into the Lamb's own song of thanksgiving to the Father.

A Veil Pulled Back

It is possible we can see these three images as perspectives on one reality. I will offer some more systematic theological comments here, in the space we have left. These are intended to be generative, given the constraints of this chapter, and as directions for further reflection.

For Stephen S. Smalley, Revelation occupies a genre of its own. It stands in a Jewish apocalyptic tradition, in which the seer is given

---

61. See, for instance, Osborne, *Revelation*, 564; Aune, *Revelation 6–16*, 872–73; Beale, *Book of Revelation*, 793.

62. Aune, *Revelation 6–16*, 872.

63. Every other use of the phrase "of the Lamb" in Revelation has this possessive sense. See Rev 6:16 (wrath); 7:14; 12:11 (blood); 13:8 (book of life); 14:10 (presence); 19:7 (marriage); 19:9 (marriage supper); 21:9 (wife); 21:14 (apostles); 22:1, 3 (throne).

64. Similarly, most if not all uses of the phrase "of God" in Revelation have a possessive sense. See Rev 1:2, 9; 2:7, 18; 3:1; 4:5; 5:6; 6:9; 7:15; 9:4; 10:7; 11:1; 12:17; 14:12, 19; 15:1, 3, 7, 8; 16:1, 9, 14; 17:7; 19:9, 13, 17; 20:4, 6; 21:3, 11, 23; 22:1, 3.

a glimpse of divine truth hitherto veiled from human sight.[65] It is also Christian prophecy.[66] John speaks "God's word of judgment and salvation" in Christ to his community.[67] He "reaches backwards, and into the present and future, to interpret God's word to his own circle and to the world beyond; but he does so with the ability to perceive and uncover the end of salvation's drama."[68] The first three chapters of Revelation find the church in a dark night. John's is an age of imperial opposition, including persecution and martyrdom of Christians, as well as resistance from Judaism and sore internal conflicts.[69] Yet, in the spirit, John is given to see what is secure in heaven and ultimately real.

What John sees is the victory of God over his enemy, and the consummation of his kingdom. What he hears is the voice of redeemed humanity through all history, caught up in the song of the Lamb: a song of wonder, gratitude, and joy, lifted to the one on the throne, the giver of life.

It is an eternal song. It is the song of Christ: he who was present in God's saving act in the Exodus and in Israel's first joyful response; he who was present in the psalmist who sang again of God's steadfast, enduring love. His song to the Father is embodied and perfected at the Last Supper, and will be fulfilled at the consummation of history, beside a sea of glass and fire. The song is a musical, poetic offering of thanks. In the incarnation, Thomas F. Torrance reminds us, the Word assumed human nature and ranged himself alongside humanity as a worshipper of God.[70] His worship is complete, a gift of himself to the Father, his song part of a life offered gratefully, freely, in response to the Father's love.

Christ is our High Priest. The song of the church is taken, by the Spirit, into his song, becoming "a participation in his [worship] before the

---

65. Smalley, *Revelation to John*, 6; see further Moo, *Letters*, 250. For the prophet Jeremiah, the prophet is defined as one who has been present in the council of heaven (Jer 23:18) (Aune, *Revelation 1–5*, 313).

66. Smalley, *Revelation to John*, 6.

67. Smalley, *Revelation to John*, 7.

68. Smalley, *Revelation to John*, 7.

69. On imperial opposition, see Smalley, *Revelation to John*, 3–4. On pressure from Judaism and internal strife, see Smalley, *Revelation to John*, 4–6, 359. John's core concerns are true worship, love, and unity in Christ's body, in the face of threats to its integrity.

70. Following Cyril of Alexandria. See Torrance, *Theology in Reconciliation*, 176–78.

throne of the Father in heaven."[71] The redeemed not only experience and respond to the reality of God's love when they sing this song; they enter into the relationship and loving response of Christ vis-à-vis the Father, by the power of the Spirit. The song in Christ—on the lips of the disciples in the upper room, of Paul and Silas in prison (Acts 16:25), of an embattled church in Revelation—is, finally, a participation in the incarnate Son's self-offering to the Father. God gives the Lamb and accepts him as the church's true worship. Christ is "the Priest and the Sacrifice, the Offerer and the Offering."[72] He is the Singer and the Song.

The song in Revelation 15 is an eschatological reality, and so it is also a *present* reality that may be touched in the musical, poetic language of song, even in the darkest night. In Mark and Matthew, on the night he is betrayed, Jesus sings a song Israel has sung since the day of their deliverance, and he leads the song of the eschatological people of God. He does both at the same time, because it is the same song. It is *his* song. YHWH is God. He has redeemed a people. Now he is their God, and they are his. As Jesus steps into the night, he lives in an unending story, in a profound, eternal act of trust.

> You are my God, and I will give thanks to you;
> you are my God, I will extol you.
> O give thanks to the Lord, for he is good,
> for his steadfast love endures forever. (Ps 118:28–29)

Two Stories and a Plea

My singing has changed since the year I joined my friends in their fight against slavery. There has been sorrow and joy in this work. We have seen wondrous things: thousands brought to freedom; light breaking into broken lives. But the world has felt dark at times. There have been evenings when my spirit is dull, weighed down by encounters with greed and unimaginable loss. On those nights, I finish work, go home, light a candle, pick up my guitar, and sing the old hymns. Sometimes, I sing for hours. New melodies form and take flight, mostly wordless: always a new song, yet ever the same. More often than not, after a time, I will touch something eternal. It is the love of God and the joy of my salvation. And the darkness? It falls away.

---

71. Torrance, *Theology in Reconciliation*, 175, 214.
72. Torrance, *Theology in Reconciliation*, 176.

There is power in the song in the night. This musical, poetic, beautiful language leads me into God's story with my entire, human, being. I sing the old songs and remember the reality of his steadfast love. I see the cross. I stand in the knowledge of his victory: recalling glimpses I have seen in my lifetime and touching, by the Spirit, the unseen reality of its consummation. I experience all of this again. I soak in what it means, and I respond with joy. But there is more—or so I am coming to believe. Because by the Spirit, I sing in *Christ*, indwelling the truth of the Father's love and of Christ's own loving response, in communion with the Godhead. We stand together on the shore. There is nothing more real, or more secure, than this.

Song can seem a marginal thing, to those in social vocations as well as to theologians. I understand this. Singing might not feel like a "practical" thing to do when we are hard pressed, when our actions "for others" are urgent and often involve facing fully into human brokenness. I want to suggest, though, that singing is not a heart-warming extra in Christian life. The songs of God offer an anchor in these very nights, "when darkness seems to hide His face." They usher us, again, into the story—the *reality*—of the unfailing love of God, with all of our being. We stand and live in this story as we sing in Christ. We need to keep singing.

I spent my most recent years in anti-slavery work in another, even larger city, with a newer and smaller team. We were comprised of Buddhists, Muslims, Hindus, and Christians, gathered around a mission to turn the tide against forced labour in their nation. The work was heavy, and we met each morning to pray. Soon, we started to sing to end our times together. We took turns leading the song, and one morning, when it was my turn, I chose the hymn "The Steadfast Love of the Lord Never Ceases." We sang it three times—then we sat still, in silence and in peace.

"The Steadfast Love" would become our anthem. I was asked by people of every faith to sing it in our morning meetings, for the remainder of my time with these friends. It dawned on me, as I was preparing this chapter, that this is the song Jesus sang in the upper room. He stepped into the night to lead his people out of slavery and onto a new shore, remembering, again, the unending love of YHWH for his people, and offering his life in response. Our voices joined his as we sang the same, eternal story. As we stepped out into our days, and our nights, we went with Jesus, his song on our lips and in our heart.

Bibliography

Aune, David E. *Revelation 1–5*. WBC. Dallas: Word, 1997.
———. *Revelation 6–16*. WBC. Nashville: Thomas Nelson, 1998.
Austin, John. *Philosophical Papers*. 3rd ed. Oxford: Oxford University Press, 1979.
Beale, G. K. *The Book of Revelation: A Commentary on the Greek Text*. The New International Greek Testament Commentary. Grand Rapids: Eerdmans, 1999.
Begbie, Jeremy S. *Music in God's Purposes*. Edinburgh: Handsel, 1989.
———. *Voicing Creation's Praise: Towards a Theology of the Arts*. Edinburgh: T&T Clark, 1991.
Bicknell, Jeannette. *Philosophy of Song and Singing: An Introduction*. New York: Routledge, 2015.
Burridge, Richard A. *Four Gospels, One Jesus? A Symbolic Reading*. 3rd ed. Grand Rapids: Eerdmans, 2014.
———. *What Are the Gospels? A Comparison with Greco-Roman Biography*. 2nd ed. Grand Rapids: Eerdmans, 2004.
Chosen People Ministries. "A Messianic Family Haggadah." In *Messiah in the Passover*, edited by Darrell L. Bock and Mitch Glaser, 263–74. Grand Rapids: Kregel, 2017.
Cole, R. Alan. *The Gospel According to Mark: An Introduction and Commentary*. 2nd ed. Grand Rapids: Eerdmans, 1989.
Davies, W. D., and Dale C. Allison Jr. *A Critical and Exegetical Commentary on the Gospel According to Saint Matthew*. Vol. III, *Commentary on Matthew XIX–XXVII*. London and New York: T&T Clark, 1997.
Dowley, Tim. *Christian Music: A Global History*. Minneapolis: Fortress, 2011.
Dyrness, William. *Poetic Theology: God and the Poetics of Everyday Life*. Grand Rapids: Eerdmans, 2011.
Edwards, James R. *The Gospel According to Mark*. Grand Rapids: Eerdmans, 2002.
Feldman, Larry. "The Gospel in the Passover Seder." In *Messiah in the Passover*, edited by Darrell L. Bock and Mitch Glaser, 195–207. Grand Rapids: Kregel, 2017.
Foley, Edward. *Foundations of Christian Music: The Music of Pre-Constantinian Christianity*. American Essays in Liturgy. Collegeville: Liturgical, 1996.
France, R. T. *The Gospel According to Matthew: An Introduction and Commentary*. Grand Rapids: Eerdmans, 1985.
———. *The Gospel of Mark*. Oxford: Bible Reading Fellowship, 1996.
Friedmann, Jonathan L. *Music in Biblical Life: The Roles of Song in Ancient Israel*. Jefferson: McFarland, 2013.
Hays, Richard B. *Echoes of Scripture in the Gospels*. Waco: Baylor University Press, 2016.
Hurtado, Larry W. *At the Origins of Christian Worship: The Context and Character of Earliest Christian Devotion*. Grand Rapids: Eerdmans, 1999.
Keener, Craig S. *A Commentary on the Gospel of Matthew*. Grand Rapids: Eerdmans, 1999.
Lane, William L. *The Gospel According to Mark*. Grand Rapids: Eerdmans, 1974.
Moo, Douglas J. *The Letters to the Colossians and to Philemon*. Pillar New Testament Commentary. Grand Rapids: Eerdmans, 2008.
Morris, Leon. *The Book of Revelation: An Introduction and Commentary*. Tyndale New Testament Commentaries. Leicester: InterVarsity, 1987.
———. *The Gospel According to Matthew*. Grand Rapids: Eerdmans, 1992.

Osborne, Grant R. *Revelation*. Baker Exegetical Commentary on the New Testament. Grand Rapids: Baker Academic, 2002.

Scott, R. B. Y. *The Psalms as Christian Praise*. London: Lutterworth, 1958.

Sendrey, Alfred. *Music in Ancient Israel*. New York: Philosophical Library, 1969.

Silva, Moisés. "*Hymnos; Hymneō*." In *New International Dictionary of New Testament Theology and Exegesis*, edited by Moisés Silva, 547–48. Grand Rapids: Zondervan, 2014.

Smalley, Stephen S. *The Revelation to John*. Downers Grove: InterVarsity, 2005.

Smith, John Arthur. *Music in Ancient Judaism and Early Christianity*. Burlington: Ashgate, 2011.

Stainer, John. *The Music of the Bible: With an Account of the Development of Modern Musical Instruments from Ancient Types*. London: Novellow, Ewer & Co., c. 1880.

Thomas, John Christopher, and Frank D. Macchia. *Revelation*. Grand Rapids: Eerdmans, 2016.

Torrance, Thomas F. *Theology in Reconciliation: Essays Towards Evangelical and Catholic Unity in East and West*. London: Geoffrey Chapman, 1975.

Vanhoozer, Kevin J. *The Drama of Doctrine: A Canonical Linguistic Approach to Christian Theology*. Louisville: Westminster John Knox, 2005.

Watts, Rikki E. *Isaiah's New Exodus in Mark*. Grand Rapids: Baker Academic, 2000.

Witherington, Ben, III. *The Gospel of Mark: A Socio-Rhetorical Commentary*. Grand Rapids: Eerdmans, 2001.

Wright, Christopher J. H. *To the Cross: Proclaiming the Gospel from the Upper Room to Calvary*. Downers Grove: InterVarsity, 2017.

Wright, N. T. *Jesus and the Victory of God*. Minneapolis: Fortress, 1996.

Chapter 3

Found by Love

Lex S. McMillan

Introduction

IN THIS CHAPTER I consider Jesus' invitation to a specific kind of relating illustrated in the story of his encounter with Zacchaeus in Luke 19:1–10. I do this in order to build towards a theological vision for relating, so that practitioners of the social sciences might have an end goal in mind for their work. I see represented in the Zacchaeus story a hope that threads its way through the Jewish and Christian scriptures. This is the hope that people—who in some way experience themselves as "outsiders"—might be found by love expressed in very practical ways.

In my work as a relationship therapist I am concerned with the way people sometimes lose touch with themselves, with one another, and with wider community concerns as they traverse the various seasons of life. In the light of this I am interested in how our work might reverse movement towards relational fragmentation. While it is inevitable that life's challenges—such as caring for young children, financial struggle, working long hours, and coping with illness and other forms of loss—sometimes erode connection, I do not think it is inevitable that people need to remain isolated. Naming disconnection as an issue, and developing practices with which to engage it, are important because as time passes loss of connection can take a similar toll on the strength of a relationship as osteoporosis does to bones—weakening them from the inside out. Further, I wonder what a vision of relational encounter shaped in the style of Jesus' life—cruciform love—might have to offer our therapeutic work with relational disconnection?

Typically, people consult with me about their relationships when their experience of loss of connection threatens to become unbearable. I am suggesting that useful therapeutic responses might be formed through developing a Christ-centered imagination. This is an imagination that offers insight into how we might understand *and* engage experiences of disconnection. In practice I find that while on the one hand desire for connection urges people towards vulnerability, on the other hand shame and fear hold them back. Put another way, experiencing love inevitably brings up experiences of vulnerability. For example, one day someone might feel safely loved, and then the next day find themselves afraid to trust when painful memories of rejection surface again.[1] My contention here is that when working with people who find themselves caught in ongoing cycles of desire and fear, hope and loss, and acceptance and rejection, social science practitioners may look to love shaped relationality as a telos[2] for the work, and practices that incarnate love as a means to assist people toward engaging such a goal.[3] Furthermore as Browning proposes, because all therapeutic approaches represent large culturally agreed to stories about life, our concern should not be whether underlying stories exist, but rather if their versions of normal fit with people's hopes for themselves.[4]

I am aware that in my promotion of one particular story—the Jesus one—I am risking affronting personal freedom to choose. Doing so has almost become an anathema in this relativistic, postmodern era.[5] However, I am not content to follow the recent trend of attempting to disconnect practice and story. This is not because I am unconcerned with justice, but because in my view the style of loving at the center of the Jesus story has the potential to safeguard its adherents from violating difference. Put another way, the Jesus story creates space for the infinite to

---

1. Johnson, *Emotionally Focused Couple Therapy*, 14–61.
2. *Telos* is a Greek word used initially by Aristotle meaning "end," "purpose," or "goal."
3. Balswick et al., *Reciprocating Self*, 27–118.
4. Browning, *Fundamental Practical Theology*.
5. Webster, "Grand Narrative of Jesus Christ."

enter the particularity of people's lives and relationships without perpetrating violence on the particular.[6]

I hope that it will now be clear that in drawing attention to the existence of large stories that give coherence to each therapeutic approach, my aim is to make it possible to evaluate their usefulness in terms of sketching a vision of wellbeing. This evaluation moves beyond *what* we do to include *why* we do it. While it is usual for practitioners of the social sciences to represent one—or, increasingly, an eclectic blend—of the main schools of counseling psychology, beyond the alleviation of pain and suffering it is less usual for practitioners to consider the kind of person that is being shaped in the therapeutic process.

To illustrate what I see as the limited way counseling psychologies can be used without awareness of the vision of wellbeing they represent, I will cite four prominent examples. First, a psychodynamic approach interprets human behaviour in the light of underlying psychological forces, and seeks to provide insight into, and connections between these.[7] I wonder if consideration could also be given to which interpretations and connections may be more likely to contribute to wellbeing. Second, social psychology interprets people's thoughts, feelings, and behaviors in the light of the influence of others and seeks to develop personal agency in response.[8] Again, through locating the use of this approach alongside a preferred meta-story, such as the Jesus one, a person's search for wellbeing could be more substantially resourced. Third, practices based on humanist psychology aim to re-prioritise individual human need and values above the needs and desires of other humans.[9] Might the effectiveness of a therapist's work be enhanced through gaining inspiration from the Jesus story's concern for understanding people from a larger community and social canvas? And fourth, cognitive psychology intends to shape internal mental process to achieve desirable feelings and behaviors.[10] Might further consideration be given in the light of the Jesus story to *which* thinking is more likely to lead to experiences of wellbeing?

My overall proposal here is that each approach to counseling might be enhanced by locating their use within the larger canvas of the Jesus

---

6. Volf, *Exclusion and Embrace*, 1–24.
7. Lemma, *Introduction to the Practice of Psychoanalytic Psychotherapy*.
8. Deaux and Snyder, *Oxford Handbook of Personality and Social Psychology*.
9. Rogers, *On Becoming a Person*.
10. Beck, *Cognitive Behavior Therapy*.

story's invitation to practice love. Put another way, while each therapeutic approach arguably represents important insights of human life, their use would be enhanced by considering *why* their use contributes to a person's capacity to move away from experiencing distress ("hell") towards experiences of wellbeing ("heaven"). In the light of this, my hope in looking to the Jesus story is that we will find a vision of heaven as a satisfactory telos for human development.

Sketching Jesus' Call to Encounter

Central to the Jesus story is a call to recognise that relations are central to human life, and to accept the invitation to participate in the shared life of God towards a restoration telos.[11] God's hope for human relating is represented across the span of the Jewish and Christian Scriptures, including in the many sub-stories about Jesus' relating. Together, these stories of encounter recast the familiar assumption that people merely choose—or not—to engage *in* relations. Instead they suggest that people exist *as* relation just as the Father, Son, and Holy Spirit exist in relations.[12] And so, the Jesus story, together with my practice observation, support the view that quality of relating needs to be one of the central concerns of social science practitioners. And further, quality relating has something to do with engaging in the way Jesus does.

These insights lead me to conclude that our primary ethical task as social scientists who claim Christian identity must involve asking what cruciform love looks like in the detail of day to day life. Furthermore, for those who do not wish to be associated with the Christian religion—where love is understood personally—love can also be understood ethically as an implicit faith category. By "implicit faith" I mean local human commitments, beliefs, and values that are represented in people's actions. While these commitments may have their roots in religion, these links typically remain invisible. This is much the same methodology Paul Tillich uses with regard to the categories of guilt, meaninglessness, and despair.[13] In his work Tillich attempts to make these ethics available for everyone to engage with, regardless of religious affiliation. When viewed in these ways, whether practitioners of the social sciences claim Christian

---

11. Grenz, *Social God and the Relational Self*.
12. Torrance, *Christian Doctrine of God*.
13. Tillich, *Courage to Be*.

identity or not, cruciform love can be freely embraced by all. My hope in suggesting this is to inspire engagement in this form of practical theology that sets up dialogue between questions that emerge in practice with answers drawn from faith stories. In this case an aspect of the Jesus story is represented in the Gospel of Luke's telling of the encounter between Jesus and Zacchaeus.

The Zacchaeus Story and Three Relational Themes

> He entered Jericho and was passing through it. 2 A man was there named Zacchaeus; he was a chief tax-collector and was rich. 3 He was trying to see who Jesus was, but on account of the crowd he could not, because he was short in stature. 4 So he ran ahead and climbed a sycamore tree to see him, because he was going to pass that way. 5 When Jesus came to the place, he looked up and said to him, "Zacchaeus, hurry and come down; for I must stay at your house today." 6 So he hurried down and was happy to welcome him. 7 All who saw it began to grumble and said, "He has gone to be the guest of one who is a sinner." 8 Zacchaeus stood there and said to the Lord, "Look, half of my possessions, Lord, I will give to the poor; and if I have defrauded anyone of anything, I will pay back four times as much." 9 Then Jesus said to him, "Today salvation has come to this house, because he too is a son of Abraham. 10 For the Son of Man came to seek out and to save the lost" (Luke 19:1–10 NRSV).

We can assume that, as a collector of tax for the occupying Romans in first century CE Palestine, Zacchaeus is not generally popular. We can also assume that he is ostracized, and without many friends. It interests me that in the Luke 19:1–10 account, the writer has chosen an outcast as the recipient of Jesus' attention. This choice appears to contradict with whom we might expect an esteemed visitor to the Palestinian village to converse. However, it is Zacchaeus, a man generally perceived as a greedy, ambitious, and manipulative businessman who we see Jesus pausing on his walkabout to speak with.

While we might not be familiar with the intricacies of the cultural lore—including financial arrangements under the occupying Romans—it is not difficult to recognize, and perhaps even identify at some level with Zacchaeus' familiarity with social isolation. When we reflect a little deeper on Zacchaeus' experience, we can recognize that relational isolation and alienation—whether it is imposed by the community or maintained by the choices we make—is a familiar human experience. Like many of us, Zacchaeus appears caught in an isolating cycle. As readers we first meet Zacchaeus at a potential turning point in his story, a place that is inconsistent with what we might expect given his history of choosing money over relationship. In v. 5 we read: "when Jesus came to that place [beside Zacchaeus in a sycamore tree], He looked up and said, 'Zacchaeus, hurry down, for I must stay at your house today.'" Unaware of this approaching moment, Zacchaeus has positioned himself geographically just close enough to see Jesus, but far enough away to avoid face to face contact. As a shrewd entrepreneur, Zacchaeus appears open to any advantage the visiting Jesus might afford him, while attempting to remain firmly in control.

Zacchaeus is not alone in exercising this kind of caution in his exposure to others. It is at this point in the story that love visits in the person of Jesus, and as C.S Lewis reminds us in *The Four Loves*, "to love at all is vulnerable, love anything and your heart will certainly be wrung and possibly broken."[14] We can observe that this is precisely the point when Zacchaeus makes himself vulnerable to something new: love encounter in the person of Jesus. I wonder what it was that drew Jesus to Zacchaeus? Perhaps it was recognizing his longing for meaningful connection that he typically directed towards making money. Here we have an invitation for practitioners to follow suit, to recognise people's longing for connection and respond by incarnating love in the form of hospitality. In doing so we might also engage our clients at points when they take timid steps towards encounter. This initial part of the Zacchaeus story invites us to allow love to do its work, through gently offering things like recognition of longing, acceptance, and hospitable presence.

My hope is that together these practices of love offer a richer form of presence than the impoverished forms of relating our clients may typically settle for. Recently the New Zealand Herald newspaper ran a story about a growing phenomenon that in "an era when dating is at your fingertips very few Japanese young people are choosing to go on a date, or even get intimate with another person." According to an investigation by SBS News The Feed, "millions of people under 30 simply turn to masturbation clubs or robots for intimacy."[15] Luke's account of Jesus meeting

---

14. Lewis, *Four Loves*, 169–70.
15. "Why Young Single People in Japan Are No Longer Having Sex," para. 6.

Zacchaeus is just as relevant today as it was when it was written. I claim this because it represents a time worn explanation for why longing for relationship can become misdirected, and insight into how to engage people's longing in ways more likely to lead to experience of personal and relational wellbeing.

This relevance is because it engages a fundamental dilemma we all face: how to experience encounter when we are so accustomed to staying safe at the same time. For Zacchaeus climbing the tree to watch, he unwittingly risked more than he foresaw. I like to observe that it was in response to Zacchaeus having taken this tentative first step that Jesus responded, speaking to him directly. Now, we witness the unexpected. This time Zacchaeus takes a conscious risk and accepts the invitation to host. James Olthuis refers to these kinds of deliberate steps towards encounter as *beautiful risk*.[16] *Risk* because acting with regard to relational longing inevitably exposes us to fear and shame, and *beautiful* because the call of love when it is enacted personally proves to be the antidote to life crippling and inhibiting experiences.

The Zacchaeus story is just one of many places we can observe this love orientated relational anthropology reflected throughout the Jewish and Christian Scriptures. As the creation story unfolds in the early chapters of Genesis, we hear that God creates Adam and Eve in God's image, to reflect their glory and to enjoy fellowship. However, Adam and Eve turn from God in the mistaken belief that they can experience a similar quality of flourishing alone. As a result of this mistake, they become enslaved by shame and fear, and flee into the garden's shadows. In this more secluded part of the garden, we see Adam and Eve trying to resist meeting God coming as usual to walk with them in the cool of the evening. God's response to Adam and Eve's isolation is expressed in his call, "where are you?" (Gen 3:9). Adam answers, "I heard you in the garden, and I was afraid because I was naked, so I hid" (v. 10). Brad Jersak and others observe that this exchange represents "the fundamental relational shape of God's nature."[17] Luke refers to the same love-shaped relations in the life of Jesus at the end of the Zacchaeus story: "The Son of man came to seek and to save the lost" (Luke 19:10). I think we as practitioners of the social sciences are invited to remember this shape of love in action, identifying longing and responding by using all of

---

16. Olthuis, *Beautiful Risk*.
17. Jersak, *More Christlike God*.

the therapeutic technologies at our disposal to assist us as we incarnate cruciform love.

Based on the Jesus I see represented in the Zacchaeus story, I cannot help reading the Genesis 3 reference to "saving the lost" through a relational lens. In this way "saving" involves being personally found by practical love in the midst of all the ways we are lost from relationship with ourselves, God, one another, and the natural world. This lostness is the core human condition that the church has long referred to as *incurvatus in se*. While we are constantly being urged not to remain turned in on ourselves, and instead stand up straight, and look out in order to encounter God and others, and ourselves through one another, the struggle with shame and associated self-sufficiency remains until someone comes on behalf of love to find us. Based on all that I have said so far, it seems appropriate to draw a parallel between the sycamore tree and a counseling room because they are both places people arrive at in response to deep longing for relationship.

I see two further implications here for us as practitioners of the social sciences. The first is the need to be skilled observers for the many subtle ways our clients position themselves to "see" something new, particularly when it involves movement towards encounter and away from isolation. If we take seriously the notion that personhood is fundamentally relational, then this must be one of our central concerns. In other words, we need to give priority to listening for relational longing, and to the development of conversations in which people's longing for love is privileged.

The second implication for us as social practitioners is that, like Jesus, we need to be ready to exceed our clients' limited view of relating. Like Jesus, this "more" needs to be more personal than expected. More personal in two practical ways: first because it has us *recognising* the uniqueness of the client-person's struggles to relate; and second because it involves us making ourselves personally vulnerable. As a key feature of incarnated love, this vulnerability enables others to similarly risk vulnerability and thus to experience more significant relational presence. In the story we see Jesus going home to dine at Zacchaeus' home. Before offering himself as a host to Zacchaeus's relational meal, Jesus invites Zacchaeus into the role of host: "I see you, and would like to dine with you." In practice, then, for love to lead to personal transformation, it must be preceded by interpersonal transformation characterised by the sharing of mutual vulnerability.[18] We can only speculate on the exact shape of the resulting personal transformation in Zacchaeus' life, but we do hear in v. 8 that he pursued reconciliation with those he had wronged. In practical terms, power must be shared if love is to prosper.

Joining Forces with Love

The last aspect of the story I want to draw attention to is the different levels on which change appears to have taken place. These are important because together they represent the holistic nature of our incarnational anthropology. The first change is the one we have already been discussing: interpersonal transformation. We read in v. 6 that Zacchaeus "came down at once and welcomed him gladly." While we don't typically have trees in our offices, we can read "coming down" and "glad welcome" as desirable relational changes resulting from our therapeutic work. The second site of transformation is intrapersonal. Resulting from Jesus' offer to lovingly and vulnerably encounter reciprocally, as both guest and host, Zacchaeus clearly undergoes a change of mind and heart that results in changed actions. The third level of transformation evident in the story concerns Zacchaeus' social context. In v. 8 we read that Zacchaeus stood up and said, "Here and now I give half of my possessions to the poor, and if I have cheated anybody out of anything, I will pay back four times the amount." Again, I am merely speculating, but my contention is that this kind of change in behaviour from someone who the community usually experienced as selfish and possibly even dangerous would have changed aspects of the social fabric of their community. And so, while practitioners might be accustomed to viewing people from more atomised or reductionist perspectives, surely the lead Jesus takes in showing what love looks like when incarnated into real lives and relationships challenges us to take a broader approach, one that invites us to seek personal, relational, and social transformation.

I want to emphasize that Zacchaeus transformation did not come from hearing objective talk about love. Instead, he experienced it personally in his encounter with the person of Jesus. I am convinced that at the heart of God's call of love is a call to subjectivity. This implies that therapeutic practice needs to be as personal as it is professional. Jesus' example is a challenge to me in my counseling practice. For example, I

---

18. Volf, "Trinity Is Our Social Program."

do not believe Zacchaeus only changed because of the things Jesus said; the strength of his contribution lay in the gift of his presence. This can be difficult for us as modern practitioners of the social sciences to grasp well. In spite of all of this I continually find my work shaped by Descartes' invitation to prioritize change of the mind as the path towards people experiencing wellbeing.[19] This has me emphasizing thoughtful conversation at the expense of attending to interpersonal dynamics. With this insight I want to invite practitioners—and theologians—to reflect on their own therapeutic presence. The story of Jesus invites us as practitioners to shape our therapeutic presence in the style of love. Neil Pembroke summaries this point well: "Tender love is at the heart of healing relationships. This is a love that is characterized by empathy, vulnerability, suffering with, deep respect, and strong affirmation. We are able to love in this way when we are lit up by the love of the Spirit of Christ."[20]

In Conclusion

C.S. Lewis offers a creative illustration of this distinction between subjectivity and objectivity in his "Meditation in a Toolshed."[21] Here, he uses the terms "looking at" and "looking along" to distinguish between observation and experience. He asks his readers to imagine a dark toolshed with a shaft of light streaming in through a hole in the roof, and draws attention to two possibilities. The first is to look at the shaft of light and the things in the shed it illuminates. The second possible stance is to place our heads in the shaft of light and look along it to the things outside the shed, including the source of light. Part of God's call to us as practitioners in the Zacchaeus story is to follow Jesus' example and place ourselves in the way of the light, to look along it towards its source. Here, in doing so we develop our capacity to love—that is to engage relationships more fully—and to offer those who come in contact with us the opportunity to do so too. This might look like being welcomed with tenderness, being called by name, having power shared with, and being honored as a person to be known not merely as an object to be judged and used, but as someone with a name who can and needs to be known. The extent to which we risk being encountered by love is the extent to

19. Descartes, *Discourse on Method*.

20. Pembroke, "Trinitarian Perspective on the Counseling Alliance in Narrative Therapy," 20.

21. Lewis, "Meditation in a Toolshed."

which we will be able to offer the people we work with this same gift of welcome and presence, so that they might also have the opportunity to choose the beautiful risk of being found by love.

Bibliography

Balswick, Jack O., Pamela Ebstyne King, and Kevin S. Reimer. *The Reciprocating Self: Human Development in Theological Perspective*. Downers Grove: InterVarsity, 2016.

Beck, Judith S. *Cognitive Behavior Therapy: Basics and Beyond*. New York: Guildford, 2011.

Browning, Don. *A Fundamental Practical Theology*. Minneapolis: Augsburg Fortress, 1991.

Deaux, Kay, and Mark Snyder. *The Oxford Handbook of Personality and Social Psychology*. Oxford: Oxford University Press, 2013.

Descartes, René. *A Discourse on Method*. Oxford: Oxford University Press, 2018.

Grenz, Stanely J. *The Social God and the Relational Self: A Trinitarian Theology of the Imago Dei*. Louisville: Westminster John Knox, 2001.

Jersak, Brad. *A More Christlike God: A More Beautiful Gospel*. Pasadena: Plain Truth Ministries, 2016.

Johnson, Sue M. *Emotionally Focused Couple Therapy with Trauma Survivors*. London: Guilford, 2005.

Lemma, Alessandra. *Introduction to the Practice of Psychoanalytic Psychotherapy*. 2nd ed. Hoboken: Wiley, 2016.

Lewis, C. S. "Meditation in a Toolshed." In *God in the Dock: Essays on Theology and Ethics*, 212–15. Grand Rapids: Eerdmans, 1970.

———. *The Four Loves*. New York: Harcourt Brace Jovanovich, 1960.

Olthuis, James. *The Beautiful Risk: A New Psychology of Loving and Being Loved*. Eugene, OR: Wipf & Stock, 2006.

Pembroke, Neil. "A Trinitarian Perspective on the Counseling Alliance in Narrative Therapy." *Journal of Psychology and Theology* 24 (2005) 13–20.

Rogers, Carl. *On Becoming a Person*. London: Constable, 1961.

Tillich, Paul. *The Courage to Be*. New Haven: Yale University Press, 1952.

Torrance, Thomas. *The Christian Doctrine of God, One Being Three Persons*. Edinburgh: T&T Clark, 1996.

Volf, Miroslav. *Exclusion and Embrace: A Theological Exploration of Identity, Otherness, and Reconciliation*. Nashville: Abingdon, 2019.

———. "'The Trinity Is Our Social Program': The Doctrine of the Trinity and the Shape of Social Engagement." *Modern Theology* 14 (1998) 404–21.

Webster, John. "The Grand Narrative of Jesus Christ: Barth's Christology." In *Karl Barth: A Future for Postmodern Theology?*, edited by Geoff Thompson and Christiaan Mostert, 29–48. Adelaide: Australian Theological Forum, 2000.

"Why Young Single People in Japan Are no Longer Having Sex." *NZ Herald*, September 27, 2018. https://www.nzherald.co.nz/lifestyle/why-young-single-people-in-japan-are-no-longer-having-sex/NRCA3DQSVTZEPBCQDIRZN6I7M4/.

Response 1: Wellbeing

Formation through Friendship, Love, and Song

Jonathan Rivett Robinson

In all people-centerd work, whether understood as social practice or Christian ministry (or for many of us, both), it is a truism that *who* we are is even more important than *what* we do. The formation of the self has such a huge impact on our ability to relate to others, that any technical practical skill and knowledge can easily be undermined by poor character, emotional reactivity, or a lack of empathy. The question of personal formation is then an essential one, even as it is a deeply personal one that cannot be addressed by "one-size-fits-all" approaches. Likewise, the same character issues that so powerfully affect the Christian social practitioner equally hinder the client in their lives and relationships. Thus, the preceding three essays have touched on a critical aspect of Christian social practice: how do we become who we are called to be? And, how do we help others become who they are called to be?

Friendship

Anne-Marie Ellithorpe has provided us with a compelling exploration of friendship as "integral to the faithful outworking of social vocations within communities of practice." Rooted in our experience of the friendship of God "this friendship impacts other dimensions of life, as it spills over into concern for and friendship with others, earth, and self." Friendship is understood as "mutuality and equal regard," but also a "premoral good" (i.e., a basic human need).

Most fascinating to this reader is the argument that friendship has become the victim of neoliberal social forces. Ellithorpe writes, "The elevating of instrumentalist, materialist values over relational values, and the detaching of individual freedom from communal responsibility, continues to have a negative impact on relationality in general, and on friendship in particular." She rightly notes how long work hours and time spent on technology absorb time that could otherwise be spent relating positively to our fellow human beings.[1] Yet, friendship also seems to be the antidote to such societal sickness, as friendship can generate "a willingness to help others in times of crisis" and actively challenges "various forms of injustice, including unjust laws, and social customs."

Ellithorpe argues that parental metaphors for God should be supplemented by images of friendship. Here, several scriptural texts come to mind which might support and also nuance Ellithorpe's argument. Abraham is called a "friend of God" in Isa 41:8 and Jas 2:23. God speaks to Moses as to a "friend" in Exod 33:11. And Jesus calls his disciples "friends" in John 15:13–15. In each of those texts, no one claims for themselves to be a friend of God or of Jesus.

Indeed, there is a marked asymmetry in any relationship between God and his creatures. It is not healthy to worship your friends. In a good friendship there is an equal exchange of benefits. But how can we benefit God? The asymmetry of the parent-child relationship seems to be a more appropriate image, and it is certainly more frequently employed in Scripture. Likewise, the words of Jesus, which seem most readily available for a wider application, are striking in this regard: "You are my friends *if you do what I command*" (John 15:14, emphasis added). I would not want a human friendship like that, but with Jesus that is as it should be.

---

1. I initially wrote this prior to the COVID-19 crisis. Now I edit this under New Zealand's "level 4 lockdown," and have to admit the power of technology to allow relational connection without physical proximity. As well as pastoral care, prayer meetings, and online lectures and seminars, technology such as Zoom and YouTube have allowed church leaders to not just connect with their church but also with diaspora, people who have moved away or friends and family of congregation members, and—most significantly—the housebound. Our small Dunedin online gatherings are now attended by people from around the country and even overseas! None of that, of course, diminishes Ellithorpe's point. Indeed, the vast increase in people watching Netflix at this time attests to how technology can take us away from human interaction—even from those "in our bubble"—while we relate to fictional characters on the screen who do not even know we exist.

The problem here is applying a non-scriptural model of friendship to a biblical passage. I am not suggesting Ellithorpe has done this, but it shows the difficulty of using friendship as a static concept.

Perhaps this is what Ellithorpe is arguing when she calls pastors to form "multi-dimensional friendships that serve as schools of love, hospitality, freedom, wisdom, and compassion, and foster civic friendship." Friendship is then a loose idea of mutual regard and benefit (more biblically, of love) which must be adjusted to many different situations. Another scriptural text which mentions friendship is Jesus' enigmatic parable of the shrewd (or dishonest) steward (Luke 16:1–15). There Jesus states, "I tell you, use worldly wealth to gain friends for yourselves, so that when it is gone, you will be welcomed into eternal dwellings" (Luke 16:9, NIV). While friendship has sometimes been used as a *means* of evangelism, I much prefer to think of friendship as a *goal* of evangelism. Ellithorpe perhaps implies agreement with this in her comment, "communities of faith will benefit from considering their identity as an open community of friends, modelling the open welcome and hospitality of God."[2]

Friendship presents as a powerful and essential Christian spiritual discipline, one we practice within the church, and with those outside. By practising mutuality of regard we avoid the one sided paternalism that has so often marred the history of Christian evangelism in the modern era. Recently, as a pastor of a church, I was on the end of the pastoral care team's sympathies—after a bereavement in my extended family. I felt awkward, but it was actually really good that they saw me not just as there for them but that they were to be there for me too, and that is surely friendship (the evocation here of the theme song from *Friends* was accidental, but seems apposite). It was humanizing, as well as humbling, to be the receiver and not just the giver of pastoral care.

Friendship requires a posture of humility and equality between the parties, and exposes us to other, often transformative, points of view. Friendship with people too similar to us is after all not real friendship, but only a form of self-love. A challenge both my local and national church context currently faces is dealing with difference. We have representatives in our church of many points on the theological spectrum, and the instinctive Protestant reliance on a doctrinal statement for unity is no

---

2. I wonder if Ellithorpe has considered the Quaker movement, also known as "the Religious Society of Friends" or even "Friends Church," and how their self-conscious designation as "friends" has impacted their ecclesiological praxis?

help to us. Perhaps recognizing friendship with God and with each other as our unifying principle, rather than "right belief," could be a way ahead for us. It is certainly what unites my local church at present; we *like* each other, even though we struggle with our diversity (i.e., not *being like* each other) at many points.

Found by Love

Ellithorpe frames Christian love and mutuality as friendship. In Lex McMillan's essay Jesus' friendship for the outsider is advanced as a model of love for us to follow in counseling practice.

McMillan explores the goal, or telos, of psychotherapy when it is specifically shaped by the Christian story. Rather than, as in Ellithorpe's essay, the friendship of others serving the formation of the practitioner, McMillan focuses on the way that personal, subjective, and loving relational connection with the client can lead to the "personal, relational, and social" trans-formation of the client.

McMillan rightly argues that social vocation cannot be simply a matter of alleviating "pain and suffering" but must have a greater goal. For the Christian practitioner this telos should emerge from our understanding of the gospel, what McMillan calls "the Jesus story." Problematically, McMillan appears to suggest that the Jesus story is just one story among many metanarratives which might address suffering and hope. He justifies the application of the Christian metanarrative, at the expense of other possible stories, on the basis that it is mitigated by "the hospitable essence of love that forms the primary ethics within the Jesus story." If all we need is a "hospitable essence of love," why should we bother with (the rest of) the Jesus story at all? While the Gospel story is no less than Jesus' loving and inclusive praxis towards outsiders, it is far more than that, and its truth and benefit to the believer is surely far more than that. Indeed, Jesus' exclusive claim over the believer is fundamental to the liberation the gospel brings—only by belonging completely to Christ are we set free (e.g., John 8:31–36). But that is a conversation for another day.

If we are to do more than alleviate suffering then a vision of human flourishing is required. The gospel vision of human flourishing stands in sharp contrast to materialistic individualistic consumerist values of Western society, at the heart of which is the avoidance of pain and inconvenience and the pursuit of pleasure and comfort. But in the Christian vision it would seem our suffering can be something to accept or even celebrate. For example, in Matt 5:11–12 Jesus tells his disciples to "rejoice and be glad" when reviled, persecuted, and slandered, because such treatment gives them solidarity with God's prophets. In Rom 5:3–4 Paul describes Christian joy in suffering, because of the way it deepens Christian character and experience of the Holy Spirit. Likewise, in 2 Cor 11:16–33 Paul boasts about his own suffering as authenticating his apostleship. And in 1 Pet 2:18–25 willingness to suffer unjustly is part of the Christian calling to walk in the footsteps of Christ.[3]

Beyond issues of human connection and suffering is the gospel call to be children of God. McMillan perhaps hints at this when he writes, "the Jesus story creates space for the infinite to enter the particularity of people's lives and relationships without perpetrating violence on the particular." At the heart of the gospel vision of human flourishing is the restored relationship between humanity and the "infinite" divine, that we should be reconciled to God through Christ (2 Cor 5:11–21). Of course, it is often inappropriate for a Christian counselor to urge a client to be reconciled to a God they might not even believe in, and I approve McMillan's instinct to be respectful of other worldviews. What I would ask for though, is a fuller account of human flourishing, a telos beyond loving human connection—as important as that is.

For McMillan, this telos, of "love shaped relational development," is demonstrated and illustrated by the story of Jesus and Zacchaeus (Luke 19:1–10). He identifies in Zacchaeus someone who had directed a longing for personal connection into the pursuit of money and who was avoiding relational closeness by climbing up a tree to see Jesus. In counterpoint to McMillan, I would suggest a different reading of the story. Luke states that Zacchaeus was a chief tax collector and rich (Luke 19:2). He was therefore in a powerful and privileged position within a network of tax collectors, not an isolated outsider but a wealthy insider. Luke also makes it plain that Zacchaeus climbed the tree because he was vertically challenged (Luke 19:3), not because he was shy, an unlikely personality attribute for a chief tax collector. Further, rather than loneliness, curiosity is given as his motivation ("he was trying to see who Jesus was," Luke 19:3).

---

3. For in-depth studies on this deeply counter-cultural theme, a good starting point is the edited volume, Kilby and Davies, *Suffering and the Christian Life*.

Zacchaeus' joyful response to Jesus' self-invitation (Luke 19:5) likewise does not evidence any relational awkwardness or feelings of unworthiness to be a host; instead he welcomes him happily (19:6). It is only when the crowd grumble against Jesus, that "he has gone to be the guest of a sinner" (Luke 19:7), that Zacchaeus shows any sign of self-consciousness. In the presence of Jesus, the words of the crowd evidently convict Zacchaeus of his sins and he immediately resolves, in a promise to Jesus, that he will make things right (Luke 19:8).

Yes, Jesus' grace filled invitation to relationship was transformative, but so were the hard words of the crowd who questioned his worthiness. In the context of Jesus' acceptance, Zacchaeus was able to accept the painful challenge of the crowd. As far as we can tell from the account in Luke (and psychologizing biblical stories is fraught with danger)[4] it is only in the context of Jesus' acceptance that Zacchaeus is able to comprehend his need to reconcile to the community he has exploited, and, as a sinner, to God. The telos of the encounter was Zacchaeus' reconciliation; the loving relationship with Jesus was the means by which that end was achieved.

McMillan issues a vital challenge: that Christian counselors "consider the kind of person that is being shaped in the therapeutic process." Surely, this is a radical and difficult call and goes beyond counseling, to our personal interactions in any sphere of life (as well as other social vocations). The Zacchaeus story, in the reading I have proffered, suggests that one telos for counseling is the restoration of broken relationships. Within a Christian vision of human flourishing that telos must include that the client is reconciled towards God in Christ. The security and grace of the counseling relationship may create a transformational space where the client can hear, perhaps for the first time, the complaints of those they have hurt and comprehend their nature as a sinner. In terms of formation, the ability to recognise our own failings and contribution to the relational disconnection that causes us pain is a fundamental step forward in emotional maturity and for the maintenance of relational wholeness. It is also a fundamental step in the process of Christian conversion.[5] The therapeutic relationship thus does not become a substitute for the relationships that are broken, but is theorised as a space of grace where

---

4. For a particularly egregious example of this, see in Robinson, "To See Your Face Is Like Seeing the Face of God."

5. In traditional theological terms we would call this "conviction of sin" and "repentance." See here Oden, *Classic Christianity*, 561–82.

the client can experience a reorientation in their lives towards right relationships with others and with God.

A Song in the Night

McMillan has highlighted for us the importance of metanarrative, the big story that shapes our telos and praxis. Ryan Lang's essay explores the way that song can help us connect our life and work with the metanarrative of Christian Scripture. Lang has given us a deeply personal autobiographical account of his own experience of being sustained and formed in Christian social practice through "a song in the night." His own experience of formation through song is placed within a scriptural frame of reference as he argues that Israel was a people "born in song," that Jesus himself sang "a song in the night," and that this song recurred throughout the scriptural story, eventually being reprised in Revelation 15 beside the sea of glass and fire. For Lang this song is "the voice of the church, gathered into the Lamb's own song of thanksgiving to his Father."

As a biblical scholar, I find myself hesitant at a key point. When I look at Mark 14:26, "When they had sung the hymn" (NRSV), it seems a lean and cursory note. In fact the Greek here has no noun for hymn; the word Lang cites (*hymneō*) is a verb. There is no emphasis on "the hymn" or "a hymn" but only a description of them (Jesus and the disciples) singing. An absolutely literal translation would be "when they had sung"; the hymn is only implied. Further, the earliest ancient source that suggests that Jesus might have sung Psalm 118 is the third century CE *Mishnah* (*Pesaḥim* 10.5–7). There is no such identification in either Mark or Matthew. Lang has thus made something of a theological mountain out of an exegetical molehill. But Lang's argument has a poetic force; I can't resist it. And anyway, what else would Jesus have sung?[6]

In Lang's argument, song allows the singer not just to recount a story but to experience it for themselves. It is an engagement of the whole person, body, mind and emotions, with the story of God. Thus, he writes, "that singing is not a heart-warming extra in Christian life. The songs of God offer an anchor in these very nights." Singing such songs leads us from one place to another. In other words, they can be used to form our character, emotions, and self-understanding. For Lang, the "song

---

6. Psalm 118 is certainly prominent earlier in the passion account, e.g., Mark 11:9; 12:10–11.

in the night" is a mode of transportation. It is a way to relive salvation history and, vitally, to discover the singer's own place within that story. Lang's experience allowed him to realize that he was part of something bigger than his own limited life and contribution. The "song in the night" connected his particular situation to the universal salvation story of Christian faith.

Lang's argument is not simply about the power of music, but the power of music to relay to us a larger story and connect us into it. His brief but stimulating overview of the song in Scripture shows how essential our knowledge of the scriptural story, both Old and New Testaments, is to the formational process. The song allows the whole person to grasp what might have been only an intellectual proposition before. But importantly, we have to know what that story is, otherwise we might as well be singing *Dancing Queen* or *Bohemian Rhapsody*. At the risk of stating what is obvious, the importance and power of scriptural song and of knowledge of the scriptures for the formation of the Christian practitioner, is affirmed.

This insight may seem to be undermined by Lang's recounting of a second experience; this time singing served to unite a religiously (and presumably, culturally) diverse group of workers and encourage them in their task. Even though the group were working from different faith stories, his experience there reveals the power of song to mediate spirituality across such divides and to foster group bonding (or friendship!). This "song in the night" was not just a personal method of coping but a way of sustaining and unifying a whole group in difficult and draining cross-cultural social practice. But what of the particularity of the gospel story? I'm reminded here of the extraordinary story of Imam Din Shahbaz, a Punjabi poet who translated the entire Psalter into Punjabi within the metrical system of Indian classical music in the late nineteenth century (he lost his sight in the process).[7] Recently, Pakistani Christians have rediscovered these Psalm settings and begun to use them for their own discipleship and worship. But the resurgence of Psalm singing among Pakistani Christians has also opened up relationships with Muslim musical scholars and Sufi mystics, creating a safe avenue for the Christian minority in Pakistan to share their spirituality and engage in inter-religious dialogue.[8]

---

7. See, e.g., Sadiq, "Precious Gift."
8. See the first-hand account of Sarwar, "Psalms, Sufis and Peacemaking."

Despite the power of song, in many ways a song is a less threatening way of holding forth truth claims. People can object to you preaching at them on the street (perhaps reasonably so?). They are less likely to complain if you sing a gospel song; a heartfelt rendition of Amazing Grace, for example, is appreciated whether the hearer, or even singer, is a believer or not. I am not sure that Lang's second anecdote is an effective example of a scriptural "song in the night." *The Steadfast Love of the Lord Never Ceases* is sufficiently vague and universal in its lyrics (Lam 3:22–23) that I imagine any of the world religions could sing it happily to whoever they consider their "Lord" to be. The salvation story of Scripture and the claims of the God of Israel are not explicit in that song. However, it remains a powerful example of the spiritual and formational power of a singing faith.

In Col 3:16 we read, "Let the message of Christ dwell among you richly as you teach and admonish one another with all wisdom through psalms, hymns, and songs from the Spirit, singing to God with gratitude in your hearts." This, among other clues in the New Testament, is highly suggestive of the central place singing took in early Christian communities, as well as the expectation of its formative effect. It seems to me that the most prevalent contemporary concept of Christian singing is as worship which is directed from the individual to God. This misses out the impact that singing can have on us, and the way it can change who we are. It is possible that this habit of singing *to each other* is in need of rediscovery. Lang's essay helpfully points us in that direction.

Conclusion

I am an extrovert—I love making friends; and I am a musician—I love singing and making music. It is easy for me to embrace the theses of these different essays. For those not so inclined, I hope they do not dismiss these insights out of hand. Each chapter highlights a fundamental aspect of Christian discipleship.

These disciplines of receiving and giving loving friendship and of sacred song might seem somewhat soft and wishy-washy in our contemporary world, focused as it is on performance indicators, budgets, and time-sheets. But for those who care to look, there is also unequivocal evidence from scientific studies of the psychological and health benefits of both friendships and singing. In utilitarian and materialist terms, investing in singing and friendships will make you a better worker. Encountering love and grace in the therapeutic relationship and/or discovering a larger story which gives meaning to life will no doubt improve the client's outcomes. But these are perhaps poor incentives to the Christian.

I would prefer to state that investing in our own friendships can bring us closer to God and help us as we seek to be an extension of God's friendship to others; that extending grace-filled loving friendship to others humanizes them and us, and creates possibilities of redemptive transformation; and that participating in sacred song can reform our identity in the story of God's salvation and strengthen us against the attrition of loving and serving others in a broken world.

All three essays are in some sense about bringing ourselves, and our efforts to do good, into the wider context of the reality of God's goodness, the gospel story, and the saving power of Jesus Christ. It was a pleasure to read and interact with them. My brief comments here could not hope to do justice to either the essays or their subjects, but I hope I have respectfully and helpfully furthered some aspects of the conversations, or at least provided a constructively contrasting voice. For their scholarship, bringing to our attention and provoking thought about ways of further becoming who we are called to be and of helping others to become who they are called to be, Ellithorpe, McMillan, and Lang deserve our thanks.

Bibliography

Kilby, Karen, and Rachel Davies, eds. *Suffering and the Christian Life*. Edinburgh: T&T Clark, 2019.
Oden, Thomas C. *Classic Christianity: A Systematic Theology*. New York: Harper, 1992.
Robinson, Jonathan R. "'To See Your Face Is Like Seeing the Face of God': Pastoral and Systemic Reflections on Forgiveness and Theosis in the Jacob Story." In *The Art of Forgiveness*, edited by Phil Halstead and Myk Habets, 55–65. Louisville: Fortress Academic, 2018.
Sadiq, Yousaf. "A Precious Gift: The Punjabi Psalms and the Legacy of Imam-ud-Din Shahbaz." *International Bulletin of Missionary Research* 38, no. 1 (2014) 36–39.
Sarwar, Eric. "The Psalms, Sufis and Peacemaking: Creative and Critical Contextualized Musical Approach in Pakistan." Paper presented at the American Society of Missiology Annual Conference 2016, University of Northwestern–St. Paul, St. Paul, Minnesota, June 17–19, 2016. https://www.fuller.edu/wp-content/uploads/2018/01/Sarwar-ASM-2016-Psalms-and-Sufi-ggs.pdf.

Part II

FORMATION

Chapter 4

Towards a Christian Spirituality for Counselors

Neil Pembroke

For a long time now I have been interested, along with many others, in approaching personal and spiritual formation in a holistic manner. In 2007 I published a book entitled, *Moving Toward Spiritual Maturity: Psychological, Contemplative, and Moral Challenges in Christian Living.*[1] Though the book was intended for all Christians and therefore covered spiritual formation in a general way, I have had teachers of counseling contact me to thank me for my contribution and to inform me that it is on the list of required readings in their courses. They clearly share my conviction that for Christians in the counseling field spiritual formation plays a very significant role.

In this essay, I want to briefly reflect on five qualities that I contend play a vital role for counselors committed to personal and spiritual growth. These qualities span the domains of spiritual character, moral character, and positive psychology. I refer to vulnerability, compassion, availability, integrity, and wholeness. Clearly, there are more attributes that could be added to the list. Let me simply say that in my experience, and with confirmation from the writers I engage below, the ones I have identified are absolutely central. Even if a counselor decided that these were the only ones they would concentrate on, they would have more

---

1. Pembroke, *Moving Toward Spiritual Maturity*.

than enough to keep them challenged for their entire working life (and beyond).

Before moving to a discussion of the five select attributes, I want to briefly mention some of the work by pastoral theologians and others who join me in acknowledging that spiritual formation is a multi-domain activity. They write from the perspective of companioning others, but it is of course implied that a holistic approach will be adopted by the counselor/caregiver in their own quest for personal and spiritual maturity.

Many years ago now, Don Browning argued that along with the psychological orientation there is also a moral context in pastoral care.[2] The proposal for a shift from concentrating exclusively on intrapsychic, interpersonal, and developmental dynamics to including moral issues has been very influential.[3] William Schmidt, for his part, attends to the spiritual horizon of psychology. Schmidt helpfully acknowledges the contribution of the spiritual practice called "pilgrimage" in facilitating healing and recovery for persons suffering from grief and loss.[4] Also significant is the argument mounted by Jean Stairs that a comprehensive approach to caring for others requires the integration of theological and psychological insights with wise teaching on the spiritual life.[5] Stairs discusses the nature of the close relationship between pastoral care and the ministry of spiritual direction.

More recently, this theme has been developed in two important collections edited by Peter Madsen Gubi entitled *Spiritual Accompaniment and Counselling* and *What Counsellors and Spiritual Directors Can Learn from Each Other*.[6] The contributors present a psychologically informed approach to spiritual companioning and a spiritually attuned method for pastoral counseling. Highly significant issues such as building an effective relationship in spiritual companioning, prayer in counseling, and dialogue between counselors and religious pastoral carers are discussed, along with topics that stretch across the moral and spiritual domains such as forgiveness, spiritual abuse, and sexual abuse.

---

2. See Browning, *Moral Context*.

3. See Noyce, *Minister as Moral Counselor*; Miles, *Pastor as Moral Guide*; Capps, *Life Cycle and Care*, 33–52; Graham, *Moral Injury*.

4. Schmidt, "Transformative Pilgrimage."

5. Fairchild, "Guaranteed Not to Shrink"; Stairs, *Listening for the Soul*; Moon and Benner, *Spiritual Direction and Care*, 171–244; and Louw, "'Habitus' in Soul Care."

6. Gubi, *Spiritual Accompaniment and Counselling*; *Counsellors and Spiritual Directors*.

In his pastoral theology, Daniël Louw similarly rejects a narrow perspective on supporting personal and spiritual growth.[7] Louw construes the work of pastoral counseling as helping people correct unhealthy personal schemas.[8] He points out that the categories that make up a schema are moral, psychological, and spiritual in nature. The psychiatrist, Len Sperry, tackles the issue in his own particular way in his book *Transforming Self and Community*,[9] but he ends up at the same general place that the pastoral theologians do. The central principle is that helping people move toward spiritual and moral maturity requires a holistic approach. The corollary is that when it comes to attending to their own spiritual growth, counselors similarly need to include multiple domains.

Vulnerability

In coming now to reflection on five attributes spanning the domains of spiritual character, moral character, and positive psychology, I begin with vulnerability. For a very long time in my pastoral ministry I struggled to come to grips with my own fears, inadequacies, and short-comings. I wished that I could simply throw them off and be the strong, confident, calm, in-control person that I imagined the best counselors were. Finally an important moment of insight came: accepting my weaknesses and limitations, embracing my farcical humanity, is a positive. Such an attitude is an asset for a counselor. Counselor and author, Jeanne Ellin, gives sound advice when she says this: "Acknowledge your weakness and make it work for you; it can be a source of strength, a resource for you, whether it makes you aware of your humanness or is a source of increased sensitivity to the varied ways in which people respond to painful or stressful situations."[10]

The spiritual theologian, Henri Nouwen, tells the story of taking a group of final-year seminarians on retreat in preparation for their ordination. One of the students, feeling anxious about his future ministry, said, "I just hope that I'll be strong enough to be a good priest." To which

---

7. See Louw, *Mature Faith*; "Philosophical Counselling."
8. See Louw, "Philosophical Counselling."
9. See Sperry, *Transforming Self and Community*.
10. Ellin, *Listening Helpfully*, 32.

Nouwen responded, "I don't think your strength is really the issue. The question is whether or not you are weak enough for priesthood."

So what did Nouwen mean by this paradoxical reference to weakness as a strength in ministry? Well, for a start, it is evident that he is *not* connecting with the Pauline approach to the value of weakness. Recall what Paul says in 2 Cor 12:8–10:

> About this thing, I have pleaded with the Lord three times for it to leave me, but he has said, "My grace is enough for you: my power is at its best in weakness." So shall I be very happy to make my weaknesses my special boast so that the power of Christ may stay over me, and that is why I am quite content with my weaknesses, and with insults, hardships, persecutions, and the agonies I go through for Christ's sake. For it is when I am weak that I am strong.

Paul is here extolling the virtue in the apostle embracing his weakness in order to manifest the greatness of God. That God can change lives via the vehicle of "damaged goods" shows just how majestic God is. In this text, Paul is presenting an important gospel truth, but it is not what Nouwen has in mind. Rather, what we have is a theme that comes through quite often in Nouwen's writings, and especially in his classic book, *The Wounded Healer*.[11] That theme is that an inflated, unrealistic sense of one's personal strength keeps us apart from others. An unavoidable part of being human is to live with confusion, fear, destructive urges, deceit, failure, shame, and guilt. To pretend to ourselves and to others that we are always strong emotionally, spiritually, and morally is futile, silly, dishonest, and destructive. Our weakness is part of our common humanity. It is only when it is acknowledged and accepted that we can relate to others in an honest and real way. Moreover, it is through being in touch with our weakness that we release within ourselves a flow of compassion and understanding. It is not that a counselor must have experienced precisely the same kind of suffering or loss as the other person. Rather, it is that through her own painful experiences, whatever they may be, she entered for a time into that place of shadows in which the other person now finds himself. In the pastoral conversation, we find two fellow travellers who have passed the same way and feel a bond of communion. Alastair Campbell puts it well when he says that "[t]he wounded healer heals,

---

11. See Nouwen, *Wounded Healer*.

because he or she is able to convey, as much by presence as by the words used, both an awareness and a transcendence of loss."[12]

It is when we feel a bond of solidarity with another, borne out of a common journey into the shadowlands of human existence, that there is confidence, trust, and openness, and beyond that, hope. An important gift that a counselor can offer a person in pain, confusion, and despair is a re-kindling of hope. A person in the depths suffers under the awful burden of the thought, so powerful and all-pervasive, that they will always be there. The presence of the counselor, usually without them needing or wanting to make a specific reference to transcendence of similar experiences, becomes a sign of hope.

Compassion

I have been alluding to the link between woundedness and a capacity for compassion. It is now time to explore compassionate presence more fully. In the case of compassionate understanding, we draw the pain and distress of the other into our ownmost sphere. The biblical writers, in describing compassion, use the images of the womb, the bowels, and the heart to communicate this. They identify a deeply personal act in which the hurt the other suffers is experienced in that space which is most intimately our own.

Dianne Bergant observes that in the cluster of Hebrew words for compassion, *rhm* is the most prominent.[13] It has the primary meaning of "cherishing," "soothing," or "a gentle attitude of mind." It refers to a tender parental love. The word *rehem*, meaning womb, is also derived from this root. Hence, Bergant concludes that this Hebrew word-group indicates a bond like that between a mother and the child of her womb.[14]

The New Testament writers often use *eleos* (mercy) when speaking of compassion.[15] A form of the verb *oiktirō* (connoting sympathy) also appears. However, when reference is made to the compassion of Jesus, *splanchnon* is always used. In early Greek usage, the word denotes the "inward parts" of a sacrifice.[16] Later, it was used to refer to the "inward

12. Campbell, *Rediscovering Pastoral Care*, 42.
13. See Bergant, "Compassion."
14. See Bergant, "Compassion," 154.
15. See Bergant, "Compassion," 156.
16. This discussion of *splanchnon* in pre-NT and NT usage is informed by Köster, "Splanchnon."

parts of the body," and finally to the womb. We also find the noun form used in the *Testaments of the Twelve Patriarchs*. There it denotes "the center of feelings" or "noble feelings." Once the verb is used to indicate mere emotion, but it generally refers to the inner disposition which generates acts of mercy. The adjective, *eusplanchnos* (tender-hearted), denotes human virtue and the disposition of "pity."

The noun appears in three of Jesus' parables: the Good Samaritan, the Prodigal Son, and the Unmerciful Servant. Of particular interest for our reflection is the way Paul describes compassion. Only the noun occurs in his writings. He uses *splanchna* not merely to express natural emotions but as "a very forceful term to signify an expression of the total personality at the deepest level."[17] It occurs twice in Philemon (vv. 7, 20); reference is made to the refreshing of the *splanchna*. In v. 12 of that letter, Paul says that in Onesimus he is, in effect, coming in person with a claim for Philemon's love. Philippians 1:8 contains a unique phrase. Paul declares that "God can testify how I long for all of you with the affection (*splanchna*) of Jesus Christ." The reference is to "the love or affection which, gripping or moving the whole personality, is possible only in Christ . . ."[18]

In these various uses of the word "compassion" by the writers of the Scriptures, there are a number of key features. First, the idea of tenderness comes out in several places. Secondly, compassion is associated with an instinctive, intimate relationship; it is like the loving, soothing action of a mother or father. Finally, it refers (most clearly in Pauline usage) not just to an emotion, but to the deepest part of one's personality. This depth dimension is indicated by the cluster of inner parts identifying the seat of the emotion, namely the womb, the bowels, and the heart. We moderns naturally take these organismic references as metaphorical. It seems, however, that the Semitic view of emotion was very definitely psychosomatic.

In a study of the foundational role of compassion in pastoral care and counseling, Arthur Becker identifies both the intensity of emotion and the somatic base we have been discussing. For the writers of the Scriptures, he observes, compassion entails "a perception of another's pain, hurt, sorrow, longing, so intense and vivid and organismic that you

---

17. Köster, "*Splanchnon*," 1068.
18. Köster, "*Splanchnon*," 1068.

feel it 'in your guts.'"[19] Feminist pastoral theologians use expressions such as "the weeping womb" in their evocative descriptions of compassion.

Availability

The condition of the possibility of a compassionate presence is personal availability. The term "availability" refers to a willingness to dispose of oneself for the sake of the other. It indicates a readiness for self-giving in the service of others. The French philosopher, Gabriel Marcel, rightly says that it is simply another name for the Christian virtue of *caritas*. He also points out that there is a very close link between availability and receptivity to the other's experience—especially her pain and distress.[20] Marcel establishes the link between the two terms using the metaphor of "in-cohesion." To exist with others, he observes, is to be exposed to influences. It is not possible to be human without to some extent being permeable to those influences. Permeability, in its broadest sense, is associated with a certain lack of cohesion or density. Thus, the fact of being exposed to external influences is linked with a kind of *in-cohesion*. I am "porous," open to a reality which seeks to communicate with me. Marcel puts it this way: "I must somehow make room for the other in myself; if I am completely absorbed in myself, concentrated on my sensations, feelings, anxieties, it will obviously be impossible for me to receive, to incorporate in myself, the message of the other. What I called in-cohesion a moment ago here assumes the form of disposability . . ."[21]

Disposability, then, is closely associated with receptivity. Receptivity involves a readiness to make available one's personal center, one's ownmost domain. Marcel uses a different metaphor to capture this phenomenon; he refers to inviting others to be *chez soi* (at home). He observes that we receive others in a room, in a house, or in a garden, but not on unknown ground or in the woods. Receptivity means that I invite the other to "be at home" with me. A home receives the imprint of one's personality; something of myself is infused into the way my home-space is constructed. Contrast this with "the nameless sadness" associated with a hotel room; this is no-one's home. To share one's home-space is

---

19. Becker, "Compassion," 145.
20. See Marcel, *Creative Fidelity*, 87–91.
21. Marcel, *Creative Fidelity*, 88.

disposability or availability because "[t]o provide hospitality is truly to communicate something of oneself to the other."[22]

The meaning of hospitality can also be broadened to include receiving into oneself the appeal of another for understanding and compassion. When I open myself to the call of the other to be with her in her pain and confusion, I am able to spontaneously feel with her. The intonation of my words, my posture, and my facial expressions say to her that I am with her in her suffering.

Integrity

The fourth spiritual quality I wish to comment on is integrity. "To possess integrity is to be incapable of compromising that which we believe to be true . . . To possess integrity is to have a kind of inner strength which prevents us from bending to the influence of what is thought expedient, or fashionable or calculated to win praise; it is to be consistent and utterly trustworthy because of a constancy of purpose."[23] A person of integrity chooses convictions and personal consistency over satisfying the craving for popularity and conflict-free relations.

A number of psychologists refer to the true or authentic self and the false or conforming self. They contend that values are the primary factor in establishing a coherent sense of selfhood.[24] The suggestion is that when a person acts in accordance with their value structure they feel in touch with their core self. That is to say, living true to their deepest values leads to a sense of authenticity. A person whose words and actions are congruent with their value structure feels as though they are living out of their true self. It goes without saying that such authentic living is difficult to enact.

Living out of the true self means being unafraid to speak the truth. For most, if not all, of us, that's a big challenge. In his book *Who is Worthy?* Father Ted Kennedy opens his deeply challenging reflections on the church's relationship to gay and lesbian persons and to Australia's First Peoples with this comment: "Some time ago I suffered a stroke which triggered in me a decision to live the rest of my life as if I were already dead. I am now more inclined to state things as they are, or as I

---

22. Marcel, *Creative Fidelity*, 91.
23. Campbell, *Rediscovering Pastoral Care*, 12.
24. See Hitlin, "Values as Core of Identity."

see them, without fear or compromise."²⁵ The problem for many of us is that we can't achieve this illusion. We are very aware of being alive, and we are even more aware of the living hell others may wish to create for us!

In the context of counseling, this conversation reminds us of how crucially important it is to relate honestly and genuinely. There are times when we need to speak "an inconvenient truth" to a counselee. Counselees love us when we are empathic, understanding, and supportive; they are usually not so appreciative when we confront them about their self-deception and game-playing! It requires integrity to speak the truth as one sees it.

Integrity in the counselor also refers to her capacity to be "dependably real," as Carl Rogers so nicely put it.²⁶ Assuming the persona of the all-knowing and wise one, projecting a saintly presence, mimicking the style of another (admired) counselor, refusing to acknowledge mistakes and failings, and pretending to be deeply interested when one is actually bored silly are just some of the ways a counselor fails the integrity test.

As soon as we seriously engage with spiritual and moral qualities such as compassion, availability, and integrity, the problem of perfectionism is not too far away. As I have struggled to deal with this scourge, I have found the reflections of Carl Jung helpful. Jung eschews perfection, advocating instead for wholeness—the final attribute to be discussed.

Wholeness

In Jungian theory, the desired state for the psyche is individuation. Individuation refers to wholeness/completeness in the psyche, or realization of the Self. The Self is the term Jung uses to denote the personality as a whole (both the conscious and unconscious elements). It represents the wholeness that comes through reconciliation between psychic opposites such as the persona (one's conventional public representation) and the shadow (representing one's moral inferiorities), the male (*Logos*) and female (*Eros*) aspects, and the thinking and feeling selves.

It's interesting to note that when Jung searches for a symbol of the completeness that comes through individuation, he turns to Christ.²⁷ "He

25. Kennedy, *Who Is Worthy?*, 27.
26. Rogers, *Reader*, 119.
27. See Jung, *Aion*, 36–71.

represents a totality of a divine or heavenly kind, a glorified man, a son of God *sine macula peccati*, unspotted by sin."[28] Since the Self represents the totality of personhood it can only be symbolized through "antinomial" or oppositional terms (such as persona and shadow). In order to make the connection between the Self and Christ, Jung needs to find "antinomial terms" in the Christ symbol. He identifies two quaternions of opposites.[29] The first is comprised of the matched sets unitemporal-eternal and unique-universal. The Son entered human history at a particular time in the person of Jesus of Nazareth and in him adopted a unique set of human characteristics. We can therefore refer to him through the terms "unitemporal" and "unique." But at the same time, Christ is divine and therefore eternal and universal.

To describe the other quaternion of opposites, Jung uses the following matched pairings: good-evil and spiritual-material. In Christ there is no evil, but the Christian tradition acknowledges the opposition of Satan. As Jung puts it: "[I]f theology describes Christ as simply 'good' and 'spiritual,' something 'evil' and 'material'—or 'chthonic'—is bound to arise on the other side, to represent the Antichrist."[30] This is so for Jung because inherent in human existence is a need for balance through opposition. Hot is defined by cold, high by low, and light by darkness; this is the nature of our world of experience.

In positing Christ as the symbol of the Self, Jung is aware of the possibility that some will want to turn things around. That is, there will be those who put the Self as the archetype of Christ.[31] Here we see at work the strong human propensity to raise ourselves to the sphere of the divine.[32]

Jung has already indicated how he resolves this issue. He also goes on to identify the problems associated with assigning the archetype of the Self the preeminent role. Anyone who reverses the real situation fails to recognize the considerable difference between perfection and wholeness. Though Christ represents perfection through his sinlessness,

28. Jung, *Aion*, 37.
29. See Jung, *Aion*, 63.
30. Jung, *Aion*, 63.
31. Jung, *Aion*, 68.

32. It is interesting to note that here Jung makes a reference to alchemy. He focuses on the famous *lapis philosophorum* or philosopher's stone. The *lapis* was a symbol of perfection for the medieval alchemists. Thus they naturally associated it with Christ. But the stone was elevated to a status it had no legitimate right to.

it is not this fact that makes him a symbol of the Self. Sinlessness does not typify human selfhood. The Christ symbol typifies the Self because it contains the two quaternions of opposites. These quaternions capture the completeness that is the goal of self-realization. In the reversal, this proper relation between perfection and completeness is completely lost sight of: "The Christ-image is as good as perfect (at least it is meant to be so), while the archetype (so far as known) denotes completeness but is far from being perfect."[33] In a word, only in God do we find perfection.

But what happens when we take the archetype of the Self as the real agent in the process? That is, what is the practical outcome of positing the Self as the archetype of Christ? Jung suggests, first, that it is no bad thing to strive after perfection. In fact, the moral achievements of European civilization are grounded in such a striving. There is, however, a very large shadow hanging over that civilization—one that is not sufficiently acknowledged when the archetype is assigned the active role. The crux of the matter for Jung is that we can freely choose individuation, or we can allow it to be forced on us. If we one-sidedly concentrate on our moral achievements the shadow will rise up and demand attention. The movement toward completeness is a struggle. To face one's inner opposites is no easy task. Indeed, it is like descending into "a deep pit." But we can freely take on the burden. It is better to walk into it with one's eyes open, says Jung, than to fall into it backwards. When there is a prideful elevation of the Self the unconscious rises up in protest. Completeness is something forced upon one. That is, the shadow will not be denied; it will come at you, ready or not. Here Jung makes reference to the inner struggle as depicted by Paul in Romans 7: "The individual may strive after perfection . . . but must suffer from the opposite of his intentions for the sake of his completeness. 'I find then a law, when I would do good, evil is present within me.'"[34]

Jung here brings a psychological interpretation to Paul's theological analysis of the human condition. A central idea for Jung, as we have seen, is that the Self seeks to maintain balance. Thus, a psychic thrust too far in one direction will result in a push in the opposite direction. Jung contends that this psychological dynamic is driving the spiritual conflict described by Paul. A person driven by an ideal of perfect goodness will "stir up" the shadow. Feeling slighted, he will make his presence felt. The question

---

33. Jung, *Aion*, 68–69.
34. Jung, *Aion*, 69.

arises: does Paul advocate pursuit of moral perfection? I don't believe that he does. Indeed, the clear implication of his theology in Romans 7 is that it is folly to strive for perfect goodness. One should seek to advance in goodness, but the fact that the law of sin has such a strong hold means that moral and spiritual perfection are impossible goals.

In another place, Paul teaches: "Do not conform yourselves to the standards of this world, but let God transform you inwardly by a complete change of your mind. Then you will be able to know the will of God—what is good and is pleasing to him and is perfect" (Rom 12:2). In his commentary, Matthew Black has this helpful reflection to offer: "True dedication of spirit is to engage powers of the mind, in the quest for perfection, or rather for the perfect will of God for us."[35] The divine will is perfect; we are not. We should be attempting to embrace God's perfect will ever more fully, but Paul knows that we will never live it to perfection. The sinful self is like a squatter who has taken up residence in the soul (to use an Australian metaphor). We may wish to evict him, but try as we might he simply will not budge. Once we catch hold of this, we free ourselves from a futile, and ultimately quite unhealthy, drive to perfection.

Above I referred to the fact that for Jung a crucially important job of work in the journey into wholeness is giving the shadow his due. The first task in moving toward a reconciliation of the opposites within is to recognize and acknowledge what is really there. Up to this point, we have cast the shadow in completely negative terms. It is important to recognize that as well as being an expression of evil impulses, it is also a source of dynamism and creativity. "[T]he unconscious man, that is, his shadow," writes Jung, "does not consist only of morally reprehensible tendencies, but also displays a number of good qualities, such as normal instincts, appropriate reactions, realistic insights, creative impulses, etc."[36] But of course it is the "morally reprehensible" qualities that are the difficult ones to acknowledge. If we try to ignore or deny these, the shadow will rise up against us.

More than insight it takes courage to acknowledge the shadow. Looking the negative self squarely in the face always results in an assault on self-esteem. It is for this reason that we tend to gloss over the differences

---

35. Black, *Romans*, 151.
36. Jung, *Aion*, 266.

we have with the dark side. However, there can never be any progress toward reconciliation when we settle for an easy accommodation.

While some Jungians advocate tolerance and even occasional acquiescence to the shadow,[37] Jung himself suggests that we need to correct it: "Everyone carries a shadow, and the less it is embodied in the individual's conscious life, the blacker and denser it is. If an inferiority is conscious, one always has a chance to correct it. Furthermore, it is constantly in contact with other interests, so that it is continually subjected to modifications. But if it is repressed and isolated from consciousness, it never gets corrected."[38]

This approach fits much better with gospel values. Given that Christians are called to aim for conformity to Christ, it should not be our intent to accede to morally inferior impulses. Sometimes, of course, our human frailty is to the fore and we do in fact give in. This is Paul's point: "I find then a law, when I would do good, evil is present within me." Our aim is always to align ourselves more closely with the way of Christ; sometimes we miss the mark. From a Christian perspective, reconciliation with the shadow involves recognition, honesty, and understanding. The idea that part of the process is to sometimes choose to give in to the shadow seems contrary to the gospel ethic.

Jung's point in all of this is that while it is right to seek to correct the moral inferiorities that constitute our dark side, wholeness rather than perfectionism is the goal. Reconciliation between the persona and the shadow, rather than total obliteration of the dark side, is the desirable aim.

Conclusion

I'm very aware that this discussion on a Christian spirituality of the counselor is both incomplete and inadequate. This vitally important topic deserves a much fuller treatment. At least some crucially important dimensions have been covered.

In closing I wish to reiterate my strong conviction that what we bring as persons contributes at least as much to the quality and effectiveness of counseling as does our skilful technique. The conscientious, professional counselor constantly works on enhancing knowledge, skill, and technique.

37. Von Franz, "Process of Individuation."
38. Jung, *Aion*, 240.

But just as importantly for those who are Christians, there is a continual openness to the Spirit of God in the journey into stronger faith, deeper compassion, more positive personal psychology, and firmer character.

Bibliography

Becker, Arthur. "Compassion: A Foundation for Pastoral Care." *Religion in Life* 48 (1979) 143–52.

Bergant, Dianne. "Compassion." In *The Collegeville Pastoral Dictionary of Biblical Theology*, edited by Carol Stuhlmueller, 154–57. Collegeville: Liturgical, 1996.

Black, Matthew. *The New Century Bible Commentary on Romans*. Grand Rapids: Eerdmans, 1984.

Browning, Don. *The Moral Context of Pastoral Care*. Philadelphia: Westminster, 1976.

Campbell, Alastair. *Rediscovering Pastoral Care*. 2nd ed. London: Darton, Longman, and Todd, 1986.

Capps, Donald. *Life Cycle Theory and Pastoral Care*. Eugene, OR: Wipf & Stock, 2002.

Ellin, Jeanne. *Listening Helpfully*. London: Souvenir, 1994.

Fairchild, Roy W. "Guaranteed Not to Shrink: Spiritual Direction in Pastoral Care." *Pastoral Psychology* 31 (1982) 79–95.

Graham, Larry. *Moral Injury: Restoring Wounded Souls*. Nashville: Abingdon, 2017.

Gubi, Peter M., ed. *Spiritual Accompaniment and Counselling: Journeying with Psyche and Soul*. London: Jessica Kingsley, 2015.

———, ed. *What Counsellors and Spiritual Directors Can Learn from Each Other*. London: Jessica Kingsley, 2017.

Hitlin, Steven. "Values as the Core of Personal Identity: Drawing Links between Two Theories of Self." *Social Psychology Quarterly* 66 (2003) 118–37.

Jung, Carl. *Psychological Reflections*. London: Routledge and Kegan Paul, 1974.

———. *Aion*. Princeton: Princeton University Press, 1978.

Kennedy, Ted. *Who Is Worthy?* Sydney: Pluto, 2000.

Köster, Helmut. "*Splanchnon*." In *Theological Dictionary of the New Testament*, edited by Gerhard Kittel and Gerhard Friedrich, 1067–69. Grand Rapids: Eerdmans, 1985.

Louw, Daniël J. "'Habitus' in Soul Care: Towards 'Spiritual Fortigenetics' (*Parrhesia*) in a Pastoral Anthropology." *Acta Theologica* 30 (2010) 67–88.

———. *A Mature Faith: Spiritual Direction and Anthropology in a Theology of Pastoral Care and Counseling*. Louvain: Peeters, 1999.

———. "Philosophical Counselling: Towards a 'New Approach' in Pastoral Care and Counselling?" *HTS Teologiese Studies/Theological Studies* 67, no. 2 (2011). Doi: 10.4102/hts.v67i2.900.

Marcel, Gabriel. *Creative Fidelity*. Translated by Robert Rosthal. New York: Noonday, 1964.

Miles, Rebecca. *The Pastor as Moral Guide*. Minneapolis: Fortress, 1998.

Moon, Gary W., and David G. Benner, eds. *Spiritual Direction and the Care of Souls: A Guide to Christian Approaches and Practices*. Downers Grove: InterVarsity Academic, 2009.

Nouwen, Henri. *The Wounded Healer*. New York: Image, 1979.

Noyce, Gaylord. *The Minister as Moral Counselor*. Nashville: Abingdon, 1989.

Pembroke, Neil. *Moving Toward Spiritual Maturity: Psychological, Contemplative, and Moral Challenges in Christian Living.* London: Routledge, 2007.

Rogers, Carl. *The Carl Rogers Reader.* Edited by Howard Kirschenbaum and Valerie L. Henderson. Boston: Houghton Mifflin Harcourt, 1989.

Schmidt, William S. "Transformative Pilgrimage." In *The Spiritual Horizon of Psychotherapy*, edited by William S. Schmidt and Merle R. Jordan, 65–76. New York: Routledge, 2010.

Sperry, Len. *Transforming Self and Community: Revisioning Pastoral Counseling and Spiritual Direction.* Collegeville: Liturgical, 2002.

Stairs, Jean. *Listening for the Soul: Pastoral Care and Spiritual Direction.* Minneapolis: Fortress, 2000.

Von Franz, Marie-Louise. "The Process of Individuation." In *Man and His Symbols*, edited by Carl Jung, 158–229. New York: Doubleday, 1964.

Chapter 5

Conversation Partners: Stories of Integration

LISA SPRIGGENS

I HAD NOT THOUGHT a great deal about the integration of theology and counseling until I was required to teach it in an undergraduate programme at an evangelical theological college. When I trained as a counselor my Christian faith was kept separate from my counseling practice. It was something valuable to me, but not something that I considered part of my counselor identity. I imagined my counselor-self bound by theory and ethics, not impermeable or inauthentic, but also not in active relationship with all aspects of my self. I was aware, however, that what I held valuable and meaningful in the world would be, in some way, present in my counseling work and that I valued the integrity that is possible when there is "narrative coherence" between my public/professional and private life.[1] The journey of integration I am on has become a significant part of how I undertake teaching the integration of counseling and theology to students. In this essay I will reflect on my own journey of integration as I engaged with theology and my counseling practice. Drawing on a relational model of integration I will suggest an integration that holds both theology and counseling in dialogue, reflecting a relational epistemology.[2] In the practice of holding space for

---

1. Lee, "Integration and the Christian Imagination."
2. Sandage and Brown, *Relational Integration of Psychology and Christian Theology*.

the other and an openness to being changed by the other, integration is experienced in a way that holds complexity and nuance without an expectation of resolution. Using examples from my counseling work and as a counselor educator I will explore how I navigate the complexity and nuance experienced in this integration journey and how I use this to inform my teaching. My hope is that this serves as an example of how theology and counseling can speak to and shape each other.

What Is Integration?

Defining what is meant by integration in this context is critical. In the counseling context integration can refer to a variety of intra-psychic processes connected to self-awareness and identity, so it is important to clearly define what is meant by integration for the purposes of this essay. The integration of social sciences, particularly psychology, with theology has been developed extensively; however, as I have taught in this field, I have witnessed students struggling to connect a theory of integration with their expression of this in practice.[3] Integration of a theology with a theory of counseling which reflects some similar values may initially appear to be obvious and uncomplicated, but I have experienced a significant degree of complexity and nuance underlying both the theory and practice of integration. The articulation of an integration of theology and professional practice poses a challenge to honor each without the subjugation of the other. This challenge can be experienced by an individual, but also in institutional and community spheres.

Eck provides a framework within which to understand the different approaches to the integration of theology and psychology.[4] For the purpose of this chapter, I am using these theories in the context of counseling theory and practice. Within his framework Eck pragmatically defines the relationship between theology and psychology identified by nine different models of integration. While models and theories have continued to be developed since the publication of Eck's article, understanding the nature of these theoretical relationships is a critical initial step for students as they begin to articulate their own integration.

---

3. For examples, see Palmer and Woolfe, *Integrative and Eclectic Counselling and Psychotherapy*; Eck, "Integrating the Integrators"; Shults and Sandage, *Transforming Spirituality*; Sandage and Brown, *Relational Integration of Psychology and Christian Theology*; McMillan et al., *Stories of Therapy, Stories of Faith*.

4. Eck, "Integrating the Integrators."

A relational model of integration will be discussed later in this essay, but I think it is important to note that any model of integration implies some form of relationship. It is the nature and characteristics of the relationship which are key. My counseling practice and theology have always been in relationship, but it was not one which reflected the nature of relationship I value. In choosing to actively consider the relationship between theology and counseling I am more aware of the way in which it may be expressed in my counseling work. Students are likewise invited to consider the nature of the relationship they wish theology and counseling to have, the values this relationship represents, and the outcome this has on their counseling work.

Arguably, the work of counseling focuses on relationship. This could be the relationship with self, other, or God. Understanding integration in light of relationship provides a familiar framework for students, and also a common language to use when identifying the relational dynamics.

Relational Integration

Steven Sandage and Jeannine Brown propose a relational approach to integration in their book *Relational Integration of Psychology and Christian Theology*.[5] I have found this concept of relational integration reflects key characteristics of the theology and counseling integration project I undertake in my own practice, and teaching. It is consistent with the characteristics of both social Trinitarian theology and the models of counseling I use, those being person-centered counseling and narrative therapy.

It makes sense, to me, to view the integration of theology and psychology as occurring in relationship. The nature of this relationship reflects the nature of the participants. A social Trinitarian anthropology provides a model of being-in-relationship which, I argue, supports the kind of relating described in the relational integration model.[6] This is a relationship of reciprocity, of welcome to other in recognizing both difference and similarity. Counseling using person-centered and narrative therapies also engages in relationship in particular ways. Features of this relationship include unconditional positive regard, empathy, congruence,

---

5. Sandage and Brown, *Relational Integration of Psychology and Christian Theology*.
6. Balswick et al., *Reciprocating Self*; King, "Reciprocating Self."

an awareness of power and social relationships, and an awareness of the constructive nature of relationship.[7]

Integration in this manner positions theology and counseling in an egalitarian relationship. It is a dialogical relationship—in that the conversation generated by the integration of theology and counseling is generative, non-prescribed, and the participants engage with an openness to being changed in that engagement. The challenge of a relationship of this nature is maintaining a posture of welcome and openness, reminiscent of Volf's "embrace."[8] A dialogical space which is less focused on resolution than relationship invites theology and counseling to truly make space for the other. Sandage and Brown describe this as a "third space" which holds the integration conversation.[9] This space creates some separation between the person and the ideas which can make possible a more critical, less defended, conversation. This third space can help address any tensions and anxieties that will inevitably emerge in a conversation between parties with differing modes of knowing and learning. This is a delicate holding. It is easy to hold the intent of integration in this manner, but maintaining an extended liminal space is challenging in environments which rely on definitive positions and declarations of truth. This is not to say that these don't emerge out of relational integration, but that this is not the telos of relational integration.

It is this image of relationship and dialogue which holds how I experience the integration of theology and counseling. It is a dynamic conversation where each participant makes room for the other, recognizing the uniqueness they bring and engaging in a transformative conversation. My experience of relational integration supports a relational epistemology, that is, knowledge is understood to be "something that is socially constructed by embedded, embodied people who are in relation with each other."[10]

---

7. Tolan, *Skills in Person-Centred Counselling and Psychotherapy*; McMillan, "Social God, Relational Selves."

8. Volf, *Exclusion and Embrace*.

9. Sandage and Brown, *Relational Integration of Psychology and Christian Theology*; Sandage and Brown, "Relational Integration, Part I."

10. Thayer-Bacon, "Nurturing of a Relational Epistemology," 245.

Embodied Integration

Sandage and Brown warn against the abstraction of integration. This abstraction is recognized in two ways: firstly, where an individual practitioner attempts interdisciplinary integration within their own body of work, a "single-integrator model" of integration.[11] They argue for integration between people, that is, theologians and counselors in dialogue with each other. An embodied conversation of this nature allows for people to speak from their area of expertise, avoiding the common integration pitfalls of overreach, misinterpretation, or inappropriate use of concepts from another discipline. This is an attractive model of integration in that it, quite literally, invites you in to relationship with an other. The reality, though, is that most counselors will not have contact with a theologian prepared to engage in dialogue of this nature. Likewise, theologians may also find themselves equally wanting for a conversation partner. The embodied nature of this model, through encouraging conversation between people engaged in the different discipline, does have the effect of bringing to our attention relational dynamics that when understood by the individual practitioner can invite them in to a deeper understanding of integration in their practice. These relational dynamics include acknowledging the inevitability of conflict, that anxiety will be present, that desegregation alone will not achieve relational integration and that existing social hierarchies will influence integration.[12]

The second caution with regard to abstraction is limiting the conversation to abstract concepts, both in theology and counseling theory, rather than grounding the conversation in the particular. Embodied integration attends to the particular, making space for both difference and similarity. This is applicable in "actual" conversations where individuals with different specialties come together, and also for the one person navigating their way through a conversation with theology and counseling. The challenge is to make space for the other as you enter the embrace.[13] In my experience of integration this has led me to recognize difference and value it as such, rather than seeing difference as a "sticking point" I need to address.

11. Sandage and Brown, *Relational Integration of Psychology and Christian Theology*, 51.

12. Sandage and Brown, *Relational Integration of Psychology and Christian Theology*, 53–60.

13. Volf, *Exclusion and Embrace*.

The challenge I experience as a counselor educator is to find opportunities for integration conversations reflective of those proposed by Sandage and Brown in order to deepen my own integration of theology and counseling and those of the students I teach, but also to find a way of teaching integration which counseling students can practically engage with. I do not want to teach them what the end result of integration should look like, but rather offer a way of doing integration for themselves: a transformative, rather than formative process.

Examples of Practice

An aspect of my counseling practice in which I experience the integration of theology and counseling is when working with survivors of sexual violence. In this work I can see how theologically-integrated counseling practice supports victim/survivors in "living on" after an experience of sexual violence.[14] I have written previously about practices of hope in counseling work which reflect an integration of theology and counseling theory.[15] In this I identified aspects of my practice when working with survivors of trauma which I felt reflected an integration of theology and counseling theory.

I want to offer two examples of counseling practice which I consider to be integrated with theology in my work. These are the practices of witness and of holding hope.

Witness

Trauma fractures language, and survivors can struggle to find the words to describe their experience.[16] It is hard to continue living while carrying an event which has caused so much disruption. Often what can arise is a deep desire to understand why an event has happened: "Why me?" In these moments deep questions exploring suffering and theodicy emerge. Moltmann's description of a God who "suffers with" provides, for me, a particular kind of witness position.[17] In the role of witness, the counselor deeply connects with the experience of the survivor, hearing not just the

---

14. Derrida, "Living On," 75–79.
15. Spriggens, "Christian Hope."
16. Herman, *Trauma and Recovery*.
17. Moltmann and Moltmann-Wendel, *Passion for God*.

story of the trauma, but also the distress, the harm, the ongoing effects of the event. Witnessing, with empathy, also requires a response from the counselor, an acknowledgment of what we have witnessed which includes an acknowledgment of how we, as the counselor, have been affected by the story.[18] I see a strong relationship between the "suffering-with" proposed by Moltmann and the witnessing practices used in counseling.

Holding Hope

Entering the suffering of another requires vulnerability. I risk being changed by my witnessing of another. For both my client and myself, holding hope for life in the aftermath of trauma is a key therapeutic practice. Shelly Rambo offers a theology of remaining using the "inbetween" space of Easter Saturday as a metaphor for life following trauma.[19] Easter Saturday represents the life with death which is experienced by survivors of trauma. The trauma event has taken something, or someone, but life is still present. As counselor I accompany my client in their efforts to discover what living on looks like and in doing so hold hope for my client. Weingarten talks about reasonable hope, hope that is done in relationship, aware of what is influenceable, and open to be changed.[20] Reasonable hope allows for doubt, fear, uncertainty, pain. I think we might find this hope in Easter Saturday. I start with hope when I acknowledge that the person I am sitting with is a survivor, and that I am privileged to be walking this journey with them. Hope is found in the small moments of counseling conversation where a woman states a preference for life, where she notices that this week wasn't as difficult as the last. Hope is when I hear stories of people reaching out and connecting with those disconnected from relationship. Hope is in the bigger moments, when people gather and make public declarations against violence, against the social norms that encourage it. In the practices of holding hope I experience the relationship between my counseling practice and theology. Both shape how I understand and undertake my work in these moments.

18. Weingarten, *Common Shock*.
19. Rambo, *Spirit and Trauma*.
20. Weingarten, "Reasonable Hope"; Weingarten, "Witnessing, Wonder, and Hope."

A Vignette

Jill is a third-year counseling student who feels strongly that her counseling work is a context within which she should be explicit about her Christian faith. Jill decided to become a counselor out of a deep desire to guide people towards better lives, informed by the biblical principles she considers key in achieving this. During her counseling training she has learned that the goal of counseling is not to fix or cure a person, rather to build a therapeutic relationship within which clients can grow in understanding of themselves and explore the challenges they face in life and the skills they have to address these. She is clear that her intention is not that her clients might experience some form of conversion, rather she desires for her clients to have an experience of God's love and acceptance, regardless of the decisions they make about their life, but also for her clients to understand that her counseling work is guided by some fundamental principles about what a "good life" should look like. There have been occasions where clients have asked her to pray at the conclusion of their session and she considers this to be a huge honor and a great opportunity for her client to experience the healing power of God in their life. Jill has been aware that in the final year of her degree she will be learning about how to integrate theology and counseling. She's not certain exactly what is meant by this but is excited to see how she can bring more theology in to her counseling and hopefully fulfil her desire to be the counselor she has always imagined she'd be.

Teaching Integration

As a counselor I value theology which can flex and move with the complexity of human experience. I have started many sentences with the phrase "I'm no theologian, but . . ." in the hope of absolving myself of the inevitable misstep that will follow, so I am always a little tentative talking into this space. While it is easily arguable that we are all theologians, I am not inclined to embrace this position while working alongside much more learned colleagues. I have also been known to meet with aforementioned theologian-colleagues to request from them a theology which would support a particular counseling-informed view I hold, or wish to include in my teaching. I've lectured to students the need to be tentative and open in engaging with differing ideas while myself refusing to engage with other positions in relation to highly valued beliefs. In disclosing this small vignette I want to make explicit my experience that the integration of theology and counseling is complex, conflicting, and messy. Teaching integration in ways which sit comfortably with the discomfort integration can bring, I argue, is key. It develops the relational skills needed to sit in unresolved spaces.

At the outset of each academic year when I meet with third-year Bachelor of Counseling students to introduce them to integration, I start by revealing that they will not finish the year as integrated counselors; rather this is a recognition of a journey of integration where the intended destination is a dynamic conversational and relational space. I also acknowledge that they are already on this journey. Integration, of some kind, is already happening. The intent of our work together, that they undertake as part of their counseling training, is to apply a theoretical framework and to develop an articulation of their integration of theology and counseling. I could draw some conclusions about how this introduction is received by students but I suspect they may mirror my own experience of teaching this course, over a number of years. If I were to extend the journey metaphor a little further I would draw attention to the unknowable nature of a journey, the anticipation that might be present, perhaps alongside uncertainty. Every year there is an anticipation of what this might look like, and every year as we journey together the integration stories that emerge from students reflect diversity, and a common experience: relationship. As their guide in this experience, the common adage of staying one page ahead of the class feels very applicable. There is, of course, another way of understanding what happens during this course. The collective storying of the integration of counseling and theology makes room for imagination and invites students to personalize their learning. Formalizing an integrative framework in this manner is less theoretical, and more of a relational experience. There is, regardless, some need for a framework to guide students through. There is a tension between providing structure and creating space for the dialogue and relationship that this approach to integration is based on.

Tim Bond's "pond" metaphor, created to provide a framework for theoretical models, gives a basic structure from which students can articulate the integration emerging in their practice.[21] Grounding the theory of integration, it provides a guide for students to articulate how the integration of theology is evidenced in their work with clients. It is important for trainee counselors to be able to articulate the "why" informing their

21. Bond, "Integration and Eclecticism in Counselling Theory," quoted in Horton, "Principles and Practice of a Personal Integration."

practice, and in this instance where the integration of theology forms such an integral foundation to counseling practice this is key. Identifying individual practices and connecting them to larger theological and philosophical standing places strengthens these connections, as does tracking the journey from the theological and philosophical standing places towards the practices engaged with in the counseling room. Bond's Pond model supports students to articulate an embodied integration so they can identify aspects of their counseling practice which reflect the relationship between theology and counseling.

Using Bond's Pond Jill (see vignette above) is able to start developing an articulation of her integration of theology and counseling. Jill recognizes that Trinitarian theology underpins her understanding of being invited in to a relationship of love with the Father, Son, and Spirit and that, as a counselor, she is committed to extending this love to her clients on behalf of a particular vision of wellness which she can see being offered in the relationship of the Trinity.[22] Jill starts to see the connection between this theological position and counseling theory she has learned. The Rogerian principle of Unconditional Positive Regard invites the counselor in to a position of acceptance and regard for the client, acknowledgement of the inherent value of their humanness.[23] The core condition of Empathy positions her with compassion for the client and directs her towards hope for wellbeing. Understanding the connections between her theology and counseling theory, Jill is then able to envision how theology is in conversation with counseling theory, both shaping and informing her practice with her clients. As a consequence, Jill has noticed she feels differently about her counseling practice, with a greater sense of God's presence with her as she works and an understanding of the "why" which is directing her words and actions in her counseling conversations.

One might reasonably argue that the client would experience similar words and actions from a counselor trained in the same counseling modality, who is not also integrating with theology. I propose, however, that a counselor who is more deeply connected with the "why" of their work is one who can offer a deeper relational encounter to their client. When this "why" is informed by a telos of wellness and flourishing underpinned by a commitment to a theology of relationship and

---

22. McMillan, "Social God, Relational Selves."

23. Thorne, *Counselling and Spiritual Accompaniment*; Tolan, *Skills in Person-Centred Counselling and Psychotherapy*.

participation in the life of the Trinity, the counseling relationship offered to the client will inevitably direct them towards love and flourishing.

Navigating Complexity

It is, of course, a comfortable relationship between theology and counseling practice when there is a shared intention of love and acceptance. Relationships inevitably encounter some conflict, and we can expect the same in this instance.[24] Creating a dialogic relationship, where there is room for multiple perspectives to exist simultaneously establishes integration as an ongoing conversation between theology and counseling. In this space I can hold the tension and complexity of conflict, while striving towards the telos I hold in my counseling work.

Conclusion

At the end of each academic year graduating students participate in a conversation which requires them to speak to their counseling practice: the ethics that guide it, the theories that inform it, their counselor identity that is being shaped. These conversations start with the same invitation: to articulate a description of themselves as a counselor. It's a huge question, one that often causes students to pause. After the pause students start to share the commitments which underpin their work. These are varied, from a desire for people to have a voice, or to experience acceptance and hospitality, or to counter injustice and bring peace. It is deeply moving and rewarding to hear an articulation of commitments which reflect an integration of theology and counseling. These are dynamic, thoughtful, and meaningful for the student. Relational integration offers a literal and figurative conversation space for theology and counseling to meet and encounter each other, in ways which reflect the encounter of counselor and client.

---

24. Sandage and Brown, *Relational Integration of Psychology and Christian Theology*.

Bibliography

Balswick, Jack O., Pamela Ebstyne King, and Kevin S. Reimer. *The Reciprocating Self: Human Development in Theological Perspective.* Downers Grove: InterVarsity, 2005.
Derrida, Jacques. "Living On." In *Deconstruction and Criticism,* edited by Harold Bloom, Paul De Man, Jacques Derrida, Geoffrey H. Hartman, and J. Hillis Miller, 75–176. Translated by James Hulbert. New York: Seabury, 1979.
Eck, Brian E. "Integrating the Integrators: An Organizing Framework for a Multifaceted Process of Integration." *Journal of Psychology and Christianity* 15 (1996) 101–15.
Herman, Judith Lewis. *Trauma and Recovery.* Rev. ed. New York: Basic, 1997.
Horton, Ian. "Principles and Practice of a Personal Integration." In *Integrative and Eclectic Counselling and Psychotherapy,* edited by Stephen Palmer and Ray Woolfe, 315–28. Thousand Oaks: SAGE, 2000.
King, Pamela Ebstyne. "The Reciprocating Self: Trinitarian and Christological Anthropologies of Being and Becoming." *Journal of Psychology and Christianity* 35 (2016) 215–32.
Lee, Cameron. "Integration and the Christian Imagination." In *Integrating Faith and Psychology: Twelve Psychologists Tell Their Stories,* edited by Glendon Moriarty, 246–64. Downers Grove: InterVarsity Academic, 2010.
McMillan, Lex. "Social God, Relational Selves." In *Stories of Therapy, Stories of Faith,* edited by Lex McMillan, Sarah Penwarden, and Siobhan Hunt, 3–17. Eugene, OR: Wipf & Stock, 2017.
McMillan, Lex, Sarah Penwarden, and Siobhan Hunt, eds. *Stories of Therapy, Stories of Faith.* Eugene, OR: Wipf & Stock, 2017.
Moltmann, Jürgen, and Elisabeth Moltmann-Wendel. *Passion for God: Theology in Two Voices.* Louisville: Westminster John Knox, 2003.
Palmer, Stephen, and Ray Woolfe, eds. *Integrative and Eclectic Counselling and Psychotherapy.* Thousand Oaks: SAGE, 2000.
Rambo, Shelly. *Spirit and Trauma: A Theology of Remaining.* Louisville: Westminster John Knox, 2010.
Sandage, Steven J., and Jeannine K. Brown. *Relational Integration of Psychology and Christian Theology: Theory, Research, and Practice.* New York: Routledge, Taylor & Francis Group, 2018.
———. "Relational Integration, Part I: Differentiated Relationality between Psychology and Theology." *Journal of Psychology and Theology* 43 (2015) 165–78.
Shults, F. LeRon, and Steven J. Sandage. *Transforming Spirituality: Integrating Theology and Psychology.* Grand Rapids: Baker Academic, 2006.
Spriggens, Lisa. "Christian Hope: Ethical Responses to Trauma." In *Stories of Therapy, Stories of Faith,* edited by Lex McMillan, Sarah Penwarden, and Siobhan Hunt, 114–28. Eugene, OR: Wipf & Stock, 2017.
Thayer-Bacon, Barbara J. "The Nurturing of a Relational Epistemology." *Educational Theory* 47 (1997) 239–60.
Thorne, Brian. *Counselling and Spiritual Accompaniment: Bridging Faith and Person-Centred Therapy.* Chichester: Wiley, 2012.
Tolan, Janet. *Skills in Person-Centred Counselling and Psychotherapy.* London: SAGE, 2017.

Volf, Miroslav. *Exclusion and Embrace: A Theological Exploration of Identity, Otherness, and Reconciliation*. Nashville: Abingdon, 1996.

Weingarten, Kaethe. *Common Shock: Witnessing Violence Every Day*. New York: Dutton, 2003.

———. "Reasonable Hope: Construct, Clinical Applications, and Supports." *Family Process* 49 (2010) 5–25.

———. "Witnessing, Wonder, and Hope." *Family Process* 39 (2000) 389–402.

Response 2: Formation

Quests and Questions

Sarah Penwarden
(with found poetry by Yael Klangwisan)

While in their work therapists accompany human beings on their journeys of struggle and potential growth, therapists are themselves works in progress, pursuing their own quests over time. One key quest for the therapist is integration. Integration can mean an integration of models of practice with each other,[1] integration between a counselor's personal and professional selves, or integration between their Christian faith and counseling work.[2] This section of the book has focused on the integration of faith in practice/practitioners. A therapist's aim for integration may connect with a desire for integrity, for coherence,[3] and for an interlocking of one's beliefs, attitudes, and actions.

Lisa Spriggens and Neil Pembroke write about their own quests for integration. They raise questions along the way. I read Spriggens' quest as being that, while acknowledging the importance of holding theology and counseling equally in dialogue, in practice, how does one tolerate the discomfort of difference (theology) within the comfort of sameness (counseling)? Pembroke's quest is also embodied. The question I hear him ask is, how can I live in some degree of comfort with my own "farcical humanity," full of shadows and sin, while I journey with others? Both

---

1. Horton, "Principles."
2. Sandage and Brown, *Relational Integration*.
3. Sandage and Brown, *Relational Integration*.

writers express something of the unease of integration: the realisation that integration is not a model to learn, but rather actions to take. Integration is a practice, "lived out in real lives, embodied in the person of the psychotherapist."[4]

For me, Spriggens' chapter highlights both the aspirations of integration, and the potential threat of it: its invitation to discomfort. Spriggens advocates for a relational integration in which counseling and theology are in dialogue. Even more than that, integration can be seen in the light of the Trinity, where each discipline is particular and different to the other, and yet there is "mutual recognition" between them, rather than subjugation of one to another.[5] Spriggens values a space where "theology and counseling… truly make space for the other."

In a resonant example, Spriggens writes about how, in conversations with people who have experienced sexual abuse, she witnesses to suffering *and* holds hope. This is a *being in* Holy Saturday—in a place of death with the faint hope of new life. She knows the God who "suffers with."[6] This is a sacred space where her faith and work interlock, and from which flows witnessing, compassion, and hope.

> The why of the work
> Deeper relational encounter
> Shared intentions
> Of love and connection
>
> Holding hope for life
> I risk being changed
> By my witnessing
> Easter Saturday
> I am sitting with
> A survivor
> Hope is found
> In the small moments.[7]

For Spriggens, this holding of faith, hope, and love in places of trauma is a place of integrative ease. Vibrant theology is present here, supporting

---

4. Neff and McMinn, *Embodying Integration*, 52.
5. Sandage and Brown, *Relational Integration*, 52.
6. Moltmann and Moltmann-Wendel, *Passion for God*.
7. Found poem written as a response to Spriggens' chapter by Yael Klangwisan. This prose reflection incorporates poetic responses (found poetry) by Yael Klangwisan.

her finding hope in bleak places: inbetween spaces of loss and what might yet be.

However, she also acknowledges places of integrative discomfort; times when holding both theology and counseling in mutual recognition is very difficult:

> I have also been known to meet with aforementioned theologian-colleagues to request from them a theology which would support a particular counseling-informed view I hold, or wish to include in my teaching. I've lectured to students the need to be tentative and open in engaging with differing ideas while myself refusing to engage with other positions in relation to highly valued beliefs. In disclosing this small vignette I want to make explicit my experience that the integration of theology and counseling is complex, conflicting, and messy.

Writers on integration offer ideas for managing the anxiety of integration, through having a "spirit of exploration," an "ability to tolerate ambiguity,"[8] as well as "welcoming curiosity" and practicing "perspective-taking."[9] But reading Spriggens' chapter reminds me of the embodied challenge of remaining open and "patient with difference" when it comes to integration between counseling and theology.[10] I personally find this task of being "patient with difference" particularly difficult when, for example, a student's faith position of certainty around what is true clashes with professional counseling ethics and with my own position. How then can I engage with another's perspective, another's difference, without subsuming it? The challenge remains one of tolerating difference and seeking to keep open spaces for dialogue both with those whose positions differ and with different ideas themselves.

My wondering from Spriggens' writing is whether there is something to be gained from noticing times of *particular* discomfort, times of real jarring between theology and counseling (for example, in discussing concepts such as sin). I also wonder whether being able to sit in this "third space"[11] and unpack the discomfort, might offer unexpected gifts and learnings otherwise not gained.

---

8. Brown et al., *Becoming Whole and Holy*, 21–22.
9. Neff and McMinn, *Embodying Integration*, 24.
10. Fuller Studio, "Fuller Dialogues."
11. Sandage and Brown, *Relational Integration*.

Pembroke's challenges in integration are of a different hue: how to relate theologically to oneself as a human being and a counselor. In Pembroke's chapter, I read both the hope and challenges of humanness: a human being as potentially offering "vulnerability, compassion, availability, integrity, wholeness" to the client, and a human as a person who wrestles with a "sinful self [who] like a squatter has taken up residence in the soul." A counselor's journey is thus with *their own* multi-faceted human being.

If a human being is seen as a verb not a noun,[12] human being is always in process, in movement. A counselor, while accompanying others, is, as Pembroke says, on "their own quest for personal and spiritual maturity": a journey in their own humanness in which they too grow and change. Pembroke writes about his own struggles: "For a very long time in my pastoral ministry I struggled to come to grips with my own fears, inadequacies, and short-comings. I wished that I could simply throw them off and be the strong, confident, calm, in-control person that I imagined the best counselors were. Finally an important moment of insight came: accepting my weaknesses and limitations, embracing my farcical humanity, is a positive."

In his writing, Pembroke exhibits a number of positions on humanness: accepting one's human weaknesses (for oneself and also to invite others to do likewise), seeing humanity as "farcical," and wrestling with a "sinful self." He sees this wrestling is important—to have a "firmer character"—but he also sees the fruitlessness of being caught in a never-ending drive for personal perfection.

In reading this chapter, I could relate to these positions. My own journey has been one of seeking to notice how grace and law (Rom 6:4) both flow through my embodiment as a person of Christian faith. In my mid-twenties, I had an epiphany when I realised how hard I had been working to try to please God. I sought from then on to *be* in my faith rather than to work hard: to inhabit it, and grow in it without laboring at it. My life journey for the past ten years has also been one of getting to know and live more in my humanness (which relates to ill health); accepting my humanness and seeing its value, because "it is through being in touch with our weakness that we release within ourselves a flow of compassion and understanding." Through entering our own "shadowlands of human existence," we can companion others in their own journeys. I see these

---

12. Combs and Freedman, "Relational Understanding."

journeys of self-acceptance and *being* in relationship with God as interlinked.

I warmed to Pembroke's compassion towards his own humanness as a value in the work.

> Common journey
> Into the shadowlands of existence
> The awful burden of thought
> A sign of hope
> Pain and the distress of the other
> Drawn into our ownmost sphere
> The womb, the bowels, the heart
> Hurt most intimate.
> The nameless sadness
> in the home and the soul
> journey in continual openness
> to the Spirit of God[13]

Yet I also found myself reflecting critically on the notion that one should not "accede to morally inferior impulses" but rather grow into a "firmer character." While we are seeking to grow in love, I see this as a growing in humanness, rather than in moral character/superiority. The notion of humans carrying an intrinsic dark side which we must "correct" carries echoes of both legalism and essentialism, and a tiring slog of working one's way to heaven through moral actions. Rather, human beings can be seen as teleological creatures with the potential to grow in love, knowledge of self and other, and capacity for deep relationships. Humans are also in positions to have to choose again and again to do love and not harm to others, to turn towards God and away from violence, no matter how small.[14] One part of this telos of growth is to grow in love for and acceptance of oneself. Pembroke's writing reminded me again of the value of moving *towards* rather than away from one's humanness—finding "the strength to be human"[15] rather than wrestling with moral character towards trying to be *sine macula peccati*, without blemish.

Reading Pembroke has reminded me again of my own journey into my humanness: to find and know a God who "suffers with"[16] and to know Christ—who is in my embodiment and also calls me to grow

---

13. Found poem written as a response from Pembroke's chapter by Yael Klangwisan.
14. Cone, *Black Theology*.
15. Moltmann, *God in Creation*, 273.
16. Moltmann and Moltmann-Wendel, *Passion for God*.

and change. In this way I can join, with humility, those whom I counsel on their journeys in humanness and into new growth. Reading both these authors has highlighted again that whoever I am travelling with in my counseling, I too am on my own path. Perhaps this journey is more prominent at some times than others; perhaps at times it is cloaked by clients' journeys, and at other times more plain. Yet, I too am on a personal quest in seeking that both counseling and my Christian faith can be dialogical partners which both call me into becoming.

Bibliography

Brown, Jeannine, Christine Dahl, and Wyndy Corbin Reuschling. *Becoming Whole and Holy: An Integrative Conversation about Christian Formation.* Grand Rapids: Baker Academic, 2011.

Combs, Gene, and Jill Freedman. "Narrative Therapy's Relational Understanding of Identity." *Family Process* 55 (2016) 211–24.

Cone, James. *A Black Theology of Liberation.* Maryknoll: Orbis, 2012.

Fuller Studio. "Fuller Dialogues on Relational Integration." YouTube video, 3:09. May 10, 2017. https://fullerstudio.fuller.edu/fuller-dialogues-relational-integration/

Horton, I. "Principles and a Practice of Personal Integration." In *Integrative and Eclectic Counselling and Psychotherapy*, edited by S. Palmer and R. Woolfe, 329–40. London: SAGE, 2000.

Moltmann, Jürgen. *God in Creation: An Ecological Doctrine of Creation.* London: SCM, 1985.

Moltmann, Jürgen, and Elisabeth Moltmann-Wendel. *Passion for God: Theology in Two Voices.* Louisville: Westminster John Knox, 2003.

Neff, Megan, and Mark McMinn. *Embodying Integration: A Fresh Look at Christianity in the Therapy Room.* Downers Grove: InterVarsity, 2020.

Sandage, Stephen, and Jeannine Brown. *Relational Integration of Psychology and Christian Theology: Theory, Research, and Practice.* London: Routledge, 2018.

Part III

HOSPITALITY

Chapter 6

Food, Table Fellowship, and Human Flourishing in Luke

Theresa Lau

Introduction

Luke-Acts together has an extraordinarily large number of food and meal scenes.[1] We can find this theme in every chapter of Luke's Gospel.[2] Luke, in particular, enjoys using the image of food and the act of eating to communicate Jesus' identity and vocation. This chapter intends to explore the background and rationale behind Lukan "foodology"[3] (i.e., how Luke employs "food" as a concept to communicate theology) and "tableism"[4] (i.e., how Luke uses "table fellowship" to communicate theology). Our key questions are: how does evangelist, historian, writer, and doctor Luke write about Jesus? Especially, as a doctor rooted in Hippocratic energetic

---

1. Luke 5:27–32, 33–39; 7:36–50; 9:10–17; 11:37–54; 14:1–24; 16:19–31; 17:7–10; 22:14–38; 24:28–32; Acts 2:42–47; 4:32–37; 6:1–6; 15:1–29; 16:25–34; 20:7–12; 27:33–38; 28:23–29.

2. Karris listed at least sixty such passages. See Karris, *Eating*, 16–20.

3. "Foodology" is defined in this chapter narrowly as the utilization of the ideology associated with food or anything edible to convey a deeper philosophical meaning.

4. "Tableism" in this chapter means, narrowly, the attitudes and styles of eating a meal. This term is inspired by the title of a music CD released in Australia in August 2011 by Ministry of Sound, with mixed musical style from Deep House, Breaks, Ambient, Downtempo to Disco. I find the CD's description of its title "tableism" interesting and a most appropriate illustration for our study.

medicine[5]—or what we now call holistic (body and mind) medicine—and, as a writer rooted in a Greco-Romans psychological narrative,[6] how would Luke present the gospel of Jesus? Can we see Luke's physician plus psychologist background in the Gospel narratives? If we can, what would this first century doctor-psychologist prescribe for human flourishing?

Background: Luke and Psychological Narrative

Starting from the very beginning of the Gospel, Luke has taken care to highlight Jesus' ability to reveal human heart conditions. In Luke 2:34–35, Simeon's prediction anticipates Jesus' vocation: *"that this child is destined for the falling and the rising of many in Israel, and to be a sign that will be opposed. So that the inner thoughts of many will be revealed."* Many have pointed to the importance of this verse in the narrative and believed that Luke has the intention of using these verses as a map to show readers how he will write about Jesus.[7] John A. Darr even states that,

> in the Lukan story the determinative factor in whether a character recognizes and/or responds correctly [to Jesus] is the status, or quality, of that character's 'heart' . . . Characters who have hearts that are not fully right fail to grasp the message . . . The ability to perceive correctly, which is a prior necessity for correct response, is thus tied directly to one's value system and inner orientation.[8]

John Drury notes the special attention Luke pays to revealing characters' internal monologues (what we today called "self-talk").[9] While Drury regards the frequent use of self-talk as Luke's personal style, scholars like John R. Donahue, Philip Sellew, and John Darr find the revealed self-talk as an intentional narrative device adopted by Luke for formation purposes. Let me cite Donahue here:

> For Luke, the human condition is a stage on which appear memorable characters . . . Luke invites us into this world by frequent use of soliloquy . . . where we are made privy to the inner

---

5. Bernie-Hurbin, "Common Principles," 1–3.

6. Walsh, "Surprised by Self," 1–21; Malherbe, "Hellenistic Moralists," 267–333; Halliwell, "Traditional Greek Conceptions of Character," 32–59.

7. Dinkler, "Thoughts of Many Hearts," 373–99.

8. Darr, *On Character Building*, 58.

9. Drury, *Parables in the Gospels*, 108–20.

musings of the characters. Luke eschews allegory and expresses realistic sympathy for the dilemmas of ordinary human existence. His memorable characters offer paradigms of discipleship for daily Christian existence.[10]

This style of writing has its root in the teaching of the philosophers, as Sellew has spelled out:

> When a narrator renders his or her characters' thoughts and decision-making processes so directly, the reader or dramatic audience is able to grasp their self-understanding and moral dilemmas with increased psychological depth and empathy. Awareness of this technique and its effects is not just a modern event. The distinction between a distanced or "plain" narration [*haplē diēgēsis*] and imitative narration [*mimēsis*], where the narrator speaks in the person of a character, was already a matter of interest for Plato.[11]

Bringing Greco-Roman thought into the discussion can help clear up some misconceptions and open up new horizons for deciphering Lukan rhetoric. Bruce J. Malina has popularized the view that ancient people were less concerned about psychological development because as "dyadic personalities," in collective societies, they seldom if ever experienced an autonomous self. Hence, ancient communities tended to avoid introspection.[12] However, studies of ancient writers such as Homer, Plato, Vergil, Ovid, Apollonius, Longus, and Xenophone of Ephesus reveal abundant introspection. Of course, we must acknowledge that ancient "self-knowledge" differs from our modern one, but they are by no means "anti-introspective."[13]

Researchers into this area have uncovered some interesting ancient rhetorical exercises as a means for psychotherapy or healing. The rise of narrative criticism in biblical studies has opened up new possibilities for interpreting the story of Jesus. New Testament narrative criticism focuses

---

10. Donahue, *Gospel in Parable*, 126.

11. Sellew, "Interior Monologue," 240. Unlike Bruce Malina (see below) or others who argue that ancient collectivistic societies are not interested in interiority.

12. It is commonly believed that ancient people were allocentric (defined by their relations to others) and post-modern (especially Western) people are idiocentric (defined as autonomous individuals). Malina, *New Testament World*, 68–69; *Portraits of Paul*, 169, 227–31; Malina and Neyrey, "First Century Personality," 67–96. See also Gill, *Structured Self*, 29–40.

13. Dinkler, "Thoughts of Many Hearts," 377–80.

on studying a text or story through the rhetoric of plot and characterization; it aims to understand the world of the implied reader, and thus its implied author. The study of psychological narratives, which is also a part of narrative criticism, focuses on studying how an author structures the inner world of the characters in the story.

Michal Beth Dinkler has shown that in Luke's time, Greco-Roman writers frequently employed psychological narratives to convey their message.[14] Josh Stigall uses Aesop's Fables as example to discuss psychological narratives and apply them in Lukan narrative.[15] Abraham J. Malherbe and others turn to an ancient rhetoric known as psychagogy for insights into early Christian texts.[16] Psychagogy, according to Darr, "involved the moral, spiritual, and psychological formation of budding philosophers through wide-ranging dialectical interaction with their philosopher-mentors, and was understood not simply as a pedagogical tool, but as an intimate form of personal therapy, the cure of souls through words." Darr has summarized this technique succinctly thus:

> Most striking to a relative newcomer to this material is the frequency and conviction with which Greco-Roman philosophers of many stripes referred to what they were doing as therapy. Andre-Jean Voelke sums up this sentiment: "One encounters in most ancient philosophers the idea that philosophy is therapy. This idea takes the form, for example, of comparing the philosopher to the physician, the ignorance of the non-philosopher to an illness, and philosophical learning to healing." What ails humans is never simply of the body, as Hippocrates knew. Full and true healing occurs with the aid of "physicians of the soul," that is, authentic philosophers who use words to cure all manner of intellectual, spiritual, and moral ills. Pedro Lain Entralgo observes that philosophers as divergent as Plato and Aristotle agreed that "by persuasively arousing new beliefs in the mind of the hearer, or by modifying with art and tact those in it that might already exist, the psychagogic word creates in that mind a new order, more 'natural' and proper than the one existing prior to the speech, or corrects the disorder (ametria) from which the constitution of the psychic life may have been suffering." According to Malherbe, a wide spectrum of philosophical groups

---

14. Dinkler, "Thoughts of Many Hearts," 380–84.

15. Stigall, "Progymnasmata," 350.

16. Malherbe, "Hellenistic Moralists," 267–333. See also *Paul*. However, most of Malherbe's studies focus on Paul and his letters.

(eg., Epicureans, Stoics, Pythagoreans, Platonists, Cynics, Peripatetics) were utilizing psychagogical means to engender moral reform in their students by the first century CE; prominent practitioners included the likes of Zeno, Dio Chrysostom, Epictetus, Seneca, and Plutarch.

What were these philosopher-physicians (or psychagogues) up to? Malherbe maintains that psychagogy was a well-known and well-developed system of care designed to promote the growth and welfare of those seeking the philosophical life. This system included what today is meant by spiritual exercises, psychotherapy, psychological and pastoral counseling. Clarence E. Glad observes that a person's turn to philosophy (not unlike the process of conversion in Paul's churches) often required "radical reorientation" involving social, intellectual, and moral transformation. To effect such transformation, philosophers in the soul-molding business utilized a variety of psychagogical tools: persuasion and dissuasion, negative and positive examples (exempla), exhortation, criticism, reproach, and comfort. Glad envisions psychagogy operating in a specific educational context: intimate and personal interaction between a mature person (the philosopher-teacher) and a neophyte (the student in need of various kinds of formation). In this scenario, psychagogy involved "guidance of neophytes at the early stages of liminality," but was also applicable to more mature followers in danger of lapsing. The psychagogue's challenge was to assess a student's individual needs and then craft a rhetorical strategy to address those needs. Hence, flexibility and variety were integral to the practice of psychagogy.[17]

Growth in the field of psychology in the past decades has contributed to many new insights in biblical interpretation. In particular, advances in the field of cognitive science have opened doors to more nuanced and novel understandings of religious behaviours, traditions, rituals, extraordinary experiences, and Christian narratives. István Czachesz even claims that the field of biblical studies is witnessing a cognitive turn.[18] Exciting as this may be, we must beware of the danger in projecting our modern psychological concepts into the first century. Nevertheless, when applied with caution, the rich insights from a study of psychological narratives will open up new doors for biblical interpretation. They allow us

---

17. Darr, "Narrative Therapy," 338–39.

18. Czachesz, *Cognitive Science*, 8–23. Czachesz and Risto Uro have co-edited a book based on this new approach. See Czachesz and Uro, *Mind, Morality and Magic*.

to take an inside path to understanding how a person, for example Luke, perceives and interprets his world and experience.[19]

Embedded within the first century worldview is a holistic health concept of a connected body and mind. It would be unthinkable to picture Luke as a doctor, writer, and evangelist in the first century not following naturally his rich background of holistic medicine, philosophy, psychagogy, and narrative therapy in his gospel telling, writing for the detoxification of the heart and the cleansing of the mind, to help correct distorted understandings of reality and provide for the healing of the whole person. Hence, I do not think it is too absurd to explore the possibility that Doctor Luke may have tried to write his gospel as a type of narrative therapy or prescription, introducing a special cure for age old common human ailments of the hearts and minds.[20] And, our more difficult question now is: if Luke had indeed attempted such an exercise, how do we know he had? If he had, how would Doctor Luke write down his prescription to help his possible "patients" with heart and mind afflictions? Can we read Luke as a type of "narrative therapy" to bring about healings of the heart?

The answers to these questions call for a whole new reading of Luke using these new lenses and approaches. If Doctor Luke did write his gospel as a prescription for the nourishment of the heart and mind, and if we are to answer this question, we must look at the whole narrative of Luke. Such an extensive study is beyond the scope of this paper. However, though we cannot enter this exciting door for now, I hope we can at least take a glimpse through it. We do not have the luxury to be exhaustive; instead, we will limit ourselves to a few sampling studies of Lukan foodology and tableism.

---

19. Schiff, "Function of Narrative," 45. Even though in general, narrative psychotherapy is not used in this way, we can still draw insight from the methodology to understand how Luke perceives and retells the story of Jesus as a third person.

20. "Narrative therapy" is used here simply to denote the restructuring of stories and memories, in particular the story and memory of Jesus, in a therapeutic way to bring about healings by inviting positive changes in people's perception of reality and themselves, empowering listeners to engage their problems by providing a healthy alternative solution and reimagining their identities. It is different from the modern psychotherapy with the same name.

Aspects of Lukan Foodology

Luke 1–2

When we open the Gospel of Luke, we first discovered Jesus being served to the readers in a food container: the manger. Careful study shows that Luke has intentionally orchestrated this spectacular entrance of Jesus. After much announcement and preparation in ch. 1 (viz, 1:1–2:6), the stage is set for the appearance of the main character in ch. 2. When the spotlight turns to Jesus, there is the image that is related to food: a baby lying in a manger. Manger as food container holding the fragile, unassuming but life-giving savior is a stunning first image crafted by Luke for his reader. Note especially that the name "Jesus" has not even appeared in the narrative, yet the image of a child lying in a manger is being repeated three times (2:7, 12, 16). Verses 11–12 give us a clue to decode the puzzle of this design: "to you is born this day in the city of David a Savior, who is the Messiah, the Lord. This will be a sign for you: you will find a child wrapped in bands of cloth and lying in a manger."

In close proximity to the "food image" of Jesus are the three most important titles of Jesus: *Savior, Messiah,* and *Lord* (v. 11). Subtly and powerfully Luke is preparing his readers to understand what a Savior, Messiah, and Lord means: Jesus is the God-given spiritual food that is essential for life and human flourishing. He will satisfy humanity's deepest hunger. The image of a child lying in a manger was a sign given to the shepherds so that they might find Jesus in history; it is also a sign given by Luke to his readers across history, so that they may be successful in locating Jesus as the "ultimate health food," served on a unique "platter," as a unique cure to their life long hunger. It is a unique foreshadowing of what the abstract titles *Savior, Messiah,* and *Lord* will mean in their everyday lives.

In antiquity, food was associated with power. Governments frequently used food to control their subjects. The rich and the powerful used food to pay, to please, and to punish. Physicians used food to bring about healing and wellness.[21] This form of power is linked especially to Jesus' power to bring peace. Within this first introduction of Jesus, Luke already summarized the vocation of Jesus through the announcement of the angels: "Glory to God in the highest heaven, and on earth peace among those whom he favours!" (2:13) This vocation is related to the

---

21. Garnsey, *Food and Society,* 22–33.

larger picture in the Gospel of Luke where Jesus' healing and life-giving power is manifested in various scenes of miracles and soul-guiding teaching. Food sustains life and brings about growth and well-being. Notably, "peace" in both Hebrew and Greek carries the connotation of well-being and wholeness. Without food we will not survive. The Christology of Jesus as "food" conveys the message that his mission and vocation is to provide for personal and community survival, which includes growth, healing, renewal, and wholeness.

Luke 9:7–20

In the miracle of the "Feeding of the Five Thousand" (9:10–17), Luke again skilfully crafts his presentation of Jesus as the essential "food" that satisfies hunger. Luke is the only one of the four evangelists, who all record this incident, to present it in a sandwiched structure, with discussions concerning Jesus' identity acting as two breads and Jesus' feeding miracle as the center piece in the sandwich. Before recalling how Jesus feeds the five thousand in the field of Bethsaida, Luke narrates Herod's perplexity concerning Jesus' identity: "because it was said by some that John had been raised from the dead, by some that Elijah had appeared, and by others that one of the ancient prophets had arisen" (9:7–9). The three identities—John the Baptist, Elijah, and ancient prophets—recurs again after the feeding story, where again Jesus' identity is being discussed: "who do the crowds say that I am?" (9:18). Only this time, the answer comes from the disciples, representing the mass population's understanding of Jesus: "some say John the Baptist; but others, Elijah; and still others, that one of the ancient prophets has arisen" (9:19). Jesus' true identity as the Messiah of God is being spelled out openly in Peter's speech (9:20). This, and only this, miracle story appears in all four Gospels. Yet only Luke frames the feeding story within two pericopes dealing with the question of Jesus' identity. The verbatim repetition (in Greek) of "that one of the ancient prophets had arisen" (9:8, 19) in the framing narratives helps to make obvious the parallel of the two frames in the reader's mind.[22]

As Howard Marshall points out, Luke deliberately couples the feeding miracle directly to the issue of Jesus' identity because it is a miracle that contributes to "a decisive revelation" of who Jesus is.[23] Here, Jesus as

---

22. Poon, "Superabundant Table Fellowship," 224.
23. Marshall, *Gospel of Luke*, 363–64.

Messiah is being linked again to a food motif. The unique A–B–A sandwich structure in Luke offers a vital key for the readers to understand the identity of Jesus: Jesus is what the soul's hunger, since creation, has been searching for (if we recall, Lukan genealogy traces back to the first human, Adam). He is the long-promised messiah, the fulfiller of human grand hunger: a perfect leader and king.

This kingly role must be understood in terms of the generous provider for the food of life. The linking of Jesus' identity as a food provider in a food-lacking desert is a subtle message to Luke's readers whereby Jesus is presented as the one who will satisfy needs, bring joy, promote healing, and sustain life. Like food, he is one of the most essential ingredients for human wellbeing and happiness. He is the powerful and hospitable ruler because he controls the food provision and gives generously with abundance left over. His provisions will be timely and overflowing. Even in a deserted place the crowds could find lavish supply. Wilson Poon observes that this miracle is done not only to satisfy a physical need, it is done to show that Jesus' identity as ruler brings about "super-abundant table fellowship," which "is symbolic of the joy of God's uncalculating forgiveness, and a pointer to the eschatological messianic banquet."[24] As it has been pictured in Isa 25:6, "On this mountain the LORD Almighty will prepare a feast of rich food for all peoples, a banquet of aged wine—the best of meats and the finest of wines. On this mountain he will destroy the shroud that enfolds all peoples, the sheet that covers all nations." Jesus' kingship is key to human flourishing. He is the generous provider of all good things, notably life-depending grace, soul-renewing forgiveness, life-preserving judgement, and an ideal kingly model of selfless service.[25]

The eucharistic overtones in the feeding story is again a rather subtle and powerful message. Luke describes how Jesus "blessed" and "broke" the bread and "gave" it to the disciples (9:16). This language looks forward to the eucharistic language in 22:16–20, and also to the Emmaus road in 24:13–35.[26] Metaphorically, Jesus is referring to himself as the bread being blessed, broken, and given. He is, both the Messiah who feeds us—the food provider—and also the food itself: blessed, broken, and given for us on the cross, in order to feed us, and nourish us towards spiritual health and peace.

24. Poon, "Superabundant Table Fellowship," 226.

25. Poon, "Superabundant Table Fellowship," 226.

26. Poon, "Superabundant Table Fellowship," 229, argues that it points primarily not to the upper room, but to the Emmaus road experience.

Luke 24:13–35

Last but not least, just as he does in the introduction, Luke crafts the ending of Jesus' earthly story carefully to shed light on the Lord's identity and to guide the readers in seeing beyond the obvious. The Emmaus meal is especially important in the Lukan narrative because it is unique, and it is the first post-resurrection meal mentioned in Luke-Acts. Again, the true identity of Jesus is revealed at last, only in close connection to the food. The disciples recognized him precisely through his very action of breaking the bread (24:30–31): "When he was at the table with them, he took bread, blessed and broke it, and gave it to them. Then their eyes were opened, and they recognized him." This eye-opening experience is so important that it is repeated again within close proximity in the disciples' recollection of the event in v. 35: "Then they told what had happened on the road, and how he had been made known to them in the breaking of the bread." The double reference here is obvious. Jesus is the bread that has been broken, and it is in this act of breaking himself open and the act of sharing a meal, that his messianic identity (i.e., as perfect leader who serves his people sacrificially) is revealed. In his bread breaking act, the disciples are brought to the knowledge of Jesus' life sharing identity and how he brings peace. Through this act comes the fulfilment of prophecy and recognition of Jesus, including his death and resurrection. The eschatological character of the meal reveals the invitation the resurrected Jesus has for his followers to participate in the meal (i.e., the practice of sacrificial service to others following their leader's perfect example), which is a proleptic celebration of the coming kingdom of peace.[27]

In summary, Jesus is being portrayed by Luke in his Gospel as both the essential food of life that brings peace, and also the powerful food provider who is himself broken, given, and shared. The combined images showcase the way of peace brought by Jesus. This powerful king and food provider does not just give good things, but, best of all, he gives himself, the ultimate good. Like all good, it is in the sacrificial giving and breaking that the food nourishes the person. This is what being the *Lord*, *Savior*, and *Messiah* means in day to day terms. This is the way of peace. These identities of Jesus point to and have been most symbolically displayed in his self-denial on the cross, offering himself to the world like bread that has been broken so that we can feed on him and partake

---

27. Arthur, *Just the Ongoing Feast*, 26–30.

in his perfect divine and human natures. This is the ultimate medicine for broken hearts and relationships, for ultimate healings and authentic human flourishing.

Food and Healing in Luke

It is only natural to link Luke's frequent usage of the food image to his medical background. A doctor's vocation is about saving life, bringing health and wellness, restoring peace to the body and mind. This vocation has a lot to do with advising what and how one eats. Especially in ancient times, as in Chinese medicines or natural medicines today, doctors would normally prescribe food as remedies to bring about health and healing.[28] It is interesting to note that Loveday Alexander, who after painstaking research into the form and genre of the Lukan preface in the wider context of Greco-Roman literature, concludes that "Luke 1:1–4 had little in common with historiographical prologues, but much in common with prefaces to technical or scientific, and more specifically, to medical treatises by the likes of Galen the physician."[29]

Not only that, Lukan fascination with food may have a deeper scriptural and philosophical significance. As Derek Flood has pointed out, the New Testament frequently portrays sin as sickness.[30] Flood devotes a whole chapter in his book to explain how in the Bible salvation often means healing. He states that, "While understanding sin in terms of legal transgression has come to be seen as the 'traditional' religious view today, this was not always the case. This legal view of sins was largely formed in the Middle Ages where theology was heavily influenced by the punitive legal thought of the time. In contrast, the understanding of the early church was much more focused on the idea of sin as sickness and salvation as healing."[31] Joel Green also states that the "larger Roman world of Jesus' day conceived of salvation as healing." In those days, the

---

28. Hippocrates, the father of Western medicine, believed that all diseases originate from the gut, i.e., what one eats. Hence, the way to healing also begins with the gut. This concept is repeated in various natural pathologies or even in natural therapeutic cookbooks today. For example, see Wszelaki, *Cooking for Hormone Balance*, 31.

29. Alexander, "Luke's Preface," 65–74.

30. Flood, *Healing the Gospel*, 17–25.

31. Flood, *Healing the Gospel*, 20.

most common usage of the term for "saved" or "salvation" was medical; to "save" was "to heal."[32]

Sin is not simply moral failure. It is in many ways a type of sickness. Many philosophers have set out to pursue the ultimate good and yet find these ultimate virtues vague and non-achievable because they cannot be achieved merely through education or understanding. Hence, in Luke's narrative, to be saved, men and women not only need to be taught about moral standards, but also to be healed. Such healing can only happen with the "right food." It is not too surprising to see Doctor Luke take good care to offer his possible patients the ultimate health food—Jesus. And this Lukan Christology of Jesus as food is in close association with the salvation theme of the Gospel.[33] Just as Hans Urs Von Balthasar has stated:

> Christian self-understanding (and therefore theology) can be interpreted neither in terms of a wisdom that surpasses the knowledge of the world's religions through a divine utterance (*ad majorem gnosim rerum divinarum*) nor in terms of man's definitive achievement of personal and social fulfillment through revelation and redemption (*ad majorem hominis perfectionem et progessum generis humani*), but solely in terms of the self-glorification of divine love: *ad Majorem Divini Amoris GlORIAM*. In the Old Testament, this glory (kabod) is the presence of Yahweh's radiant majesty in his Covenant (and through this Covenant it is communicated to the rest of the world); in the New Testament, this sublime glory presents itself as the love of God that descends "to the end" of the night of death in Christ.[34]

What Luke tries to achieve through his narrative of Jesus is not just knowledge about Jesus but a vision of the glory of Jesus, to capture the hearts for love. If sin is not just moral failure, but a type of sickness, then this sickness is the failure of a heart to love and to be loved. The cure then should start from the heart; participating in the divine recreation of a heart of love, the inner person does not shy away from love—not just any kind of love, the love of divine glory. As Balthasar continues: "Lovers are the ones who know most about God; the theologian must listen to

---

32. Green, *Salvation*, 36, cited in Flood, *Healing the Gospel*, 21.
33. Marshall, *Luke: Historian*, 77–156.
34. Balthasar, *Love Alone*, 10.

them."[35] Lukan narratives do not intend to create just theologians, but lovers of Christ who know the truth (1:4).[36] To do this, Luke has to work deep into the hearts, not just minds, though the minds are involved.

Aspects of Lukan Tableism

Served "deep into the hearts" is thus Jesus' tableism in the Gospel of Luke. Luke not only uses the motif of food to interpret Jesus' identity and mission; he also uses table-fellowship to explain Jesus' vocation to love, to befriend, to esteem. The Lukan narrative repeatedly shows how Jesus' all-embracing table-fellowship imparts divine love and esteem to all humanity.[37] Robert Karris observes that in Luke's Gospel Jesus is either "going to a meal, at a meal or coming from a meal."[38] Jesus actually eats his way through the gospel narrative! (What a vocation!) To a certain extent, Jesus' vocation in Luke can be summarized as "eating with the sinners (and Pharisees)."

To understand the rhetoric of this narrative, we need to understand the background of Roman and Jewish tableism. Dennis E. Smith identifies "symposia" as the major meal practice of the region from 300 BCE to 300 CE.[39] While the word "symposium" is used today to refer to a conference, Luke and Jesus would refer to it as meal. The word "symposium" in Greek means simply "drinking with." It was used in ancient Greco-Roman society to refer to gatherings of community, usually festive ones, to eat,

---

35. Balthasar, *Love Alone*, 12.

36. Darr has pointed our attention to the obvious but neglected: "The formative aspect of Luke's work has too often been overlooked or downplayed by recent scholarship, which has preferred to view Luke as historian, a theologian, or a literary artist, rather than as a pastor . . . Is it possible that, in our drive to recover historical data, theological doctrines, and literary art, we have either failed to notice, or underestimated the therapeutic and catechetical thrust of Luke's project? In his preface, might Luke have been presenting himself not so much as a historian, or as a theologian, or even as a physician of the body, but rather, as a philosopher-physician—that is, as a psychagogue—and his text as therapy for readers' souls?" (Darr, "Narrative Therapy," 347–48).

37. Neyrey says, "by eating with sinners and foreigners Jesus formally signals that God extends an inclusive invitation to non-observant and sinful outsiders for covenant membership and for status as forgiven persons" (Neyrey, *Social World*, 378).

38. Karris, *Luke*, 47.

39. Smith, "Table Fellowship," 614.

drink, and chat.⁴⁰ Philosophers often use those symposia or banquets as opportunity for moral instruction.

Hence, it is sometimes believed that Luke views table fellowship merely as a literary device that has great similarity with Greco-Roman symposium literature. He employs this literary genre to make it easier for his audience to understand. Though this understanding provides essential background for interpreting the genre, the significance of Lukan tableism cannot be reduced to mere conformity to Greco-Roman traditions; Jesus' tableism is not a mere literary genre. Instead, it is a powerful demonstration of the saving feature of Jesus' ministry, as acted parable showcasing God's gifts of grace to all people to join in the eschatological banquet of reconciliation. It highlights fellowship with God and with one another. It is a vivid picture of an open invitation to all to come to the kingdom of God. We eat most frequently with the persons who are closest to us. Our choice to eat or not to eat with a person conveys our heart values. Eating together means accepting, not eating together means rejecting. It is because of this that Jesus chose to eat with sinners (15:2). To Luke, this act of Jesus clearly conveys his mission to save sinners. The meals Jesus partakes of should be correctly viewed as crucial "gospel events" in the unfolding narratives.

Furthermore, Jewish meals were monitored by their oral law and their table-fellowship was guarded by purity stipulations. There were prescriptions for (1) right foods that were properly tithed and correctly prepared; (2) right persons with whom one may eat; (3) right water and other requirements for purification rites; and (4) right seating arrangement ranked appropriately in terms of status and honor.⁴¹ It is against these backdrops that Luke recorded Jesus' unconventional style of eating. Karris claims boldly that "Jesus was killed because of the way he ate."⁴²

Luke 7:34

One of the defining statements of Jesus' vocation is phrased in terms of eating: "The Son of Man has come eating and drinking, and you say, 'Look, a glutton and a drunkard, a friend of tax collectors and sinners!'" (Luke

---

40. "In the strictest sense, the meal was first and foremost, and then followed by the drinking of mixed wine and conversation. Thus, it is named" (Karris, *Eating*, 8–9).
41. Neyrey, *Social World*, 361–68.
42. Karris, *Luke*, 70.

7:34).⁴³ The summary nature of 7:34 is self-evident from the amount of narrative space Luke has provided to depict Jesus in table fellowship with sinners, tax collectors, and even Pharisees. As S.S. Bartchy summarizes, "One distinctive feature of Jesus' ministry was his practice of a radically inclusive and non-hierarchical table fellowship as a central strategy in his announcement and redefinition of the inbreaking rule of God."⁴⁴ Jerome Neyrey says, "by eating with sinners and foreigners Jesus formally signals that God extends an inclusive invitation to non-observant and sinful outsiders for covenant membership and for status as forgiven persons."⁴⁵ The tableism in Luke bridges distinctions between people coming from all walks of life at the table of God. It highlights the hospitality and esteem of God.⁴⁶

Luke 14:15–24; 15:1–2

Jesus' parables concerning banquets in Luke 14 and his experience of the divided table vividly reveal human heart conditions and our self-centred lifestyles. Unfortunately, the divided meal table is the common description of human life. It is the most natural principle we abide by in our eating customs and in our ways of treating one another. Even within the Christian home and church, such division is often inevitable. No wonder the way of peace is so elusive to many, because we live constantly in a world of division, trying to draw lines for ourselves, for others, for God, yet forgetting that Jesus came to abolish these very sin-causing and flesh-pleasing lines (Eph 2:14–18).

When Luke describes how the religious leaders murmur against Jesus' deliberate choice in eating with sinners (15:1–2), their divisive hearts revealed in psychological narrative, he is informing us that the religious leaders would not agree with Jesus' mission, and thus did not

---

43. The context of Luke 7:34 may suggest a casual description of Jesus' act as compared to John the Baptist. But detailed studies suggest that it is an important summary statement of Jesus' general conduct. This pronouncement is not too different to the summary statement of Jesus' vocation in 19:10, "For the Son of Man came to seek out and to save the lost." The "lost" is parallel to "the tax collectors and sinners" in 7:34, the work to "seek out and to save" is parallel to the work of "eating and drinking and befriending" in 7:34.

44. Bartchy, "Table Fellowship," 796.

45. Neyrey, *Social World*, 378.

46. Byrne, *Hospitality of God*, 63–68, 122–23, 127–30.

understand the will of God. The Pharisees were concerned with rituals of cleanliness, they taxed their food carefully, and chose their eating partner carefully, selected the right seat carefully. They drew a very clear line between clean and unclean, and thought that this was the way to pursue holiness, to please God, and thus help to bring about human flourishing. They did not know that by drawing a clear line between themselves and sinners, they have drawn Jesus (the very food of life) out of their table. In their rejection of the open table, they have rejected the Lord (the very food) who could change their hearts. In contrast, Jesus opposes table division. He opposes a table that would only invite the same kind, only invite one's own friends and relatives, only invite the respected, the rich, those who could return the kindness (14:12–13).

Luke 5:27–39

In Luke 5:27–39, the quasi "mission" statement of 7:34 appears again, only this time it is in a story form. Levi's salvation and discipleship are being captured in a banquet he has thrown for Jesus, where a large crowd of tax collectors were invited. As the Pharisees and their scribes are complaining to Jesus' disciples concerning his scandalous behaviour in eating and drinking with tax collectors and sinners, Jesus seizes the opportunity to pronounce a powerful statement concerning his mission: "Those who are well have no need of a physician, but those who are sick; I have come to call not the righteous but sinners to repentance" (5:32).[47] Again, Jesus' mission to save sinners is clearly presented in the acts of eating and drinking with them. It highlights the neediness of the heart. Only a needy heart will seek a physician of the heart.

In summary, Jesus' meals with outcasts are not just an expression of his outstanding humanity and generous spirit. They are the quintessential expressions of Lukan Christology. They are the acted parables revealing God's salvation and the advent of the kingdom of peace. Luke clothes Jesus' vocation in table-fellowship imagery to express worldwide salvation. Jesus' meal table crosses the social boundary of purity and religious boundary of holiness by including those who have previously

---

47. Note that the same statement appears also in Matt 9:10–17 and Mark 2:15–22; however, only Luke uses throwing a banquet for Jesus to describe Levi's discipleship content. In Luke, discipleship is also often cast in table-fellowship language, connoting a reciprocal relationship; disciples are those who esteem Jesus with reciprocal hospitality.

been excluded from a table that had been reserved only for people who lived by the same purity codes. The meal then creates an opportunity for life changing experiences in the kingdom of God in that sinners become friends with God. This powerful and yet ordinary day-to-day imagery invites the narrative readers to rethink and envision Jesus' vocation in an ordinary day-to-day fashion, but with an extraordinary punch: God befriending human, the holy one esteeming sinners!

Conclusion

Luke's abundant use of eating motifs declares in a creative and powerful way the saving and healing work of Jesus in providing God's unconditional grace and forgiveness, while at the same time declaring judgment on the proud, and exemplifying community service to those who would be his followers. From our limited study of Lukan foodology and tableism, we can conclude that Luke does not present Jesus as a mere moral teacher at a symposium. Rather, he is a savior who eats with and befriends the lost and the needy; and he is the very "health food" that will bring peace and healing, satisfying hearts. Human flourishing should not be reduced to just moral education or social reformation; it should be something bigger. It is about God feeding human needs through Jesus, about God befriending and esteeming humanity, about being the friends of God, about divine-human companionship, about God esteem (not just self-esteem), about humans accepting the humanness in one another, about generous respect and love in communities full of brokenness and inequality, about a reformed table and heart, all made possible through a unique health tonic—Jesus.

History has witnessed humanity going through various kinds of movement, development, improvement, education, emancipation, reformation, revolution, renewal, and betterment, yet human heart conditions have not improved. Every generation witnesses our hearts coming to the same place of peace-search, dreaming of something better and larger, something beyond ourselves. Education is an important part of human development and will contribute richly to human flourishing, but it can only do so much. If we conceive the hinderance to human flourishing as a lack in education, we are misleading ourselves. Great education can only achieve so much; there is a mystical part to wholeness and healing which only the gospel can provide.

Luke's picture of Jesus as the ultimate food for life, for healing from sin and brokenness, at both individual and community levels, still speaks powerfully. "Food is definitely an important theme (in Luke) and, as such, draws the reader into Luke's faith-inspiring kerygmatic story. It is a theme which, because of its elemental nature, resonates at the depths of our contingent being."[48] Food is also a major theme in the twenty-first century. Here lies a powerful medium for Christians to communicate Christ to a food-loving health-conscious world. As health gurus often say these days, "you are what you eat!" If Dr. Luke is here today in the twenty-first century, we would most probably hear him repeating the same message to us: "feed on Jesus and you will be like him!" Through the healthy recognition, acceptance, and internalization of God-esteem, we are invited by the narrative of the Gospel of Luke to feed on Jesus, walk with Jesus, and be like Jesus.

Bibliography

Alexander, Loveday. "Luke's Preface in the Context of Greek Preface-Writing." *Novum Testamentum* 28 (1986) 65–74.

Arthur, A. *Just the Ongoing Feast: Table Fellowship and Eschatology at Emmaus*. Collegeville: Liturgical, 1993.

Balthasar, Hans Urs von. *Love Alone Is Credible*. San Francisco: Ignatius, 2004.

Bartchy, S. S. "Table Fellowship." In *Dictionary of Jesus and the Gospels*, edited by Joel B. Green, Jeannine K. Brown, and Nicholas Perrin, 796–800. Nottingham: InterVarsity, 1992.

Bernie-Hurbin, Annie. "Common Principles in Socratic Psychotherapy and Hippocratic Medicine." Paper presented at the Academia Homerica Conference, Chios, Germany, July 14–23, 2017.

Byrne, Brendan. *The Hospitality of God: A Reading of Luke's Gospel*. Strathfield: St Paul's, 2015.

Czachesz, István. *Cognitive Science and the New Testament: A New Approach to Early Christian Research*. Oxford: Oxford University Press, 2017.

Czachesz, István, and Risto Uro, eds. *Mind, Morality and Magic*. New York: Acumen, 2013.

Darr, John A. "Narrative Therapy: Treating Audience Anxiety Through Psychagogy in Luke." *Perspectives in Religious Studies* 39 (2015) 335–48.

———. *On Character Building: The Reader and the Rhetoric of Characterization in Luke-Acts*. Literary Currents in Biblical Interpretation. Louisville: Westminster John Knox, 1992.

Dinkler, Michal Beth. "'The Thoughts of Many Hearts Shall Be Revealed': Listening in on Lukan Interior Monologues." *Journal of Biblical Literature* 133 (2015) 373–99.

---

48. Karris, *Luke*, 47.

Donahue, John R. *The Gospel in Parable: Metaphor, Narrative, and Theology in the Synoptic Gospels*. Philadelphia: Fortress, 1989.
Drury, John. *The Parables in the Gospels: History and Allegory*. New York: Crossroad, 1985.
Flood, Derek. *Healing the Gospel*. Eugene, OR: Cascade, 2012.
Garnsey, Peter. *Food and Society in Classical Antiquity*. Cambridge: Cambridge University Press, 1999.
Gill, Christopher. *The Structured Self in Hellenistic and Roman Thought*. Oxford: Oxford University Press, 2006.
Green, Joel B. *Salvation*. St Louis: Chalice, 2003.
Halliwell, Stephen. "Traditional Greek Conceptions of Character." In *Characterization and Individuality in Greek Literature*, edited by Christopher Pelling, 32–59. Oxford: Clarendon, 1990.
Karris, Robert J. *Luke: Artist and Theologian*. New York: Paulist, 1985.
———. *Eating Your Way Through Luke's Gospel*. Collegeville: Liturgical Press, 2006.
Malherbe, Abraham J. "Hellenistic Moralists and the New Testament." In *Aufstieg Und Niedergang Der Romiscen Welt: Geschichte und Kultur Roms im Spiegel der neueren Forschung*, edited by H. Temporini and W. Haase, 267–333. New York: deGruyter, 1992.
———. *Paul and the Popular Philosophers*. Minneapolis: Fortress, 1989.
Malina, Bruce J. *The New Testament World: Insights from Cultural Anthropology*. 3rd ed. Louisville: Westminster John Knox, 2001.
———. *Portraits of Paul: An Archaeology of Ancient Personality*. Louisville: Westminster John Knox, 1996.
Malina, Bruce J., and Jerome H. Neyrey. "First Century Personality: Dyadic, Not Individualistic." In *Social World of Luke-Acts: Models of Interpretation*, edited by Jerome H. Neyrey, 67–96. Peabody: Hendrickson, 1991.
Marshall, I. Howard. *The Gospel of Luke: A Commentary on the Greek Text*. The New International Greek Testament Commentary. Exeter: Paternoster, 1978.
———. *Luke: Historian and Theologian*. Exeter: Paternoster, 1970.
Neyrey, Jerome H. *The Social World of Luke-Acts: Models for Interpretation*. Peabody: Hendrickson, 2008.
Poon, Wilson C. K. "Superabundant Table Fellowship in the Kingdom: The Feeding of the Five Thousand and the Meal Motif in Luke." *Expository Times* 114 (2003) 224–30.
Schiff, Brian. "The Function of Narrative: Toward a Narrative Psychology of Meaning." *Narrative Work: Issues, Investigations, and Interventions* 2 (2012) 33–47.
Sellew, Philip. "Interior Monologue As a Narrative Device in the Parables of Luke." *Journal of Biblical Literature* 111 (1992) 239–53.
Smith, Dennis E. "Table Fellowship as a Literary Motif in the Gospel of Luke." *Journal of Biblical Literature* 106 (1987) 613–38.
Stigall, Josh. "The Progymnasmata and Characterization in Luke's Parables." *Perspectives in Religious Studies* 39 (2012) 349–60.
Walsh, George B. "Surprised by Self: Audible Thought in Hellenistic Poetry." *Classical Philology* 85 (1990) 1–21.
Wszelaki, Magdalena. *Cooking for Hormone Balance*. New York: Harper One, 2018.

Chapter 7

Breaking Bread: The Power of Hospitality in the Gospel of Mark

JONATHAN RIVETT ROBINSON

Introduction: Mark 6:1–18:21 and Social Practice

THE APPROACH OF THIS essay is not an obvious one. First, *hospitality* is not a usual paradigm for considering social practice. Secondly, Christians may have historically founded social services, schools, orphanages, and hospitals, but can Christian Scripture continue to inform and illuminate contemporary social practice, which is usually theorised by sociology, psychology, or other modern, secular social-scientific disciplines? Finally, the importance of hospitality is well recognised in the Gospel of Luke,[1] but not so in Mark's Gospel. So, by way of introduction, I will briefly address these points.

I have written the reflections of this essay in conversation with two experienced Christian social workers.[2] My comments regarding social practice reflect the discussions I have had with them. I also have my own experiences of visitation, advocacy, education, and counseling from within the very different context of pastoral work as a church minister.

---

1. See, e.g., Kelley, "Meals with Jesus in Luke's Gospel."

2. I gratefully acknowledge Mike Tonks (NZ) and Morag Robinson (UK) who both took the time to read earlier forms of this paper, discussed it with me in person or on the phone and via email, and shared their own interpretations and insights. The reflections on social practice in the essay are as much their work as mine. Professor Paul Trebilco also commented constructively on an earlier form of this paper.

Theory around social practice is rightly characterized by concern for avoiding the abuse of power in the interaction between social worker/counselor/educator and client/student. Similar dynamics of power and vulnerability are also present in the practice of hospitality, as has been demonstrated in the work of philosopher Jacques Derrida.[3] We will explore these dynamics in this essay. Hospitality, then, provides a fresh lens with which to think about and critique power dynamics within a social practice setting.

Hospitality is a significant theme within Christian Scripture. The ancient practices of welcoming the stranger, sharing fellowship over a meal, and of the obligations of a host, are a frequent explicit and implicit theme in the biblical narratives (e.g., Gen 24:28–32; Judg 19; Luke 19:1–10). God also takes on the role of guest and host in both literal narrative and in more figurative prophecy and parable (e.g., Gen 18–19; Isa 25:6–10; Matt 22:1–14). The Bible, then, is one resource with which we can focus the lens of hospitality. For a Christian social practitioner, the Christian Scriptures have a special authority. Moreover, the person of Jesus has a unique attraction and paradigmatic role. Thus a study of a gospel (which tells the story of Jesus' earthly life), with a view to themes that relate to social practice, fulfils a double function of being a study of Holy Scripture and a study of the person that Christians are called, above all others, to imitate.[4] This essay is an invitation, then, for Christian practitioners to

---

3. The French-Algerian philosopher Jacques Derrida wrote a number of short works on the theme of hospitality in the years leading up to his death. His overriding concern was with the issue of immigration and xenophobia, particularly in France. Derrida's method was deconstruction, the demonstration of absurdities and contradictions in every thought, even down to the level of individual words. Hospitality was no exception: "Hospitality is a self-contradictory concept and experience which can only self-destruct (put otherwise, produce itself as impossible, only be possible on the condition of its impossibility) or protect itself from itself, auto-immunize itself in some way, which is to say, deconstruct itself—precisely—in being put into practice" (Derrida, "Hostipitality," 5). In Derrida's thought, hospitality indicates two opposing things, both an "unconditional law of unlimited hospitality" and also many "laws of hospitality. These rights and obligations always conditioned and conditional" (6). For Derrida, "It is between these two figures of hospitality that responsibilities and decisions must in effect be taken. This is a formidable challenge because if these two hospitalities do not contradict each other, they remain heterogeneous at the very moment they appeal to each other, in a disconcerting way" (6).

4. "Mark's whole story of Jesus can be read as a blueprint for the Christian life: it begins with baptism, proceeds with the vigorous pursuit of ministry in the face of temptation and opposition, and culminates in suffering and death oriented towards an as-yet unseen vindication" (Davis, "Christology, Discipleship, and Self-Understanding in the Gospel of Mark," 109).

reflect on ways the gospel story can inform and illuminate their work. And, if a reader does not share the Christian faith, it is an invitation to taste and see one possible new approach to the power dynamics of social practice. Thus, this essay is itself a form of hospitality. I invite you to try out this way of thinking. My reflections are not definitive but tentative. They are experimental rather than final. I hope that you, as my guest, feel free to take or leave what I put before you, but also that you will find something worth chewing on.

At the risk of stating the obvious, the Bible is a large book and in a short essay it is necessary to be selective if we are to study it in any depth. At the time of writing, I am in the middle of a very different and much larger project on the Gospel of Mark. Along the way, I made an intriguing discovery. The Greek word for "bread," *artos*, occurs twenty-one times in Mark's Gospel. Eighteen of those times are within the section 6:1–8:21.[5] *Artos* occurs only twice before this and only once after. This high rate of occurrence of the word "bread" in 6:1–8:21, especially in contrast to the rest of the Gospel, does not appear to be random.[6] Instead, as we will see, it is part of the author's thematic strategy where the theme of hospitality helps to unify the diverse episodes of this section.[7] This section of Mark, then, is a strong example of the importance of hospitality within the Bible and, far from being incidental, appears to have significance for the Gospel's author. This small section of Mark presents itself as a manageable

---

5. "The keyword (*Stichwort*) is bread" (Hübenthal, *Das Markusevangelium als kollectives Gedächtnis*, 403). Although I discovered this independently, I later realized Hübenthal had previously made many of the same observations, although her interpretive emphasis is somewhat different. Note: here and following, translations from German works are my own.

6. In terms of method, I should note one key assumption: that the Gospel of Mark is a coherent narrative work of literature, rich with meaning both on the literal surface of the text and in its use of allusion and symbol. This needs to be noted because not every Bible scholar would agree with me here, although many do. However, I hope the results of this study could be taken as evidence to support this assumption. I will not refer every point I make to individual commentaries, except where a point may be controversial. Two commentaries have been especially useful for their literary approach: Boring, *Mark*; and Donahue and Harrington, *Gospel of Mark*. Also, no study of Mark should fail to consult the two landmark critical commentaries: Marcus, *Mark 1–8*, and Collins, *Mark*.

7. "The questions around bread, meal and table community/ies pervade the whole section of text 6:7–8:26 from the sending of the disciples to the argument in the boat. In some form, the subject is always food and community issues" (Hübenthal, *Das Markusevangelium als kollectives Gedächtnis*, 402).

and possibly fruitful text to explore with hospitality and social practice in mind.

Daily Bread (Mark 6:1–13)

For the first five chapters of Mark's Gospel, Jesus' mission proceeds at full pace. Jesus is both the center of attention and the undisputed master of each situation. When opposition comes, whether from scribes, Pharisees, or demonic forces, Jesus brushes them aside and uses each incident to further display his authority as teacher and bearer of God's spirit. In 4:35–5:43 successive miracles demonstrate Jesus' complete power over nature, demons, health, and even death. It comes as a shock then, when in Mark 6:1–6 Jesus comes to his home town and instead of a hero's welcome they take offense at him (6:2–3). As a result he can do "no deed of power there, except that he laid his hands on a few sick people and cured them" (6:5).[8] The narrator goes on to tell us that Jesus "was amazed at their unbelief" (6:6). The implication is that the lack of faith among those of Jesus' home town prevented Jesus from doing deeds of power there. For the first time in Mark's narrative we are exposed to limits in Jesus' power. The hostility in Jesus' home town, the faithlessness of his hosts, disables him. Up to this point Jesus had been the one amazing others. Now he is the one amazed, no longer the master of the situation but the victim.

The change from guest to victim is an easy one to make. Derrida notes that the etymology of the word Hospitality breaks down into two Indo-European roots: *hospes,* meaning guest or stranger, and *potis,* meaning master, sovereign, power. From this Derrida moves to observe that the host can only offer hospitality to a guest when master of the house: "the host, he who offers hospitality, must be the master in his house, he must be assured of his sovereignty over the space and goods he offers or opens to the other as stranger . . . It does not seem to me that I am able to open up or offer hospitality, however generous, even in order to be generous, without reaffirming: this is mine."[9] Hence the offer of hospitality is both an offer to a guest and a claim to sovereignty over one's home. For Derrida this creates a contradictory situation. We see this contradiction at work in Mark 6:1–6 where Jesus is received as a teacher in his home

---

8. Here and elsewhere, Bible translations are from the NRSV.
9. Derrida, "Hostipitality," 14.

town. We would expect the law of hospitality, unconditional openness, to be at work here, especially for a returned son of the village. Will they not be pleased to have him back? Is he not a "local boy made good"? Yet when they hear him teach he clearly breaks some unwritten rule of what he is permitted to do and be as a guest in his home town. The town responds not with openness but hostility. I suspect the town's indignation at Jesus' wisdom and power is a Palestinian version of "Tall Poppy Syndrome"—a condition which Kiwis may be surprised to learn is not unique to New Zealand![10] Their attitude could be paraphrased: "we know this guy is no one special, so who does he think he is?" (6:2–3). What is perhaps most surprising to us is that, as a guest, Jesus finds himself under the power of his host's laws and his own power is diminished (6:5). Here the Gospel illustrates an etymological contradiction, noted by Derrida, that *host* and *hostile* share the same root.[11] Because in offering hospitality the host asserts power, the transition from welcoming host to hostile enemy is easily made, and so the guest becomes a victim of the host.

The social practitioner often enters the homes or contexts of others, intending to bring assistance or positive change. They find themselves, like Jesus, in the posture of guests who can be disabled in their positive intentions if the host is unreceptive. If a client is hostile or passive-aggressive they may often "play games" with the practitioner, obstructing, misleading, or confusing them. As frustrating as this is we can see two things in the Gospel episode: (1) Jesus, though amazed by their unbelief, does not use his considerable power to force his help upon them; (2) Jesus still does a few healings (6:5)—he does not allow his negative reception from the majority to prevent him seeing and helping those few who are receptive in the situation.

Having been rejected in his home town, Jesus goes out among the villages teaching (6:6). He sends the twelve disciples out two by two and gives them authority over evil spirits. Their posture as they travel is to be guests. No bread, no bag, no money, no second shirt, they are to be dependent on the hospitality of others on their mission of preaching and healing. If they are rejected, they are to leave, shaking the dust off their feet as a sign against their faithless hosts (6:11).

---

10. Of course, Luke gives a different reason (and a different chronology) for Jesus' rejection (Luke 4:16–30), but we are reading Mark and can only use the clues Mark gives us.

11. Derrida, "Hostipitality," 13.

The disciples, like Jesus, are guests. While this posture risks rejection, it also creates possibility for genuine human connection beyond the playing out of dehumanizing official roles. In social practice theory, Carl Rogers' concepts of "genuineness," "unconditional positive regard," and "empathy," are often given as an ideal.[12] By showing respect, appreciation, genuine interest, and relating as a genuine person (rather than a professional front or "just going through the motions"), trust is built in the relationship and positive development becomes far more possible. The concept of *guest* is a useful way to encapsulate this, reminding us that while we have a job to do the genuine human relationship is paramount and to the benefit of both parties. Social workers and ministers often visit in people's homes, but even in the case of a counselor in an office or a teacher in the classroom they are a guest in the client/students' lives. Their effectiveness is reliant on their welcome.

When Jesus told the disciples what to do if rejected (6:11), he showed that his own rejection was not unique but that part of being a guest is vulnerability to the possibility of rejection. To be a guest, then, is to be open to *surprise*. The surprise could be rejection, but equally it could be a more receptive welcome than anticipated. Social practitioners do not always have the option of walking away from an unreceptive client/student, and they certainly should not "shake off the dust from their feet as a testimony against them"! What they can always do is enter any new situation without prejudgement, open to the surprise of human connection and seeking to engage with the resources of their "host" instead of relying on what they bring with them (6:8–10).[13]

The Banquet of Death (Mark 6:14–29)

As the Gospel continues, the focus of the narrative shifts away from Jesus altogether, the only place in the Gospel it does so. The new (temporary) focus is King Herod as he hosts his birthday banquet. Herod's birthday party includes courtiers, officers, and local leaders (6:21), but he has another guest who is there against his will. John the Baptist had been arrested for criticizing Herod's marriage to his brother's wife, Herodias (6:17–18). But once under arrest, Herod protected him from harm (6:20).

---

12. Rogers, "Client-Centered/Person-Centered Approach to Therapy," 135–36.

13. This is highly congruent with Rogers' emphasis on trusting the client (Rogers, "Client-Centered/Person-Centered Approach to Therapy," 136–37).

Herodias, Herod's sister-in-law/wife, is the one who wishes to harm John (6:19). The opportunity to do so finally comes when at the birthday feast Herod promises Herodias' daughter anything she wants, up to half his kingdom (6:22–23). After consulting with her mother the girl requests "I want you to give me at once the head of John the Baptist on a platter" (6:25). Notice how Herod is manipulated. "At once," requires that Herod has no time to back out or change his mind. It forces him to fulfil his oath in front of his dinner guests. Without the guests there Herod will once again be lord of his home able to do whatever he wants. With the guests present Herod can lose face, be shamed, and possibly even have his position threatened if he is seen to be weak. While the presence of the guests forces Herod to do something distasteful, Herod's other guest, John, becomes part of the entertainment, even part of the meal; his head is presented on a plate (6:29). Herod's birthday feast becomes a "banquet of death."[14]

We observed before how a host can turn hostile to their guests, but now we see the opposite is also true. Derrida argues that there is a "reversal in which the master of this house, the master in his own home, the host, can only accomplish his task as host, that is, hospitality, in becoming invited by the other into his [own] home, in being welcomed by him whom he welcomes, in receiving the hospitality he gives."[15] Thus only the guest has the power to create the host as *host*. The guest consequently has power over the host, as the unwritten laws of hospitality create expectations that operate on the host as much as the guest. This principle appears to be at work in Herod's banquet. Herod is lord of his house and potentate of the region, presumably he is also master of his family and step-daughter, but because of his guests he is compelled to execute John. The laws of hospitality force him to do something he did not want to do. So we see that while the host may become hostile to the guest, equally the host can become a hostage (pun intended) to the guest.[16]

If we conceive of the social practitioner as guest, perhaps this story reminds us that the presence of someone who represents a higher authority or a powerful organization may inadvertently affect someone's behavior. A social worker may have the authority to take action that results in the removal of a child or someone's committal to a psychiatric

---

14. I am indebted for this evocative phrase to Aus, *Feeding the Five Thousand*, 131–32.

15. Derrida, "Hostipitality," 9; see also Derrida, *Of Hospitality*, 125.

16. Cf. Derrida, *Of Hospitality*, 123–25.

hospital. A counselor may be required to approve someone's ability to manage their anger or return to work. A teacher may hand out the grades that can decide a person's future. Even as much as you might seek to be sensitive and open to the client/student, the power that you hold could negatively influence their response and decisions. Herod's guests may or may not have wanted John to die, they may even have been indifferent, but their presence had a decisive effect on the outcome nonetheless (6:26). Awareness of the effect we are having on the relational systems within a family or community, while hard often to discern, is of critical importance.

Equally we can conceive of the social practitioner as host. The social worker, for instance, is often host in the sense of bringing the client as guest into an unfamiliar world of law and regulation as well as access to resources and methods and opportunities for positive change. Within that, the practitioner's felt need, to be effective in their work and to help others, leaves them vulnerable to manipulation by the clients without whom that need cannot be met. Whichever way we trace the lines of power, they are fraught with danger.

Miracle Bread (Mark 6:30-52)

After the story of Herod as host, the narrative returns to the apostles and Jesus, who now have their turn to be hosts. Jesus has become so popular with the crowd that he and his disciples do not even get a chance to eat (6:31),[17] so they go away in the boat to the wilderness to find some rest. Again, Jesus is thwarted as the crowds rush ahead of him and it seems the new crowd is even bigger than before. Is anyone host or guest out in the wilderness? Unlike Herod's invited guests, Jesus' crowd is anyone who felt like coming. When it grows late, the disciples feel responsible for the crowd and tell Jesus to dismiss the crowd so they can buy something to eat in the surrounding villages (6:35-36). But Jesus places the burden on the disciples: "You give them something to eat" (6:37). Jesus makes the disciples assume the responsibility of host. As hosts they have a duty to share what they have with their guests, but they only have five loaves and two fish.

---

17. "Obviously, *to eat* [*phagein*] does not here mean a snack between meals, but a meal that allows for community and conversation, in which one is satisfied by the community of body and soul" (Hübenthal, *Das Markusevangelium als kollektives Gedächtnis*, 403).

Jesus organises his own banquet, which Mark consciously pairs with Herod's banquet through the words *deipnon* (6:21) and *symposion* (6:39). Both words can mean banquet, but in the Greek culture of Mark's day the *symposion* (cf. symposium) was the food, entertainment, and conversation that followed a *deipnon*. That is, they were often used to refer to the two parts of a banquet: the main course and the supper.[18] Thus, the Gospel follows Herod's banquet of death with Jesus' symposium of life.[19] Jesus *takes* the bread and fish, *blesses* and *breaks* the loaves, and *gives* them to his disciples. These are the same four verbs which constitute his actions at the last supper (6:41; 14:22). Herod's banquet ends with one grisly head on a plate, Jesus' with twelve baskets full of broken pieces and fish. Then the crowd is dismissed and Jesus goes up a mountain to pray.

Something important is represented or signalled by the loaves and baskets, but we are told the disciples don't get it because when Jesus walks on the water that night they are afraid (6:51). We'll return to that later.

One reaction to the miraculous feeding is to point out that social practitioners work with limited resources; Jesus' miraculous abundance is not applicable to their situation. On the other hand, like the disciples, we too have a duty to share what we have with our guests/clients, to make our small resources accessible, regardless of our hope (or lack thereof) for a spectacular outcome. Limitations of funding, expertise, personnel, and time all conspire against those wanting the best outcomes for their clients/students. You can only do what you can do. But equally, you do not know what can come of it once it has left your hands. Rogers' insights are suggestive here. His client-centered approach "depends on the actualizing tendency present in every living organism—the tendency to grow, to develop, to realize its full potential."[20] The practitioner as host does not need to be overwhelmed by the needs of a client; they can trust that, with or without a miracle, what little they have can be used. They too can ask God to bless what is in their hands as they share it out.

---

18. On this, see Sick, "Symposium of the 5,000," 26; Smith, *From Symposium to Eucharist*, 31, 34–36, 49.

19. "Within the text [of Mark] the 'contrasting-design' to Herod's feast is as clearly felt as its prefiguring of the Last Supper. The parallels and differences to Herod's feast are so interesting, among other reasons, because one immediately precedes the other. This makes the antithetical character even clearer" (Hübenthal, *Das Markusevangelium als kollektives Gedächtnis*, 406; see also Donahue and Harrington, *The Gospel of Mark*, 209).

20. Rogers, "Client-Centered/Person-Centered Approach to Therapy," 137.

The theme of surprise also reappears in this story. For Derrida the contradiction of hospitality is contained in the figure of a door. Hospitality assumes a door, or threshold, over which the other is invited to be guest. But, "If there is a door, there is no longer hospitality . . . it means that someone has a key to [it] and consequently controls the conditions of hospitality . . . This is the difference, the gap between the hospitality of invitation and the hospitality of visitation. In visitation there is no door. Anyone can come at any time and can come in without needing a key for the door."[21] When Jesus and the disciples visit villages and towns they are not invited but simply arrive, but to perform their ministry they are reliant on a welcome (e.g., Mark 6:6–12). In Derrida's terms there is still a door. At Herod's banquet only the elite have been invited (6:21), the door is shut on those not thought worthy. This is what makes Jesus' hospitality in the wilderness so powerful. Not only is the crowd uninvited, Jesus and the disciples had gone into the wilderness to escape them (6:31–32). Yet in Jesus' meal there is no door, all who come are fed.

Although the text does not specify, (theological questions of omniscience aside) we can assume the crowd in the wilderness is a surprise to Jesus, otherwise he wouldn't have gone there! Derrida argues, "For pure hospitality or a pure gift to occur, however, there must be absolute surprise. The other, like the Messiah, must arrive when he or she wants. . .If, however, there is pure hospitality, or a pure gift, it should consist in this opening without horizon, without horizon of expectation, an opening to the newcomer whoever that may be."[22] Jesus' open hospitality in the wilderness demonstrates his "pure hospitality," his ability to be open to the other in any situation. Often in our work people can transgress boundaries, make unfair demands, turn up in the wrong place and the wrong time, and fail to observe office hours and the rules of polite society.[23] These transgressions can cause us to shut down, to close off, and to react not out of human connection but from the safety of the rules, procedures, and organizational power of our roles. Jesus' example challenges that. While we would not encourage these transgressions, when they

---

21. Derrida, "Hostipitality," 14.

22. Derrida, "Hospitality, Justice and Responsibility," 70; cf. also Derrida, "Hostipitality," 17, n. 17.

23. Of course, it is not only the client/student who is capable of transgressing boundaries. The social practitioner is also able to do so, damaging the relationship and causing the client/student to react, close off, and revert to familiar (unhelpful) patterns of behavior to cope.

happen they can be times for growth (see how Jesus teaches them, 6:34) and meaningful connections (the community formed by eating together, 6:40).[24] Our response to surprise can in fact become an opportunity to express welcome, a welcome that is all the more weighty because of its spontaneity.

However, not all surprise is to be embraced. In John's Gospel we read that the five thousand in the wilderness wanted to take Jesus by force and make him king (John 6:15). Those familiar with the first century Jewish sign prophets remembered by Josephus will realize that this is a plausible scenario.[25] The association of gathering in the wilderness and recreation of a biblical miracle (in this case the manna of Exodus 16) would signal to an occupied nation that their deliverer had arrived.[26] In Mark this idea is not explicitly mentioned, but Jesus does bring his duties as host to a seemingly sudden close: "making" his disciples get into the boat and dismissing the crowd before he goes alone to pray up the mountain (6:45–46). Jesus' hospitality has no doors, but it does have limits. The expectations and desire of the guests are a risk to the hosts. Jesus' uncharacteristically forceful removal of the disciples from the scene (6:45) possibly suggests he is worried they will be caught up by the messianic fervour of the crowd.

Derrida writes, "This is the double law of hospitality: to calculate the risks, yes, but without closing doors on the incalculable, that is, on the future and the foreigner."[27] In hospitality, the human connections formed have the ability to change those involved, but the direction of transformation may be for better or for worse. Even Jesus' hospitality, characterized by the doorless wilderness, measures risk and refuses to be changed for the worse for the sake of remaining host. When the crowd becomes a danger to Jesus' authentic mission the hospitality needs be brought to a close. Likewise, the social practitioner does not contradict their hospitality by having boundaries or protecting themselves from being manipulated by the desires of others. Understanding when and how to draw that line is a complex matter, but from my reading of Mark I would suggest that a key part of it is having a secure comprehension of

---

24. "Both food stories are—within their literary context—not only about bread, but above all about the fact that sharing and eating bread constitutes community" (So Hübenthal, *Das Markusevangelium als kollectives Gedächtnis*, 413).

25. Barnett, "Jewish Sign Prophets."

26. Montefiore, "Revolt in the Desert?"

27. Derrida, "Principle of Hospitality," 6.

your identity and vocation. When Jesus was surprised by the crowd he responded from his vocation as shepherd to the lost sheep of Israel (6:34), but when he had taught and fed them it was time to move on, whether because of their growing (false) expectations or simply out of his need to care for himself and the disciples for the sake of their ongoing work. It is the same for Christian workers. We need to be individuals grounded in the same manner. Our identity is not ultimately found in our work or effectiveness, but in our relationship and calling from God. While this is an ideal rather than an always attainable reality, we will notice that we are better able to be genuinely available to others and to deal with the frustrations and complexities of our work, when we remember who (and whose) we are and why we are doing it.

Bread for the Stranger (Mark 7:1–30)

In ch. 7 the Gospel changes tack; the focus is now on Jewish traditions and ethnic boundaries. Yet the conversation still revolves around meals. The Pharisees notice that the disciples did not wash their hands before eating (7:1–5). We are not told whether the Pharisees were guests or hosts at the implied meal, but once again we have the disciples experiencing vulnerability and hostility in their role as guests. Jesus responds with a biting denunciation of pharisaic tradition (7:6–15). Later, in private with the disciples, he explains that food does not defile but only the evil intentions of the heart (7:17–23).

Next, Jesus encounters a Syrophoenician woman. Mark's redundant additional identification of her as a Gentile (non-Jew) reinforces the significance of her non-Jewish ethnicity (7:26).[28] She asks for her daughter to be delivered from a demon, but Jesus accuses her of trying to subvert the appropriate order of a meal: "it is not fair to take the children's bread (*artos*) and throw it to the dogs" (7:28). The implication is that Jews (children) are those who are entitled to Jesus' saving work, not the other nations/Gentiles (dogs). Jesus' perplexing and rude response alerts the reader to the presence of metaphor.[29] I wonder too, should we imagine Jesus saying this with a twinkle in his eye? Is he testing her? Is he joking with her? Jesus seems an ungracious host, his response harsh, but the woman has been paying attention.[30] Jesus' feasts are not characterized by

---

28. Bosenius, *Der literarische Raum des Markusevangeliums*, 227–28.
29. Bosenius, *Der literarische Raum des Markusevangeliums*, 228.
30. The preceding discussion of the question of purity (Mark 7: 1–23) also serves

scarcity but abundance, there is always some left over.³¹ She doesn't take offense, but presses on in faith. She says, "even the dogs under the table eat the children's crumbs" (7:28). Jesus recognizes her faith and rewards her with what she requests.

Again, we have an example of Jesus being surprised! Jesus is in a house in Tyre and does not want anyone to know he is there (7:24). He is surprised by this Syrophoenician woman who wants him to cast out her daughter's demon (7:25). Jesus engages her with the metaphor of a meal where first the children are fed and then the little dogs (doggies/*kunarion*, not dog/*kuōn*), that is, the household pets (7:27). If it is unlikely that a Jew would have pet dogs, and it may not be, the reader should remember that Jesus is talking to a Gentile woman and describing the scene of her own home.³² She does not disagree with him but reminds him that in the same domestic scene the dogs are enjoying the abundance that falls from the table long before they are fed according to plan (7:28). She, unlike the disciples to this point, gets it. Even if Jesus' ministry is to the Jews first, Gentiles with faith can benefit from his abundance before schedule. Jesus' hospitality has no doors, it is unconditional, and all who come can and will be fed—even, perhaps especially, the surprise visitors.

This story is often read in a different way, that Jesus is hostile to the woman and she changes his mind through her response.³³ Assuming that my reading above is correct, this shows how difficult, and easily misunderstood, humour and metaphor can be—even in the Bible! There is a clear power imbalance in the relationship. Jesus has what the woman wants, the power to heal her daughter. The woman is vulnerable, both as a woman and as a non-Jew in a Jewish home. Should humour always be avoided in such situations? I don't know, the safe answer is yes. But by challenging her with a metaphor, Jesus treats her, not as a delicate object, but as an equal, someone worthy of his wits. By allowing her to be seen

---

to prepare for this episode. Jesus' teaching that purity does not depend on external factors, but is a question of inner attitude is then taken literally by the Syrophoenician woman who does not allow the external fact of her non-Judaism (and, as such, impurity) to prevent her from accessing Jesus' saving power (Dechow, *Gottessohn und Herrschaft Gottes*, 234).

31. Hübenthal, *Das Markusevangelium als kollektives Gedächtnis*, 411.

32. In the Second Temple Period (516 BCE to 70 CE) there is evidence that some Jews were influenced by the Greek and Roman penchant for pet dogs, although it never became as common for Jews as for the Greek and Romans. See, Schwartz, "Dogs in Jewish Society."

33. In my view, this hostility to a vulnerable person would be out of character for Jesus as portrayed in Mark.

to either match him or even beat him in a battle of wits, Jesus humanizes and dignifies her and even gives her the credit for her daughter's healing (7:29).[34] Sometimes, when we treat people too delicately, when we are over sensitive, we can make things worse, and make the other person feel more isolated and helpless than they need to. Perhaps Jesus gives us an example of a better, more humanizing way?

The Message in the Bread (Mark 8:1–21)

There is another feeding miracle in Mark 8:1–10. This time four thousand are fed with seven loaves and a few small fish, and seven baskets of pieces are left over at the end. Again the crowd are dismissed. Afterwards, when the Pharisees demand a sign from Jesus, he refuses them and gets in the boat with his disciples (8:11–13). Jesus then cautions his disciples against the "yeast of the Pharisees and the yeast of Herod" (8:15). In the boat the disciples have forgotten to bring bread, except one loaf, with them (8:14) and so, absurdly, they conclude that Jesus is angry about their lack of provisions. Unlike the Syrophoenecian woman, the disciples are not good at spotting metaphors!

For Mark, the "yeast of the Pharisees" is their focus on the external and not the internal, their lack of compassion towards their family and foreigners, and their adherence to tradition instead of the spirit of God's commandments (e.g., Mark 3:1–6; 7:1–13). As hosts they only have room for a ceremonially and ethnically exclusive few. The "yeast of Herod" is the desire for status, the pandering to the elite and wealthy, indulgence of immoral desires, and the killing of the prophets (Mark 3:6; 6:14–29). He imprisons those who criticize him and murders his guests to save face. As we've moved through Mark's narrative, we have sat at their tables, we have seen the bread they serve.

For social workers, educators, counselors, or ministers these "yeasts" are real dangers. Such people work is risky and often uncomfortable. The insecurity of being host can cause practitioners to retreat into either: (1) control and legalism with no space to engage and empower the client (yeast of the Pharisees); or (2) the client can become the one who is in control and, intentionally or otherwise, dictating the responses of the

---

34. An interesting parallel is the Samaritan woman at the well in John 4:1–42. Again, there is a humorous interplay between Jesus and the woman, despite the ethno-religious and gender boundaries between them and her added vulnerability as a woman of low social status and dubious moral reputation.

host (yeast of Herod). Retaining an authentic human presence in such situations requires a third way.

Jesus' rebuke of the disciples is uncompromising and harsh: "Don't you understand?" (8:17). Jesus challenges the disciples with hard words from the prophets, accusations of hard heartedness, spiritual blindness and deafness, and forgetfulness (8:17–28). Jesus' meal is one for which there is enough for everyone; where those who give receive more than they gave—more than they could have given; where those who receive are filled and have some left over to share with others. Jesus is the host who turns no one away and always has enough.

Within the narrative of Mark 6:1–8:21 the disciples are undergoing a transformation. In the first part of the Gospel the disciples are invited by Jesus to follow him, they are invited guests of the kingdom (1:17). In 6:7–13 the disciples, for the first time, become visitors—surprise guests of the surrounding villages—but at the same time hosts of the kingdom with authority to invite people into the kingdom (i.e., preach repentance) and to share the gifts of the kingdom (i.e., exorcism and healing). The disciples become hosts again in both the feeding miracles where they are the ones who provide and distribute the food. The miracle occurs in their hands.[35]

Yet Jesus is concerned that the disciples have not properly comprehended their role as kingdom hosts and of the nature of that kingdom. There is the danger that the yeast of Herod or of the Pharisees becomes their method of negotiating the contradiction of hospitality, that the ways of Herod or of the Pharisees might flavor the bread. The disciples in the boat, thinking that one loaf is not enough, appear not to have allowed the experience of being kingdom hosts to have transformed them. They appear not to have taken on board Jesus' approach, how he manages the paradoxical power dynamics of hospitality.

Social practitioners are not (usually) miracle workers. Some of the analogies I have made may seem forced. Yet, many who are Christians will feel a sense of vocation, a "calling," that their work is not separate to

---

35. Hübenthal, *Das Markusevangelium als kollectives Gedächtnis*, 404. This raises the question as to where in the narrative the miracle is manifested—in breaking or distributing the loaves? Van Iersel states: "The story is usually read from the first view, but it is therefore possible to read it from the second, which seems to be more in line with the major part of the disciples in the story. In any case, the episode could not have been better placed than here, so soon after 6.7–13, the 'apprenticeship' of the disciples. The story shows that the training of the disciples continues and that Jesus has just taught them how the impossible can be made possible" (Van Iersel, *Mark*, 230).

but an important expression of their Christian faith. Part of their authenticity as counselors, educators, or social workers derives from that sense of calling. It is who they are.

The warning against the yeast of the Pharisees and Herod is suggestive of another (non-Markan) metaphor or parable of Jesus: "To what should I compare the kingdom of God? It is like yeast that a woman took and mixed in with three measures of flour until all of it was leavened" (Luke 13:20–21). The alternative to these other yeasts is the yeast of the kingdom of God. Only a small amount can have a widespread effect. Because of our calling, we can expect therefore that it is not just we who are at work, but that, like the unseen work of yeast, the kingdom of God is also at work in and through us.

It is *in us*, importantly, because as Christians we recognise our own need for ongoing transformation, growth into ever greater compassion, spirituality, and grace—or Christ-likeness for short. It is *through us* because we have responded to that first call to follow Jesus and now it is Jesus who sends us to bring the good news and healing of the kingdom everywhere we go. How explicit we are able to be about that will depend on our particular context, but, like yeast, God's kingdom does not have to be seen in order to be at work, it does not have to be noticed in order to bring transformation.

Conclusion

In this essay I have performed a literary reading of Mark 6:1–8:23 around the theme of hospitality. I have also reflected on how this reading might connect, support, and inform, a Christian approach to social practice. Little, if anything, has been offered which would create a form of social practice distinct from the ideal forms of secular social practice. However, for a Christian, some of the images and models suggested by the Gospel of Mark may be more helpful, compelling, or powerful, than their secular equivalents. Particularly, as social practitioners navigate the difficulties of power relationships within their work I hope I have shown how the Bible has the potential to be a resource for reflective practice and self-awareness. And finally, I hope I have shown how, as they pursue their vocation, they are on a journey of discovery and risk, which is much like that of the first disciples of Jesus. As a result they too should expect that in their hands, what little they have, when offered in faith, can be multiplied among those whom they serve.

Bibliography

Aus, Roger David. *Feeding the Five Thousand: Studies in the Judaic Background of Mark 6:30–44 Par. and John 6:1–15*. Lanham: University Press of America, 2010.
Barnett, P. W. "The Jewish Sign Prophets—AD 40–70: Their Intentions and Origin." *New Testament Studies* 27 (1981) 679–97.
Boring, M. Eugene. *Mark: A Commentary*. Louisville: Westminster John Knox, 2006.
Bosenius, Bärbel. *Der literarische Raum des Markusevangeliums*. Göttingen: Vandenhoeck & Ruprecht, 2014.
Collins, Adela Yarbro. *Mark: A Commentary*. Minneapolis: Fortress, 2007.
Davis, Philip G. "Christology, Discipleship, and Self-Understanding in the Gospel of Mark." In *Self-Definition and Self-Discovery in Early Christianity: A Study in Shifting Horizons*, edited by D. J. Hawkin and T. Robinson, 101–19. Lewiston: Edwin Mellen, 1990.
Dechow, Jens. *Gottessohn und Herrschaft Gottes: Der Theozentrismus des Markusevangeliums*. Neukirchen-Vluyn: Neukirchener Verlag, 2000.
Derrida, Jacques. "Hostipitality." *Angelaki: Journal of Theoretical Humanities* 5, no. 3 (2000) 3–18.
———. "Hospitality, Justice and Responsibility." In *Questioning Ethics: Contemporary Debates in Continental Philosphy*, edited by Mark Dooley and Richard Kearney, 65–83. London: Routledge, 1999.
———. *Of Hospitality*. Stanford: Stanford University Press, 2000.
———. "The Principle of Hospitality." *Parallax* 11, no. 1 (2005) 6–9.
Donahue, John R., and Daniel J. Harrington. *The Gospel of Mark*. Collegeville: Liturgical, 2005.
Hübenthal, Sandra. *Das Markusevangelium als kollektives Gedächtnis*. Göttingen: Vandenhoeck & Ruprecht, 2014.
Kelley, Robert L. "Meals with Jesus in Luke's Gospel." *Horizons in Biblical Theology* 17 (1995) 123–31.
Marcus, Joel. *Mark 1–8: A New Translation with Introduction and Commentary*. New Haven: Yale University Press, 2000.
Montefiore, Hugh. "Revolt in the Desert? (Mark VI.33ff)." *New Testament Studies* 8 (1962) 135–41.
Rogers, Carl. "A Client-Centered/Person-Centered Approach to Therapy." In *The Carl Rogers Reader*, edited by Howard Kirschenbaum and Valerie Land Henderson, 135–56. London: Constable, 1990.
Schwartz, Joshua. "Dogs in Jewish Society in the Second Temple Period and in the Time of the Mishnah and Talmud." *Journal of Jewish Studies* 55 (2004) 247–77.
Sick, David H. "The Symposium of the 5,000." *Journal of Theological Studies* 66 (2015) 1–27.
Smith, Dennis E. *From Symposium to Eucharist: The Banquet in the Early Christian World*. Minneapolis: Fortress, 2003.
Van Iersel, Bas M. F. *Mark: A Reader Response Commentary*. Translated by W. H. Bisscheroux. Sheffield: Sheffield Academic, 1998.

Response 3: Hospitality

Serving Sacred Food in Secular Spaces: The *Missio Dei* and Ordinary Christian Counseling

Art Wouters

I FOUND THESE CHAPTERS refreshing reading in the context of a conversation between my theologian self and my psychologist self. Both chapters engaged me on the matter of my persistent struggle with a sacred–secular split in the practice of my therapeutic work and I offer this response with this struggle in the forefront.

The struggle goes back to the formation of my early spirituality by a narrative in which I fused my own story with a theology of making it my personal responsibility to share my beliefs and save people from sin and damnation. Hence, I felt under pressure to share my faith and find opportunities to speak the words that might bring someone to Christ. When I qualified as a psychologist, the lingering theological narrative of the role of human effort and human responsibility for mission resulted in my discomfort as I wrestled with the need for congruence in my psychological work and ethical practice. Jonathan's framing of a hospitality paradigm for the relationship between Christianity and psychology speaks to this issue. It suggests a reversal of the inhospitality commonly implied in what Larry Crabb referred to as Christian counselors "spoiling the Egyptians" for useful secular concepts.[1]

---

1. Crabb, *Effective Biblical Counseling*.

I also appreciated Theresa's reflections on Luke's presentation of God's health food in the person of Jesus as a counter-script to my tendency to overemphasize human effort in engaging God's mission. I'm reminded that God's hospitality mission is more than me and a lot greater than I could ever imagine. Jesus is not just a preacher of the right words, but Luke presents Jesus as a living demonstration of "...a holistic medicine, philosophy, psychagogy, and narrative therapy in his gospel telling, writing for the detoxifications of the heart, the cleansing of the mind, to help correct the distorted understanding of reality and provide for the healing of the whole person."

Luke's announcement of the birth of Jesus in a manger takes us to the heart of the holistic mission of God and leaves no room to split sacred and secular. Theresa points out that the divine food comes to humanity in an ordinary food container for farm animals. The Lukan scheme in which God's mission of feeding humanity comes to fruition by offering the person of Jesus in a used feeding container inspires a vision of counseling as an ordinary secular food container with a capacity to mediate the Jesus food for human flourishing. Secular cultural systems ordinarily resemble what Erich Fromm referred to as a *having mode of existence* which prioritises products over people, supplies fast food, and encourages unhealthy eating habits.[2] Yet the same cultural scheme acts as a feeding trough for holistic medicine that engages individuals in alternative encounters characterised by Fromm's *being mode* and Martin Buber's *I-Thou* way of being.[3]

Jonathan's section on the Miracle Bread is compelling in the juxtaposition of Herod's banquet of death with Jesus' symposium of life. Jesus requires that his disciples take on a responsibility delegated to them as hosts in a time of need and scarcity. Jonathan reflects on this issue as being typical for social practitioners in that our resources are limited and conspire against us getting the best results for our clients. The reality of the practitioner's deficiency of resources shifts the power relationship towards clients and underpins a view of the client as the source of their healing rather than an unrealistic attribution of power to the therapist.[4] Like the miraculous multiplication that followed the disciples' distribution of their meagre resources, surprising outcomes often exceed the

---

2. Fromm, *To Have or To Be?*
3. Buber, *I and Thou*.
4. Bohart, "Client Is the Most Important Common Factor."

therapist's limitations. Jonathan notes how Carl Rogers seemed to articulate this principle specific to counseling in his client-centered approach and his reliance on the client's own self-actualizing tendency.

Psychotherapy outcome research of the last two decades reinforces the principle that healing is not primarily a function of the power of the therapist's theory and technique. Together with the counseling relationship, client factors or extra-therapeutic factors far outweigh any other components of the therapeutic enterprise. The therapeutic model or method that reflects the professional's knowledge and training only contributes around 15 percent to successful outcomes.[5]

Social practitioners have been slow to take up the reality that the client is the primary source of healing and Gordon is convinced that professionals remain unlikely to take client experience and extra-therapeutic factors seriously.[6] Apparently, clients are still the most neglected factor in counseling research, and the vast majority of literature assumes that the ingredients specific to individual models of counseling are responsible for therapeutic benefits to the client.[7] This seems to underpin the weighting of the professional's resources instead of the vision of the miracle of the bread.

On the other hand, counseling informed by a common factors perspective recognizes that what has the capacity to heal is to be found in the ordinary rather than the extraordinary.[8] The deliberate alignment of our practice with these extra-therapeutic resources that are close to the client's everyday experiences resonates with a prayerful posture of asking God to bless what's in our hands to share the miracle bread that goes beyond specific counseling sessions.

Mark's story of the miracle bread provides a context for transcending the sacred secular divide and providing a larger faith narrative for the multiplication of our meagre resources. Miracles are waiting to happen through the people, places, and things sought out by clients between sessions as we serve our meagre resources into the extra-therapeutic experiences of our clients where God is also present.

The Lukan emphasis on the personal Jesus serving as food for the soul of humanity ties in with theological reflections on the *missio Dei*

---

5. Lambert and Ogles, "Efficacy and Effectiveness of Psychotherapy."
6. Gordon, "Where Oh Where Are the Clients?"
7. See for example Duncan et al., *Heart and Soul of Change*.
8. Lambert and Ogles, "Efficacy and Effectiveness of Psychotherapy."

that point to God's relational orientation toward us: that God is for us and chooses to come and be with us.[9] God's mission is not primarily concerned with the apologetics of my past experience of trying to educate people to make them believe certain ideas about God; it is more about how and who we are in the world. "Our being bears witness to God's being. How we are oriented in relationship with ourselves and others is reflective of and bears witness to the relational character of God."[10]

Counseling and psychotherapy have the capacity to serve as a feeding trough for an I-Thou rather than an I-It way of being. Such a vision regards the client as a person rather than an object and extends the invitation to participate in this relational way of being in the world. Hence counselors do not primarily subject their clients to programmes or techniques that do something to them, but draw the participants into a way of being oriented towards others and the self that bears testimony to and mediates the relational nature of God:

> This is the missional invitation of God, that we participate in bearing witness to the very character of God that turns toward us and reaches out to whoever we may be. In this sense, all counselling attuned to the missional character of God, marked by the guidance and fruit of the Spirit is sharing our faith. One might even argue that counselling that is not specifically attuned to God still reflects God's missional nature in the world through conveying common grace.[11]

In conclusion, there is much to draw on in these hospitality chapters that inspires a vision of the spiritual nature of the counselor's work. Sacred and secular frames seem to converge in compelling narratives such as the Jesus food in the feeding trough, the miracle bread of limited resources, and the importance of clients as the primary source of healing, as well as the significance of everyday extra-therapeutic events and experiences. Being reminded of such alignment defies the pressure of responsibility to say the right words to bring people to Christ formed during my younger years. If God's very being is missional, mission is ingrained in God's nature and is not initiated by my efforts. As a result, counseling does not have to go to great additional lengths to seem to be particularly Christian. As Christian social practitioners, we participate in a remarkable mystery

---

9. Neff and McMinn, *Embodying Integration*.
10. Neff and McMinn, *Embodying Integration*, 194.
11. Neff and McMinn, *Embodying Integration*, 192.

that comes from God and is made evident by the Spirit in human form who witnesses to God's nature of moving towards us and reaching out to us wherever we may be.[12]

While assumptions about the organismic valuing process and self-actualization reflect Rogers' faith in humanity, to the counselor with faith in God these processes imply that God is already at work in the lives of our clients. Faith in the missional nature of God helps us to rest in the knowledge that God is moving our clients towards wholeness and that we are invited to notice and participate in what God is already doing in their lives, both during and outside therapy. Christian practitioners are invited into a larger view of faith and salvation, of trusting that Jesus saves us in all sorts of ways and not only by giving us eternal life.[13]

Bibliography

Bohart, Arthur C. "The Client is the Most Important Common Factor: Clients' Self-healing Capacities and Psychotherapy." *Journal of Psychotherapy Integration* 10, no. 2 (2000) 127–49.

Buber, Martin. *I and Thou*. New York: Simon & Schuster, 2008.

Crabb, Larry. *Effective Biblical Counseling: A Model for Helping Caring Christians Become Capable Counselors*. Grand Rapids: Zondervan, 2013.

Duncan, Barry L., Scott D. Miller, Bruce E. Wampold, and Mark A. Hubble, eds. *The Heart and Soul of Change: Delivering What Works in Therapy*. Washington, DC: APA, 2009.

Fromm, Erich. *To Have or To Be?* London: Bloomsbury Academic, 2013.

Gordon, Ruth. "Where Oh Where Are the Clients? The Use of Client Factors in Counselling Psychology." *Counselling Psychology Review* 27 (2012) 8–17.

Lambert, Michael J., and B. M. Ogles. "The Efficacy and Effectiveness of Psychotherapy." In *Bergin and Garfield's Handbook of Psychotherapy and Behavior Change*, edited by Michael J. Lambert, 139–93. 5th ed. New York: Wiley, 2004.

Neff, Megan Anna, and Mark McMinn. *Embodying Integration: A Fresh Look at Christianity in the Therapy Room*. Downers Grove: InterVarsity Academic, 2020.

---

12. Neff and McMinn, *Embodying Integration*, 191.
13. Neff and McMinn, *Embodying Integration*, 192.

Part IV

THERAPY

Chapter 8

Sailing with the Wind: Counseling Support in the Solomon Islands

ART WOUTERS

The Tension

THE SOLOMON ISLANDS CONSIST of hundreds of small islands and six major islands with a population of about half a million people. Roads are sparse, the majority of which traverse the area in and around the capital of Honiara on the main island of Guadalcanal. People get around in small boats from one island to another, or even sail from one part of an island to another part. Numerous signs of poverty are softened by the lush tropical vegetation and the lyrical voices that frequently punctuate the silence while walking along potholed gravel roads.

The two islands of Guadalcanal and Malaita play a defining role in the Solomon Islands' story and in the accounts of a devastating civil war between 1999 and 2003 that left more than a hundred people dead and 20,000 homeless. Many of the inhabitants are still living in the shadow of this war which is locally referred to as "The Tension." During the economic pressures of the 1990s, the people from Guadalcanal reacted to their increasing economic and political marginalization and directed their anger, not at the small group of Malaitans who had become Honiara's elite, but at all Solomon Islanders of Malaitan descent. In 1998 militant Guadalcanal youth, calling themselves the Isatabu Freedom Movement (IFM) began arming themselves with World War Two vintage rifles and home-made guns to drive Malaitans from their island. In 2000 the Malaita Eagle Force (MEF) was formed to defend the residents of Honiara from IFM attacks and to demand compensation for displaced Malaitans. Fuelled by corruption and manipulation of the conflict for selfish ends, the MEF militants eventually outgunned and drove the IFM from Honiara. A ceasefire agreement was signed in Townsville late 2000 with the help of Australia and New Zealand, although hostilities only ceased in 2003 after Prime Minister John Howard intervened with the Australian military.

Invitation

I was invited to visit Honiara in 2015 to talk with concerned Christians, assess the situation, and provide further support to a group trained in trauma healing.[1] This paper records the inner dialogue with my faith, theory, and profession while seeking to engage people helping others in the shadow of the Tension in an empowering way instead of inviting re-colonization.[2] The importance of the power issue was previously brought to my attention when I lived in South Africa during the apartheid years. Formed by the prevailing white racism of that society, a "Damascus Road" experience followed my confrontation with the reality of the torture of a number of my own clients who were members of the African National Council (ANC). I could no longer deny the political significance of being a white male and took a more radical course of political and professional action in the pursuit of justice and mercy. Proceeding on an uncertain journey with struggles of faith and political identity, I joined an organization in developing alternative approaches to treating marginalized and oppressed survivors of apartheid. Working in multi-racial teams we sought to help people to understand the nature

---

1. Hill et al., *Healing the Wounds of Trauma*.

2. With special acknowledgement to the following participants: Sister Akineti Agnes Naaru, Bethry Kwaimani, Betty Fakarii, Bruce Likaveke, John Gerhard, Mari-aLouisa Molakini, Martha Horiwapu, Pauline Radoe Firisua, and Rueben Lilo. I also received encouragement from the office of the Anglican Archbishop, the Ministry of National Unity, Reconciliation and Peace, the Melanesian Brotherhood, and Island Bible Ministries. I would also like to express my thanks to Pam Daams and Cynthia Rollins from the Trauma Healing Group, Stirling College, the Warrandyte Community Church, and the Solomon Islands Translation Assistance Group for their encouragement and support.

of the power relations that had formed and wounded them.[3] Whites were trapped in Power-over ways of political, social, and interpersonal oppression that perpetuated positions of Power-under relations for black South Africans at all levels of society. In an atmosphere of recovering from internalized oppression, we developed an alternative and empowering approach referred to as Power-with. I reflected on these memories as I set my sails to the wind on an unfamiliar course to islands and a culture I knew almost nothing about that led to five trips to Honiara.

The Melanesian Brothers

By far the majority of Solomon Islanders claim to be Christians and all the participants in conversations and workshops strongly identified with the Christian faith. On one of the visits, I spent two days with the Melanesian Brotherhood at their base outside of Honiara. The Brotherhood is an established Anglican order with an intake of about a hundred novices every two years who are trained to do mission work across the islands. The Brothers found themselves in the middle of the Tension and decided to surrender their power and serve the warring factions with absolute impartiality. Coming from a place of weakness, they risked their lives, criss-crossing battle lines to offer spiritual support and broker peace by seeking to persuade the soldiers to lay down their arms. Seven brothers were murdered in cold blood, causing tremendous grief to the nation as a whole as well as contributing to bringing an end to the civil war.[4]

The influential story of the sacrifice of the Melanesian Brotherhood for the cause of peace is inspired by the tradition of Jesus who laid aside his power to reconcile us to God. God gives up God's power in order to demonstrate triune love through Jesus the son of God. A major plot in God's re-narration is that the authority, power, and exaltation of Jesus is demonstrated particularly well in the surrender, vulnerability, and weakness of his love (Philippians 2). Consequently, everyone and every social vocation (including Western counseling and psychology) is called to practice a "peaceable psychology" that identifies with God's laying down of God's power.[5] For Dueck and his associates a peaceable psychology ". . .begins with love of enemy and refuses to collude with the empire to

---

3. Gross, "Personal Power and Empowerment."
4. Beu and Nokise, *Mission in the Midst of Conflict*.
5. Dueck and Reimer, *Peaceable Psychology*.

expand its powers. A peaceable psychology recognizes when the collusion takes place and seeks alternative ways of providing assistance."[6]

To relinquish the power of the psychological knowledge that was the stimulus for being invited seemed paradoxical. The mere fact of my academic qualifications, power, and privilege contrasted sharply with the situation of the local people surrounded by evidence of economic disadvantage, powerlessness, and a lack of privilege. The potential for abusing unearned status attributed to Western knowledge sobered me and became a challenge to remain vigilant about not taking for granted the seemingly self-evident universality of Western psychology.

Universal Science and Local Knowledge

Conversations in Honiara exposed me to certain assumptions associated with ideas about the universality of science, the uniformity of nature, and the universality and neutrality of reason, all of which can impact the power relations between a professional perceived as an expert and clients. A Christian leader spoke with me about the tendency of local people to dismiss their own ability to solve problems and look outside of themselves for help. He commented that Melanesians tend to look too highly at experts. As a result of this, people tend to swallow whole the knowledge they obtain from foreigners that then becomes difficult for them to apply.

More specific to trauma healing in the Solomon Islands, Pateson Ngalihesi, a Solomon Island researcher, argues that the Western approaches lack contextualization and cause retraumatization of trauma survivors.[7] Ngalihesi is concerned that the cultural suppression caused by monopolization by scientists and experts lacks affirmation of the healing dynamics of the cultural context.[8]

Psychology's assumption of universalism is encouraged by its enmeshment in Western utilitarianism and individualism, though in reality it represents a Western psychology that perceives and presents itself as universal.[9] Mainstream psychology is culture bound and indigenously Western instead of universal but generally fails to appreciate its cultural

---

6. Dueck et al., "Prophetic Words for Psychologists," 300.
7. Ngalihesi, *Healing the Wounds of our People*.
8. Ngalihesi, *Healing the Wounds of our People*, 33.
9. Dueck et al., "Constantine, Babel, and Yankee Doodling."

particularity. It has been proposed that the idea of the universality of psychology is as arrogant as the beliefs of the architects of the Tower of Babel who thought that they could storm heaven if only they were unified in their language and political projects.[10]

Failure to appreciate the particularity of Western psychological knowledge leads to power-over impositions on others without regard to their implicit or psychologic sensibilities. Dueck and his associates refer to this failure as the makings of a Constantinian psychology.[11] Others have used the term "therapeutic governance" to refer to the imposition of particular understandings of life, trauma, and healing through Western therapeutic language.[12] The sheer scope of personal and community problems in the Solomon Islands often traced back to the Tension makes people vulnerable to being co-opted into power-under relations through an uncritical adoption of a Constantinian psychology and therapeutic governance.

Heavy reliance on natural science creates a tendency to ignore the role that social conditions, power relations, and social institutional arrangements can play in shaping peoples' conceptualizations of illness and associated help-seeking behaviours.[13] As a result of being tied up with the status quo, the effect may be to prevent progressive social, economic, and political change and become a tool of colonialism.

Furthermore, the power of Western narratives tend to hide the fact that different societies have their own culture and knowledge systems for dealing with and responding to environmental conditions.[14] Thus, a traditional framework of diagnosable abnormalities associated with a conception of Post Traumatic Stress Disorder (PTSD) with specified treatments is likely to blind Western practitioners to the many instances of growth, mastery, drive, and insight that develop out of undesirable, painful life events.[15]

The picture painted by cross-cultural researchers and anthropologists shows that the experience of mental illness is closely related to its cultural context. Cultural beliefs, values, and stories help us make meaning of these

---

10. Dueck et al., "Constantine, Babel, and Yankee Doodling," 57.
11. Dueck et al., "Constantine, Babel, and Yankee Doodling," 57.
12. Denborough, *Retelling the Stories of Our Lives*, 43.
13. Bojuwoye and Sodi, "Challenges and Opportunities," 283.
14. Bojuwoye and Sodi, "Challenges and Opportunities," 283.
15. Schultz and Schultz, *Theories of Personality*, 483.

experiences. Whether they tell of spirit possession or serotonin depletion, the experience of the illness is shaped in surprisingly dramatic and often counterintuitive ways. We tend to ignore the valuable knowledge hidden in the diverse cultural meanings of mental health and illness.[16]

When Western counselors arrived in Sri Lanka after the tsunami disaster of 2004, faculty at the University of Colombo in Sri Lanka pleaded that the professionals refrain from diminishing the experience of survivors to a question of mental trauma and the people themselves as psychological casualties. They rejected the argument that Western ideas about trauma are universal. They stated that a victim processes a traumatic event as a function of what it means. This meaning is drawn from their society and culture and this shapes how they seek help and their expectation of recovery. They emphasized that trauma reactions are far more significant than physiological reactions inside the brain and they pointed to deeper meanings within the culture. They stated that meaningful help involves listening to the local voice of trauma and understanding what the affected people are signalling by this distress.[17] They recognized that the highly organized and overly cohesive nature of Western narratives about problems risks colonizing the public identity of people as well as their private self-concept and stealing the authorship of an individual's life story.[18] When the dominant narrative is supported by powerful persons such as psychologists, then someone contending for example, with serious trauma, may come to view themselves in negative and preemptive terms of the dominant narrative.

Positive Psychology

Two lines of thought helped me to think through these pitfalls. The first was that of Positive Psychology, by which it is assumed that effective and ineffective psychological wellness are not distinct categories but degrees along a continuum. Positive Psychology has few preconceptions about what is normal and what is supposedly not normal, which makes it suited to cultural humility in diverse contexts. Being equally interested in what goes right in life and not only what's wrong with it, the importance of validating the things that people see as making their lives worth living

---

16. Hessamfar, *In the Fellowship of His Suffering*, 178.
17. Hessamfar, *In the Fellowship of His Suffering*, 179.
18. Neimeyer, "Re-storying Loss," 74.

becomes more central. Positive Psychology introduces the notion of growth through trauma that is easily overlooked by Westerners looking for symptoms associated with Post Traumatic Stress Disorder.[19] The inclusion of Post Traumatic Growth aligns with religious beliefs about the suffering of Jesus with saving consequences for human beings.

The Post Traumatic Growth literature showed me the importance of engaging people at both the problem level as well as looking to support any signs of a growth process demonstrated by changes to the personal narrative. According to the theory there is significant disruption of the personal narrative as a result of a traumatic experience.[20] In such cases, the self-narrative could be deeply shaken and disorganized by unaccommodated images, including undigested emotion schemas operating at the level of the amygdala. These experiences are radically inconsistent with the plot structure of the person's previous life and the assumptions on which the person has based his or her narrative: for example, that the world was relatively safe, that life was predictable, that the universe was just, and that people could be trusted.[21] The invalidation of the assumptions on which the person's worldview has been premised fosters movement towards a more complex if ambivalent worldview that acknowledges the reality of death and therefore involves the process of revising, repairing, or replacing basic themes, assumptions, and goals.[22]

Passional Orientation to Knowledge

A second emerging and useful line of thought came from Smith's postmodern critique of the elevation of reason that paints a picture of the human person as cognitive and rational at the core of their identity.[23] Defining humans as disembodied rational minds can be disempowering in engaging with people from another culture by an implicit negating of the particularities of their and our embodied lives, including language, culture, religion, and those features that shape one's perspective on the world.

---

19. Calhoun and Tedeschi, "Foundations of Posttraumatic Growth."
20. Neimeyer, "Re-storying Loss."
21. Neimeyer, "Re-storying Loss," 73.
22. Calhoun and Tedeschi, "Foundations of Posttraumatic Growth."
23. Smith, *Thinking in Tongues*.

It is this confident assumption of the universality and therefore neutrality of reason that yields one of modernity's most powerful fruits: the notion of secularity and the doctrine of secularism—both of which remain powerful forces today . . . Secular becomes code for what is (supposedly) neutral, objective, unbiased, and above all, not religious. Religious belief, then becomes the very antithesis (and nemesis) of reason—and religious experience would only be worse. Indeed, the Enlightenment offered universal reason as a cure for the disease of religious belief and "superstition."[24]

The Christian significance of a more embodied rather than a cognitive view of the human person is demonstrated by affirmation of embodiment in the incarnational principle at the heart of Christian faith.[25] Not only does the Christian story of humanity begin with God making a material embodied creature and calling it good, but the affirmation of the goodness of embodiment is reaffirmed in the incarnation of God in Christ and the Word become flesh that lies at the center of God's re-narration of the world. The theme of embodiment represents a powerful statement of power-with and finds its ultimate reaffirmation in the hope of the resurrection. Smith points out that our hope is not for redemption from our bodies but *of* our bodies—undoing their brokenness to be restored to their goodness.[26]

I sought to draw on Smith's rejection of the reductionistic picture of humans that comes from privileging reason or intellect as superior to other human faculties. There is a strong case for a more postmodern, relational, and Christian "passional orientation" to the world which is much more hospitable to the integrated worldview of Solomon Islanders.[27] Their cultural construals resemble a world of experience that reflects a more pre-cognitive orientation that Christians tend to refer to as the heart, incorporating the body, music, story, spirit, dance, and visual stimulation.[28]

---

24. Smith, *Thinking in Tongues*, 56.
25. Smith, *Thinking in Tongues*, 60.
26. Smith, *Thinking in Tongues*, 60.
27. Smith, *Thinking in Tongues*, 58.
28. Smith, *Thinking in Tongues*, 58.

Not-knowing

"Not-knowing" represents a therapeutic principle associated with postmodern therapies that is significant in the creation of an atmosphere of Power-with. White proposed a therapeutic posture that prioritized the personal stories, knowledge, and skills of people seeking consultation over the knowledge and skills of the therapist.[29] The therapist's influence is not to impose an agenda or prescribe interventions based on privileged psychological knowledge about problems and their solutions, but to build a scaffold through questions and reflections. The therapist's questions and a collaborative process of co-construction makes it possible for people to become more acquainted with the knowledge and skills of their lives that are relevant to addressing their concerns.[30] I found White's ideas about negotiating experience-near definitions of people's problems helpful in the context of wanting to avoid making too many psychological generalizations about people from a different culture. Asserting the uniqueness of every predicament refuses to privilege psychological pre-knowledge and won't import existing problem descriptions into people's lives.

Listening "doubly" and for the absent but implicit is a practice congruent with a power-with position and allows for reauthoring conversations that *thicken* stories of special knowledge and skills held by the people themselves that prevent problems from completely taking over their lives.[31] These practices set the scene for helping the participants in my workshops to give voice to the skills unique to their culture, such as saying prayers, singing songs, and reading from Scripture, as well as being open to supporting the growth that has already emerged as a result of the experience of their difficulties. Participants appreciated the space that we created together for supporting identity conclusions that resonated with the desires and hopes they had for themselves.

I also drew on characteristic narrative practices such as the retellings associated with definitional ceremonies and outsider witness responses. These conversations push forward the belief that therapists have no privileged knowledge of their clients. Instead, the retellings tend to thicken

---

29. White, "Externalizing of the Problem," 5–6.
30. White, "Process of Questioning," 37–38.
31. White, "Children, Trauma, and Subordinate Storyline Development," 28.

the alternative story plots of people's lives and authenticate people's preferred ideas about their who they are.[32]

Dialogical Therapies

Dialogical or conversational therapies offer a less instrumental view of the same principle of not-knowing than is the case in narrative therapy.[33] The emphasis is on clients telling their story in their own preferred way instead of using the sequenced questions formulated as maps of narrative practice.[34] Instead of trying to fill in the missing pieces of a story with "sparkling moments" in the client's life that counter the problem story, the therapist trusts that the participants know themselves best and will talk about what is important to them and when and how. Most important is learning to understand clients from *their* perspective and preferences and to learn the lived experience and meanings associated with these perspectives. Dialogue is a reflection of a bottom-up approach to power that is characteristic of God's re-narration. Anderson describes the development of a dynamic two-way process in which people talk *with* each other rather than *to* each other and develop a sense of belonging that invites participation, ownership, and in turn shared responsibility.[35] The "dialogicality" is also described as witness therapy, and what takes place as witness practices.[36]

Anderson uses the metaphor of the client handing her a story ball to describe the beginning of an unstructured process of collaboration, and explains:

> As they put the ball toward me, and while their hands are still on it, I gently place my hands on it but I do not take it from them. I begin to participate with them in the storytelling, as I slowly look at/listen to the aspect that they are showing me. I try to learn about and understand their story by responding to them: I am curious, I pose questions, I make comments, and I gesture. In my experience, I find that this therapist learning position acts to spontaneously engage the client as a co-learner; it is as if the therapist's curiosity is contagious. In other words,

32. White, *Maps of Narrative Practice*, 167.
33. Hoffman, "Art of 'Withness,'" 64.
34. White, *Maps of Narrative Practice*, 61.
35. Anderson, "Collaborative Relationships and Dialogic Conversations."
36. Hoffman, "Art of 'Withness,'" 64.

what begins as one-way learning becomes mutual learning as client and therapist co-explore the familiar and co-develop the new, shifting to a mutual inquiry of examining, questioning, and reflecting with each other.[37]

Anderson sees this less as a theory than as a "philosophical stance," by which she means a way of being in relationship and conversation, ". . .a way of thinking with, experiencing with, relating with, acting with, and responding with the people we meet in therapy."[38] She uses the host-guest metaphor for the therapist who is a host and meets and greets the client as a guest while also being a guest in the client's life. The therapist enters the relationship as a learner who listens and responds by trying to understand the client from their perspective and in their language.

From my perspective, to adopt a not-knowing stance in the Solomon Islands with authenticity continues to be one of my greatest challenges in the context of maintaining an atmosphere of power-with dynamic. A recent illustration of the challenge is reflected in the insecurity that was expressed by a group of trauma healers I'd worked with for some time. At some point a spokesperson for the group expressed second thoughts about my writing this chapter. This came up after we had a number of conversations about the issue and I assumed that the group's concerns had been taken care of. The concern that I would use information gained from the group for my own purposes led me to adjust the paper in a way that a sense of safety would not be threatened by the reintroduction of a power-over dynamic. Not-knowing is at the heart of trusting in the uncertainty itself while things are still unresolved, hence part of the appeal to the metaphor of sailing with the wind.

Elements of Not-Knowing

I see Anderson's not-knowing stance as fundamental to any commitment to power-with relations. Anderson specifies several elements of not-knowing, of which I highlight the following.[39]

In addition to letting go of the modernist idea that you can pre-know someone in terms of general categories of knowledge discussed above, the therapist thinks about knowledge in a way that the knowledge that each

37. Anderson, "Heart and Spirit of Collaborative Therapy," 47.
38. Anderson, "Heart and Spirit of Collaborative Therapy," 43.
39. Anderson, "Collaborative Relationships and Dialogic Conversations."

person brings is equally valued. The anticipation of genuine dialogue is that what each person brings to a conversation will be influenced and changed in some way.

Anderson also describes the intention with which the counselor's knowledge is used, whether in the form of questions, comments, opinions, or suggestions. The intention is to use it as food for thought and dialogue rather than intending it to be authoritative, objective, or instructive. The way in which knowledge is used is therefore not to suppress the knowledge of others in the dialogue with authoritative knowing, but to make room for the other's voice. Knowledge is introduced in sync with the other person/s and the conversation in the moment in a tentative and provisional way, thereby giving attention not only to the timing, but also to the manner and tone with which knowledge is introduced.

Another element of the process is that therapists are public with their knowledge and invite responsive understanding.[40] This counters the influence of professionally informed inner talk on the part of therapists. In-house understandings around diagnoses, judgments, or hypotheses lead to missed understandings that do not fit with the speaker's intent. Failure to put one's thoughts into spoken words risks the talk becoming monological, contributing to a potential therapist-client monologue and an end to the criss-crossing that takes place when people are trying to understand one another.[41] On the other hand, when therapists voice their opinions, suggestions, or questions as food for thought, clients are given the opportunity to respond to the therapist's inner thought which will in turn affect the therapist's inner thoughts and invite further collaborative thinking.

These elements significantly impact group interaction with a common pursuit of power-with relationships. Creative avenues I had not previously considered began to open up, such as singing and playing music together, and conversations stimulated by pictures and videos.

Open Dialogue and the Intersubjective Space

Open Dialogue adds to the emerging practices aligned with the development of power-with relationships. Open Dialogue's specific focus is on the intersubjective space between persons. Open Dialogue is an

---

40. Boe et al., "Change Is an Ongoing Ethical Event."
41. Anderson, "Heart and Spirit of Collaborative Therapy," 51.

innovative psychiatric approach to treating patients with serious emotional difficulties in Northern Finland.[42] The Open Dialogue team of helpers appear to make no withdrawals from their psychiatric knowledge bank. Instead of experts setting the agenda and planning the treatment, two staff members start a series of open dialogues in which the team, the client, and members of his or her network speak together about the issues that are most relevant at the moment. Their responsive listening makes space for stories that are not yet told.[43] Drawing on the writings of Mikhail Bakhtin,[44] Open Dialogue appears to resemble the practice of J.K.A Smith's passional knowing.[45] It emphasizes the implicit knowing that comes from being present in the moment as embodied experience even before it is put into words. More important than explicit knowledge and the content of narratives, responsive listening creates an atmosphere that is present to the unfolding feelings in the moment as narratives are often told for the first time.[46] While this is complex in a cross-cultural situation it also seems to be particularly suited to a position of not-knowing. As facilitator or interviewer, the aim is to be responsive to every utterance, believing that intersubjective consciousness develops through dialogue and that the dialogue changes the position of everyone involved in the dialogue.

The dynamic nature of dialogue and collaboration is therefore formative and trans-formational in a genuinely power-with manner and represents a position of strong opposition to the dominant one-way perspective of power on the part of the therapist. Something new is constructed *with* each other in the collaborative conversation that continually emerges throughout the encounter and becomes the springboard for more conversation. The therapist is shaped and reshaped just as much as the client. To engage in this dynamic conversation means constructing new forms of social relation, and to construct new forms of self-other relationships is to construct new ways of being or person-world relations for ourselves.

As indicated above, therapeutic knowledge is only applied in as much as it helps to invite collaborative relationships and moves the conversation

---

42. Seikkula, "Becoming Dialogical."
43. Olsen et al., *Key Elements of Dialogic Practice in Open Dialogue.*
44. See Seikkula, "Becoming Dialogical."
45. Smith, *Thinking in Tongues.*
46. Seikkula, "Becoming Dialogical."

in the direction of a culture of mutual exploration, understanding, and knowledge sharing.[47] It involves a counselor simultaneously appreciating and respecting the different voices in the room, valuing each voice, each reality, and each expertise. Multiple voices and differences are seen, not necessarily as issues needing to be resolved, but as contributions worth exploring and learning about. Instead of counselors using the situation to apply their knowledge and theory, generative conversational processes are entered into that lead to new meanings and understandings, and that collectively create expertise and knowledge.

Open Dialogue appears to invite the possibility of regional, locally constructed psychologies and theologies in dialogue between the regions as equal partners in sharing perspectives, practices, and stories. It involves being poor in spirit and resembles what missiologists have referred to as a third space where there is mutual recognition of the value of the contribution from each party.[48] To take Dueck's metaphor further, instead of the Babylonian narrative, it aspires to "the radical particularity of Pentecost where each individual hears the Gospel in their own cultural tongue (Acts 2)."[49]

Re-storying

The human inclination for meaning making through the medium of storytelling is generally taken for granted, whether we position ourselves as the authors or the audience.[50] Storytelling has three dimensions, comprising personal, interpersonal, and broadly social or cultural. Neimeyer argues that the literature on the construction, deconstruction, and reconstruction of narratives is rich but still under-utilized.[51] People story and restory their lives to make sense of their struggles and trauma. Our training conversations focused on how to offer support to people in the changes they are making in their lives to take back their lives from the effects of the traumas they have endured.

A predilection towards storytelling is a feature of Melanesian culture. Ngalihesi describes the function of the Melanesian tradition of

47. Anderson, "Heart and Spirit of Collaborative Therapy."
48. Franklin, *Towards Global Missional Leadership*, 34.
49. Dueck et al., "Constantine, Babel, and Yankee Doodling," 57.
50. Neimeyer, "Re-storying Loss," 69.
51. Neimeyer, "Re-storying Loss," 72.

storytelling "as the fundamental way of expressing ourselves and our world to others."[52] In the context of The Tension, Ngalihesi regards storying as a vehicle for the recovery of a different life and associates storytelling with an emerging hope in the midst of hopelessness.[53] The Melanesian idea of stories is that of medicine, the particular significance given to the meaning of untold stories, the power of individual stories becoming a community narrative, and of giving one another stories as gifts. "The story-gift comes like a running flood deep in the psyche. It instructs and draws people together so that we can be able to learn about different people, their ideas and how to act upon them."[54] He goes on to describe the power of the story to transform a life shattered by hopelessness and its power to integrate acknowledged experiences into a personal or collective rebirth and social construction.[55]

Ngalihesi's approach to storytelling draws heavily on his culture and includes the creation of a "safe space" in which individuals are heard in the presence of attentive, respectful, and compassionate listeners, thus enabling the sufferers to reconnect with their lives.[56] A selected group of hearers "must enhance the confidence of the victims to tell their stories" and may include clergy, tribal representatives, and women.[57] He emphasizes the complexity of such a space from the perspective of Western scholarship in that it includes both the natural and the supernatural. These are intertwined for Melanesians. He adds: "In this space there is a great sense of belonging, strong attachments, affection, involvement and deeply felt obligation to share and to contribute something back to cherish a continuing relationship."[58] Realizing the difficulties associated with such an integrated worldview for Western psychology, he reflects that "what matters in the end is not how we are defined by others, but how we define ourselves, our boundaries, exclusions, inclusions and where we decide to take a stand. The space we take our stand is what I recommend as a safe space."[59]

52. Ngalihesi, *Healing the Wounds of our People*, 39.
53. Ngalihesi, *Healing the Wounds of our People*, 41.
54. Ngalihesi, *Healing the Wounds of our People*, 40.
55. Ngalihesi, *Healing the Wounds of our People*, 42.
56. Ngalihesi, *Healing the Wounds of our People*, 36.
57. Ngalihesi, *Healing the Wounds of our People*, 37.
58. Ngalihesi, *Healing the Wounds of our People*, 36.
59. Ngalihesi, *Healing the Wounds of our People*, 36.

Ngalihesi's work supports the importance of inviting and engaging with people's stories in an open dialogical and embodied setting, and in particular, of paying attention to the subplots of growth to support the re-storying process already in operation.

Final Reflections on Sailing with the Wind

Collaboration, dialogue, intersubjective consciousness, and witness practices have become essential principles that inform an approach that values relating in a power-with manner. This is what I have taken on board on a journey of sailing with the wind towards a psychology that is peaceable and refuses to collude with the empire. Moving in the direction of what will hopefully become a hybrid is more about *how* we make the path than knowing what it is that we have to do. Open Dialogue assumptions and practices have helped structure a way of being in relationships and learning with Solomon Islanders that aspires to power-with.

In the dialogical context, therapeutic expertise is about inviting collaborative relationships and establishing a culture of mutual exploration, understanding, and knowledge sharing.[60] Instead of using the situation to apply knowledge and theory, generative conversational processes are entered into that lead to new meanings and understandings and to unanticipated knowledge and innovation. A dialogue of this kind has resulted in respectful and collaborative mutual engagement and learning with the Islands' trauma healers and their desire for further "training." The dialogue also resembles attempts to line up with commitments, purposes, and hopes associated with the tradition of the Melanesian Brothers and with faith in God's re-narration of the world.

Stimuli for the dialogue regularly include stories, songs, and picture cards that elicit further sharing of thoughts and feelings. Videos of work in other developing nations are powerful invitations to participants to respond with their desires for what they would like to incorporate into training.

It has become something of a pattern to make initial inquiries about local knowledge, skills, and resources in the group as well as people's hopes and desires for what they wish to achieve. Sharing together in music and songs is binding, after which we dialogue about what people

---

60. Anderson, "Heart and Spirit of Collaborative Therapy."

already know, and apply, for example, listening. Instead of teaching listening skills, the knowledge and skills that are already in use become the basis for adding conversations and any useful ways of validating and expanding the practice of participants in the dialogue. Efforts are made to give voice to these skills whenever possible in English and Pijin. After many such conversations, a third space began taking shape in which contributions are more equal.

The dialogue has led us to a proposal to co-develop training for counseling support. We decided that the training group would become part of a training team who would facilitate the development of skills, resources, and strengths for others in the Islands in a similar manner to which they had entered into "training." The theme of loss has become a significant part of the programme. Narrative therapy's "tree of life" has probably become the most valuable tool explored by members of the group.[61] Between visits different trainees employed the basic ideas from the exercises in many different ways with school students, church groups, and individuals.

What excited me most was the diversity of applications by different trainees in different contexts. One example of many is the story shared by a woman participant of how she had visited a traumatized individual over many occasions and each time worked with her on creating her tree of life which eventually contributed to her return to health. Another example is a participant's applying an understanding he had come to that everyone has a different story. It helped him to listen and remain present to one of his parishioners whose values were very different to his own. It was almost as if participants continued the conversations we had during our workshops, extending them to include the voices of the people they interacted and worked with in different social settings.

Bibliography

Anderson, Harlene. "Collaborative Relationships and Dialogic Conversations: Ideas for a Relationally Responsive Practice." *Family Process* 51 (2012) 8–24.
———. "The Heart and Spirit of Collaborative Therapy: The Philosophical Stance—'a Way of Being' in Relationship and Conversation." In *Collaborative Therapy: Relationships and Conversations that Make a Difference*, edited by H. Anderson and D. Gerhart, 43–62. New York: Routledge, 2007.
Beu, Charles Brown, and Rosalyn Nokise. *Mission in the Midst of Conflict: Stories from the Solomon Islands*. Suva: Pacific Theological College, 2009.

61. Denborough, *Retelling the Stories of our Lives*, 11–20.

Bøe, Tore Dag, Kjell Kristoffersen, Per Arne Lidbom, Gunnhild Ruud Lindvig, Jaakko Seikkula, Dagfinn Ulland, and Karianne Zachariassen. "Change Is an Ongoing Ethical Event: Levinas, Bakhtin and the Dialogical Dynamics of Becoming." *Australian and New Zealand Journal of Family Therapy* 34 (2013) 18–31.

Bojuwoye, Olaniyi, and Tholene Sodi. "Challenges and Opportunities to Integrating Traditional Healing into Counselling and Psychotherapy." *Consulting Psychology Quarterly* 23 (2010) 283–96.

Calhoun, Lawrence G., and Richard G. Tedeschi. "The Foundations of Posttraumatic Growth: An Expanded Framework." In *Handbook of Posttraumatic Growth*, edited by L. Calhoun and R. G. Tedeschi, 1–23. Mahwah: Lawrence Erlbaum, 2006.

Denborough, David. *Retelling the Stories of our Lives: Everyday Narrative Therapy to Draw Inspiration and Transform Experience*. New York: Norton and Co., 2014.

Dueck, Alvin, and Kevin S. Reimer. *A Peaceable Psychology: Christian Therapy in a World of Many Cultures*. Grand Rapids: Brazos, 2009.

Dueck, Alvin, Julia P. Langdal, David M. Goodman, and Adam A. Ghali. "Prophetic Words for Psychologists: Particularity, Ethics and Peace." *Pastoral Psychology* 58 (2009) 289–301.

Dueck, Alvin, Sing-Kiat Ting, and Renee Cutiongco. "Constantine, Babel, and Yankee Doodling: Whose Indigeneity? Whose Psychology?" *Pastoral Psychology* 56 (2007) 55–72.

Franklin, Kirk J. *Towards Global Missional Leadership: A Journey through Leadership Paradigm Shift in the Mission of God*. Oxford: Regnum, 2017.

Gross, Stanley J. "Personal Power and Empowerment." *Contemporary Education* 56 (1985) 137–43.

Hessamfar, Elahe. *In the Fellowship of His Suffering: A Theological Interpretation of Mental Illness*. Eugene, OR: Cascade, 2014.

Hill, Harriet, Margaret Hill, Richard Baggé, and Pat Miersma. *Healing the Wounds of Trauma: How the Church Can Help*. Philadelphia: American Bible Society, 2016.

Hoffman, Lynn. "The Art of 'Withness.'" In *Collaborative Therapy: Relationships and Conversations that Make a Difference*, edited by H. Anderson and D. Gerhart, 63–80. New York: Routledge, 2007.

Neimeyer, Robert. "Re-storying Loss: Fostering Growth in the Posttraumatic Narrative." In *Handbook of Posttraumatic Growth*, edited by L. G. Calhoun and R. G. Tedeschi, 68–80. Mahwah: Lawrence Erlbaum, 2006.

Ngalihesi, J. Pateson. *Healing the Wounds of Our People: Trauma Healing and the Power of Storytelling: Peace Building in Solomon Islands*. Honiara: Reconciliation and Peace Publishing, 2014.

Olsen, Mary, Jaakko Seikkula, and Douglas Ziedonis. *The Key Elements of Dialogic Practice in Open Dialogue*. Worcester: University of Massachusetts Medical School, 2014.

Schultz, Sydney Ellen, and Duane P. Schultz. *Theories of Personality*. Sydney: Cengage, 2008.

Seikkula, Jaakko. "Becoming Dialogical: Psychotherapy or a Way of Life?" *Australian and New Zealand Journal of Family Therapy* 32 (2011) 179–93.

Smith, James K. A. *Thinking in Tongues: Pentecostal Contributions to Christian Philosophy*. Grand Rapids: Eerdmans, 2010.

White, Michael. "Children, Trauma, and Subordinate Storyline Development." *International Journal of Narrate Therapy and Community Work* (2005) 10–21.

———. "The Externalizing of the Problem and the Re-authoring of Lives and Relationships." In *Selected Papers*, 5–28. Adelaide: Dulwich Centre Publications, 1989.

———. *Maps of Narrative Practice*. New York: W. W. Norton, 2007.

———. "The Process of Questioning: A Therapy of Literary Merit?" In *Selected Papers*, 37–46. Adelaide: Dulwich Centre Publications, 1989.

Chapter 9

Grief as the Sounding of Multiple Notes: Grief and Loss as Seen through the Movements of the Triduum

Sarah Penwarden

To be human is to live in "the liminal space between suffering and hope."[1] We live as embodied beings, journeying towards a fullness of who we are, in relation to those we love, while experiencing losses. As human beings we mourn our losses collectively and individually. The way we grieve and remember our loved one affects the quality of the lives we continue to live. In this chapter, I offer a view of grieving that resists a linear pattern of grieving and advocates for a postmodern notion of grieving as multiple: where bereaved people grieve in ways that are socially shaped and also individual and idiosyncratic. I also seek to show how the liturgical acts of the Triduum offer a picture of life as movements which contain multiple notes of loss and hope. I then offer to pastoral carers/counselors a practical way in which they can respond with a breadth of understanding to the multiple notes of grieving sounded by a bereaved person, in the narrative therapy approach of "double-listening."[2] I show examples of how I enacted this approach in my doctoral study by listening to the multiple notes sounded within the experience of a grieving person: notes of loss, of death, love, and of hope.

1. Meadowcroft, "Finding Hope," 222.
2. White, "Narrative Practice."

The Problem of Patterns of Grieving

Grieving—the social shaped and embodied response to loss—is an area of human life densely crowded with ideas and practices. Psychology, medicine, culture, and religious thought all offer patterns for how one might grieve. Grieving may be understood as "a medical syndrome (in the case of psychiatry); as a progression through stages of adaptation (in the case of bereavement counseling); and as a spiritual journey (in the case of the clergy)."[3] In the area of psychology, grief theorists since Freud[4] have sought to devise templates for grieving, patterns that a bereaved person follows in order to be healthy and well.

Western therapeutic approaches have cast grieving as an interior journey, with the therapist as expert, guiding the client towards wellbeing.[5] In a traditional conceptualization, grief is an illness "with a point of onset, a middle course, and an endpoint of recovery."[6] A person "recovers" from grieving when the feelings of sadness and yearning for the loved one diminish. In a traditional view, therapy helps a bereaved person complete the tasks of grieving,[7] in line with therapeutic gauges and social understanding of what "good" grief is.[8]

One example of a pattern of grieving is Elisabeth Kübler-Ross's famous five stages of grief.[9] In this model, a grieving person passes through the five stages of denial, anger, bargaining, depression, and acceptance before reaching the resolution of grief. Kübler-Ross's model, although not originally intended to be read as step-by-step process, had the effect of arranging grief into a sequence. While it is the most popularly known grief process model, it has undergone recent rigorous critique and significant debunking. In particular, its oversimplification of grief, and the universality and linearity of the model has been critiqued, as has its use by therapists and others seeking to fit the diffuse, "wild" experience of grief into clearly demarcated stages.[10] Indeed, the notion that there exists a set series of stages in a grieving process which is universally applicable

---

3. Neimeyer and Prigerson, "Mourning and Meaning," 238.
4. Freud, "Mourning and Melancholia."
5. Bowlby and Parkes, "Separation and Loss."
6. Hedtke and Winslade, *Crafting of Grief*, 10.
7. Worden, *Grief Counseling*.
8. Foote and Frank, "Foucault and Therapy."
9. Kübler-Ross, *On Death*.
10. Neimeyer and Gamino, "Experience of Grief."

across cultures is now seriously in doubt.[11] As such, a linear model such as Kübler-Ross's might actually *contribute* to grieving people's sense of confusion if their experience does not conform to this model.[12]

Multiplicities of Grieving

Seen through a postmodern lens, with its "incredulity towards metanarratives,"[13] the grand narratives of grieving, such as Kübler-Ross's grief stages, are fractured. In their place comes a turn to local and contextual stories. Grief scholars influenced by postmodernism might relinquish any attempt to make universal "an experience that is incredibly personal, diverse, and often indescribable."[14] In this sense, there may not be *one* kind of grief process but many. Postmodern approaches focus on how bereaved people themselves make meaning.[15] In this ethos, "Stories take on a much greater importance than scientific truths. They become the stuff of identity projects, of relational belonging, and of cultural resonance."[16] Through stories, local truths are found and made as a bereaved person devises their own idiosyncratic narratives of grief and ways of grieving.

In this understanding, the bereaved person is walking in an unknown terrain and making meaning (stories) of the loss in and through their bodies as they communicate emotions, in their social worlds, and between them and all their relationships. They may also be making meaning in the light of their place in the cosmos, with God. The therapist listens and co-crafts stories with the bereaved person. Thus grieving is an *action* which occurs between a bereaved person and others in their communities through storied talk, as they make sense of the loved one's life, death, and continuation. In this sense, "grieving and mourning are active verbs, not merely states to be endured."[17]

Indeed, while a bereaved person may feel subject to intense emotions in grieving, there are also ways that they can actively *make*

---

11. Neimeyer, *Meaning Reconstruction*.
12. Speedy, "Failing to Come to Terms."
13. Lyotard, *Postmodern Condition*, xxxiv.
14. Ord, "Like a Tattoo," 200.
15. Rothaupt and Becker, "Western Bereavement Theory."
16. Hedtke and Winslade, *Crafting of Grief*, 44.
17. Neimeyer et al., "Social Constructionist Account," 486.

meaning of the grieving. A therapist can assist this process by listening to the bereaved person's "experience-near" expressions about their life,[18] taking up the person's own language as they describe their lives. In this way, a therapist can refuse the position of "therapist-as-gatekeeper" of the right way to grieve, and instead can position themselves as co-traveller, in a small way, with the client.

Grieving as Movements

I thus describe grieving as *movements* rather than as *work*, *tasks*, *stages*, or *processes*. A bereaved person navigates movements in liminal spaces following the loss of a loved one or other significant losses. In these liminal spaces, in the flux of grieving, there may be oscillations "between themes such as belief and disbelief, denial and acceptance, yearning and despair, disintegration and reintegration of self and the world, a sense of absence and a sense of presence" of the loved one.[19] Grieving may be chaotic, multi-tonal. A therapist can respond with a breadth of listening which can hear the range of tones sounded as the person grieves. Through this hearing, a bereaved person can come to know themselves and their values and to craft their own response to loss with a sense of agency. Here, a therapist can "craft a conversation in the shadow of death that is still about the affirmation of life. To craft something beautiful and sustaining in the face of death."[20]

Grieving as the Sounding of Multiple Notes

Grieving can be likened to the sounding of multiple notes. In caring for bereaved people, a carer may listen for both the *depth* and *range* of notes in grieving. To listen for the *depth* of notes in grieving, one may listen for the expression of raw emotions: perhaps for the darker and more discordant experiences as they are brought to speech. This bringing pain to speech might be called lament.

To lament is to pour out a range of emotions before God: emotions of anger, despair, complaint, or protest. Many of the Old Testament psalms begin with the voice of Israel expressing a depth of pain. To lament is to

18. Geertz, *Local Knowledge*.
19. McCabe, *Paradox of Loss*, 8
20. Hedtke and Winslade, *Crafting of Grief*, 169.

speak as an embodied being, to bring suffering to voice. What lament enables is the voicing of the *particularity* of one's suffering and complaint, and also the range—the full expression—of one's embodied suffering.[21] Arguably, it is in "the individual's free and full expression of his or her grief feelings" that healing can occur, as hope may rise up after lament.[22] For the psalmist, lament involved a structured movement from complaining to God, petitioning God, confessing trust in God, and then reminding oneself of God's assurance.[23] Some writers have argued that through the very *action* of lamenting, change could occur for the lamenter, as through lament they might become reorientated to life and turn again towards God.[24] Writing about Jeremiah's lament, Card, for example, focuses on the turns and movements within ch. 3 where Jeremiah quietly remembers God's steadfast love.[25]

As a pastoral carer or counselor, one can listen for the *depth* of notes within a person's grieving. One can also listen to a *range* of notes. Sadness might be a dominant note, a visceral yearning for the loved one. As might a sorrow for what has been lost, for what might not now occur, for a future hope changed or gone. Yet there are other notes. We grieve because we love. Indeed, "grief is essentially love under the condition of absence."[26] Grieving may be a testament to love. Narrative therapy pioneer Michael White wrote about how distress in the life of a traumatized person could be considered a "testimony to the significance of what it was that the person held precious" which had been trampled on in the trauma.[27] Similarly the distress and pain following the death of a loved one might testify, not only to the significance of the loved one, but to the value of love itself. Thus in notes of yearning, disappointment, and other raw emotions, one may also hear notes of love, of gratitude, of an affirmation of the importance of relationship.

A *range* of notes could also be understood as notes of *time*: of past, present, and future. Stroebe and Schut have developed a Dual Process Model which suggests two major stressors for bereaved people as they

---

21. Billman and Migliore, *Rachel's Cry*.
22. Billman and Migliore, *Rachel's Cry*, 81.
23. Fowler, *Ministry of Lament*.
24. Brueggemann, *Spirituality of the Psalms*.
25. Card, *Sacred Sorrow*.
26. Vaughn, "Recovering Grief," 40.
27. White, "Narrative Practice," 39.

navigate a world changed following the death of the loved one.[28] One is a *loss-oriented* stressor, requiring focus on and working through aspects of the loss, and the other, a *restoration-oriented* stressor, involving reorganizing life and crafting new identities following the loss.[29] Thus, a pastoral carer/counselor might hear the multiple notes sounded by a bereaved person in a focus on *time*: notes sounded as the past is told and retold, notes focusing on life in the present, and notes focusing on what the new future might mean. In this way, a counselor can hear and respond to the range of notes sounded.

Multilogue between Theology, Counseling, and Lived Experience

Thus far, I have explored postmodern notions of grieving as involving multiple movements for the bereaved person as they are both subject to grieving and also make turns and responses within it. I have proposed a particular metaphor for pastoral carers/counselors of grieving as the sounding of multiple notes, whose depth and range a counselor can hear and respond to. I now wish to weave in another thread in this chapter, a strand of liturgical theology.

The impetus of the collection of essays in which this chapter appears is to create further dialogue between theology and counseling. In dialogue, two different objects come into conversation with each other. A genuine dialogue "requires that there be two separable presences, each coming from its own standpoint, expressing and enacting its own particular specificity."[30] In this chapter, I aim to respect the integrity of both counseling and theology—their separate presences—and to bring them into conversation with the area of focus: grieving. I suggest that one might actually think of three protagonists in the dialogue or rather, multilogue, namely, counseling, theology, and the lived experience of grieving people, as I share examples of below.

In the theological thread, I have been influenced by Rambo's work on Holy Saturday.[31] Holy Saturday—the day between Good Friday

---

28. Stroebe and Schut, "Meaning Making."
29. Stroebe and Schut, "Meaning Making," 58.
30. Sampson, *Celebrating the Other*, 15.
31. Rambo, "Saturday."

and Easter Sunday—speaks of "radical suffering."[32] Holy Saturday is a space within the Triduum of both darkness and potential. It is a place to honor "the absence, the death, the impossibility of life ahead" *and also* a place to "invoke the Spirit, who creates new life and brings about new beginnings."[33] Holy Saturday allows the space for grief. In counseling a grieving person, a counselor can bear witness to this "in-between space" that is resonant both with bleakness and hope.[34] A counselor can pay attention to *both* the aspects of death in a grieving person's experience, as well as the living on beyond it.

In this chapter, I draw not only on Holy Saturday, but on the liturgical practices of the whole Triduum festival, focusing on the movements within the Triduum as one way of viewing multiple movements in grieving. In this way, both theology and counseling are brought into dialogue with each other in order to bear witness to a person's lived experience of grieving, and to create pathways towards hope.

The Triduum

Liturgy is "the work of the people."[35] It is the pattern of church worship in Catholic and Anglican churches, both across a calendar year and in the daily or weekly communal worship. Liturgies are patterns through which a person is taught and reminded about the life of Christ, and invited to participate in and be ongoingly formed in Christ's image.[36] Liturgies create meaningful spaces—through words, postures, and actions—which fashion us as we inhabit them. Thus, through the liturgy a person comes into "actual contact with the saving events that took place in the life of Christ, especially his Paschal Mystery . . . What confronts the liturgical assembly is not a force but a person. In the liturgy, the church meets Jesus Christ."[37]

Liturgies are formed around key events in Christ's life, enacted across the course of a year, with particular attention being paid to the climactic Nativity and Easter cycles. The Easter Paschal Triduum is a

---

32. Rambo, "Saturday," 234.
33. Rambo, "Saturday," 234.
34. Spriggens, "Christian Hope," 120.
35. Brown, *Being a Deacon*, 47.
36. Malloy, *Celebrating the Eucharist*.
37. Malloy, *Celebrating the Eucharist*, 70.

church festival that marks Jesus' betrayal, crucifixion, and resurrection, celebrated from Maundy Thursday to Good Friday, Holy Saturday, and Easter Sunday. Through Easter festivals many Christian churches reflect on these events which offer a path of reflection for a person where they might think on journeys from darkness to light. In this sense, a worshipper travels along with the events in the life of Christ "making the passage with Christ through death into life."[38]

The Easter cycle of liturgies are a place and time in which the church makes room for loss, emptiness, and disappointments. While some people might find the bleakness of Good Friday challenging and want to fast forward to the resurrection, I have found that this day makes visible aspects of my life experience that are not always visible within weekly church worship. I *join with* the Triduum liturgies and the life of Christ. I hear the range of notes sounded by the Triduum, some of which are notes of grief, sadness, and hope deferred. This festival highlights the "inextricably interwoven realities of suffering and salvation, of death and life" and thus the Triduum "forms the church for living the authentic Christian life."[39] The multiple notes of the Triduum—the interwoven realities of suffering and life—join with my own journey and also offer a way to understand a bereaved person's experience as containing multiple realities.

However, as I began to think about the correspondence between the Triduum and bereavement journeys, I realized that when walking with someone grieving, the movement of the Easter Triduum, when viewed too simplistically, might look like a strictly linear movement from death to life, sadness to joy, dark to light. Thus, the offering of a linear pattern of grieving to a bereaved person might actually *hinder* them in their grieving journey if they feel they are failing to live up to a grieving pattern. While the Triduum can be viewed as a journey from darkness to light, I focus here on the Easter Triduum as a movement that contains a variety of notes, where both life and death may be present at the same time.

From Darkness to Light

In a traditional celebration of the Triduum, when a person comes to church on Good Friday they find a church building stripped bare of

---

38. Evangelical Lutheran Church of America, *Evangelical Lutheran Worship*, 74.
39. Malloy, *Celebrating the Eucharist*, 73.

color and ornament. For the first three centuries CE the Paschal festival included a "night-long vigil culminating in a celebration of the eucharist as dawn broke."[40] In contemporary times, the vigil customarily begins at midnight on Holy Saturday. Then, after sunrise on Easter Sunday, a fire is lit in a brazier outside the church. The Easter Sunday service proper begins with the church in complete darkness. Then, the first of many candles are lit in the Service of Light, which symbolizes the resurrection. As the candle is carried through the church, it then gives light to "individual candles held by each member of the assembly, [thus] the light is gradually passed from this single flame into the darkest corners of the building."[41]

This description of the Triduum highlights the linear movements that arc towards light, that begin with suffering, and end with resurrection and joy. However, the Triduum can also be seen as featuring the "inextricably interwoven realities" of suffering, hope, and life.[42] In this interwoven cord, "the resurrection is celebrated not as a moment 'after' suffering and separate from it, but as a mystery born in and of suffering."[43]

Multiple Tones of Both Life and Death

As highlighted previously, one day of the three days which holds the tension of suffering and hope is Holy Saturday. Holy Saturday—the day which represents when Jesus was in the grave—is a place of chaos and transition.[44] Holy Saturday contains multiple notes: "It is the day when the pain is over and the waiting and wondering begins. Hope peeps its head above the parapet, only to be dragged back down again by doubt and fear."[45] It is a simultaneously a place of darkness and potential, and potential and darkness.

Walter Brueggemann, writing from the perspective of the Holocaust, suggests that Holy Saturday offers a blank space, a breathing space, in the journeys between death and life: "It is my simple suggestion that the Shoah—and perhaps other unbearable brutalities may qualify along with the Shoah—requires Christian faith and liturgy to pause long and deeply

---

40. Giles, *Times and Seasons*, 89.
41. Giles, *Times and Seasons*, 134.
42. Malloy, *Celebrating the Eucharist*, 73.
43. Farwell, *This Is the Night*, 7.
44. Sheppy, *Death, Liturgy and Ritual*.
45. Giles, *Times and Seasons*, 130.

on the second day."[46] Brueggemann argues for a theology which does not collapse Holy Saturday either into Good Friday or into Easter Sunday, an "already begun victory."[47] Rather, "The protection of the second day as a deep moment in God's life . . . serves to retard an all too ready Christian triumphalism when on the ground there is in fact no visible triumph."[48]

This day represents something of the human experience of bereaved people: complex movements between hope and suffering, whereby a bereaved person might be living with the finality of the loved one's death, while also there may be small shifts towards knowing how the loved one's values might continue on in those around them. Thus, this view of the Triduum as three days interwoven into one, represents some of the bereaved people's experiences of coexistent places of hope, despair, new life, and struggle.

Double-listening

To turn from liturgical theology to lived experience, those grieving a loved one can experience a wildness of grieving whereby their whole lives seem dislocated and strange. Their very selves seem in danger, irrevocably changed. There is a need to re-learn themselves, others, and the world.[49] A compassionate counselor chooses to dwell with people in these challenging terrains where both life and death are present.[50] One way a therapist can do this is through double-listening.

Double-listening is a practice within narrative therapy, a post-structuralist-inspired therapy which draws on Foucault's work on power/knowledge[51] and the writings of Bruner[52] and Geertz[53] on storied lives. A narrative therapist listens to clients as they tell both problem-saturated and alternative, hopeful stories of their lives. Through drawing forward the strands of the alternative story of a person's strengths, skills,

---

46. Brueggemann, "The Day 'In-Between,'" 110.
47. Brueggemann, "The Day 'In-Between,'" 109.
48. Brueggemann, "The Day 'In-Between,'" 110.
49. Attig, "Relearning the World."
50. Spriggens, "Christian Hope."
51. Foucault, *Power/Knowledge*.
52. Bruner, "Ethnography as Narrative."
53. Geertz, *Local Knowledge*.

capabilities and values, a person "re-authors" their story.[54] A therapist may be influential in the session through retelling a client's stories in various ways, often using clients' exact words, but with therapist selection and emphasis. In this sense a new story can be woven that promotes how a person wants to live.

Double-listening involves a therapist listening for a value that lies behind an expression of a person's distress.[55] Double-listening hears in an expression of distress a protest that things could or should be different. A value is heard that has previously been diminished or ignored.[56] In listening to people's experiences about grieving, double-listening might involve hearing the darker tones of the many facets of loss, *and also* listening for tiny glimmers of hope, for the subtle invitations the bereaved person might be aware of to live life richly. In this way, a counselor can bear witness to accounts of death, loss, rupture, pain, *and* can listen for the nearness of the loved one, for hope, love, and continuation of their influence. This is a listening which joins with a bereaved person's search for "moments of beauty among the moments of pain and loss."[57] Such a listening does not nullify the real effects of loss, but holds onto the *potential* of life in the midst of death.

In conversations with a bereaved person, I might double-listen in their conversation to hear the subtle notes which suggest hope, *and* to join with the client in growing these. I might hear a fresh remembering of a value the bereaved person has, or a realization of a quality of the loved one the bereaved person wishes to continue to hold dear. These moments can grow through being documented: turned into a written document which can capture and retell them. This documentation of "sparkling moments" in a conversation is a key feature of narrative therapy.[58]

In my doctoral research, I practiced on a particular kind of poetry therapy as a way to respond to the stories of people who had lost a loved partner.[59] I wrote poems directly from the speech of participants who had lost a loved spouse or partner, and offered it back to them to reflect

---

54. White and Epston, *Literate Means*.
55. Carey et al., "Absent but Implicit."
56. White, "Narrative Practice."
57. Hedtke, "Creating Stories of Hope," ix.
58. Speedy, "Using Poetic Documents."
59. Penwarden, "Conversations about Absence."

on. This poetry therapy is known as rescued speech poetry.[60] I share two examples here from my work with Yvonne and Jan (pseudonyms), both of whom had experienced the death of a spouse.[61]

Brick wall

A brick wall
and then you see plants growing—
from *where*?

In the middle of a brick wall
you see one starting to grow . . .
there's nothing—
no soil.

You just can't
stop life
it just carries on
in spite of yourself.

Good Friday

The sewer pipe under the house broke the other day;
it just fell down in the storm—
not a pretty sight.
All this awful stuff and broken pipes all around,
and I just stood there in the half-dark
and thought, "Oh Ed! Where are you?"

Then I knew that he wasn't there.
I had to handle it;
I had to clean it up.

It was Good Friday—
too late to ring a plumber or insurance,
so I just dug up buckets of stuff
and moved them around the garden.

It was Good Friday,
so death and dying.

60. Behan, "Rescued Speech Poems."
61. Penwarden, "Conversations about Absence."

> I was going somewhere
> and a few people knew it was the anniversary of Ed.
> I walked in, saying,
> "I've had a yucky day
> and I'm reminded
> that I'm not one of the dead,
> I'm one of the living
> and I've got to get on with it."

In these poems composed directly from two participants' speaking, there are multiple tones of death *and* life, of the unexpected emergence of life in the face of death, of creation happening again in subtle ways. In the first poem, Yvonne talks about how life continues, and this continuation is like a plant growing on a brick wall. There may be therapeutic possibilities to explore with Yvonne, both in the surprise she feels at life continuing in spite of everything, and also the small miracle of the plant growing without soil.

In the "Good Friday" poem, Jan is standing in the "half-dark." Her husband Ed's absence is keenly felt, with the mess of the broken sewer pipe. Yet there is not just death and dying, but resurrection. Jan has the epiphany that *she* is not dead, that she is "one of the living" and she has to "get on with it." This poem captures one movement she is making: towards living life after the death of her husband. In a therapy setting, one might explore with Jan the key moment of this shift, and what this meant to her, that she is "one of the living."

My work here seeks to amplify stories that contain light, to "make the light grow larger."[62] This is a work that aims to find spaces of hope within stories of loss, and *grow* these stories through literary attention. It is about subtly fomenting movements of change. This work is not at the expense of acknowledging the effects of loss, but one that hears loss and also quietly looks for glimmers of new life. It is a listening for coexistence. This double-listening hears multiplicity, a range of notes, *and* seeks to amplify the sound of particular notes of hope. This listening to multiplicity honors both the sadness of the bereaved person and also makes space for potentiality. It pays attention to both the brick wall and to the plant starting to grow, to death and re-creation.

---

62. Hedtke, "Creating Stories of Hope," 6.

An Invitation

To listen for multiplicity can be challenging for counselors/pastoral carers. Each carer brings to the listening their own historic layering with ideas—of what grief is and what good grief looks like. I am an advocate for carers seeking to acknowledge the shaping that has occurred in their own understanding of grieving, and to respond to the changes in grief theory over time. To offer an attuned listening which can hear the range of notes in grieving requires a willingness to move beyond a linear model of grieving and journey with bereaved people as they make meaning of their lives through their own experience-near stories. This kind of attuned listening also requires a willingness from the carer to notice their own embodied responses to the bereaved person. Hearing others as they express their pain illuminates one's own life. It can throw light onto our own known or half-known experiences of loss. Pastoral carers and counselors may find they grow as much as their clients through walking in these terrains, as long as there is a willingness for the carer to honestly acknowledge their own responses and to find their own sources of support. In this way, a carer's attending to their own life experiences, through reflection and supervision, can bear fruit.

The effect of embodied, attuned listening may be that a bereaved person can know they have been heard, where some raw emotions have been soothed, and stories re-woven, facilitating living life again. This embodied listening may involve a listening for the coexistence of darkness and the potential for new life in order to grow this potential. A carer/counselor with Christian faith commitments may find in the Triduum an echoing of the multiple notes of life and death, and an encouragement to hold hope for new life for a person who grieves.

Bibliography

Attig, Thomas. "Relearning the World: Making and Finding Meanings." In *Meaning Reconstruction and the Experience of Loss*, edited by Robert Neimeyer, 33–55. Washington, DC: American Psychological Association, 2001.

Behan, Chris. "Rescued Speech Poems: Co-authoring Poetry in Narrative Therapy." *Narrative Approaches*, June 5, 2013. http://www.narrativeapproaches.com/narrative%20papers%20folder/behan.htm.

Billman, Kathleen, and Daniel Migliore. *Rachel's Cry: Prayer of Lament and Rebirth of Hope*. Eugene, OR: Wipf & Stock, 1999.

Bowlby, John, and Colin Murray Parkes. "Separation and Loss Within the Family." In *The Child in His Family*, edited by E. James Anthony, 197–216. New York: Whiley, 1970.

Brown, Rosalind. *Being a Deacon Today: Exploring a Distinctive Ministry in the Church and the World*. New York: Morehouse, 2005.

Brueggemann, Walter. "Reading from the Day 'In Between.'" In *A Shadow of Glory: Reading the New Testament after the Holocaust*, edited by Tod Linafelt, 105–16. New York: Routledge, 2002.

———. *The Spirituality of the Psalms*. Minneapolis: Augsburg Fortress, 2002.

Bruner, Edward. "Ethnography as Narrative." In *The Anthropology of Experience*, edited by Victor Turner and Edward Bruner, 139–55. Chicago: University of Illinois Press, 1986.

Card, Michael. *A Sacred Sorrow: Reaching Out to God in the Lost Language of Lament*. Colorado Springs: NavPress, 2005.

Carey, Maggie, Sarah Walther, and Shona Russell. "The Absent but Implicit: A Map to Support Therapeutic Enquiry." *Family Process* 48 (2009) 319–31.

Evangelical Lutheran Church in America. *Evangelical Lutheran Worship*. Minneapolis: Augsburg Fortress, 2006.

Farwell, James. *This Is the Night: Suffering, Salvation, and the Liturgies of Holy Week*. New York: T&T Clark International, 2005.

Foote, Catherine, and Arthur Frank. "Foucault and Therapy: The Disciplining of Grief." In *Reading Foucault for Social Work*, edited by Adrienne Chambon, Allan Irving, and Laura Epstein, 157–88. New York: Columbia University Press, 1999.

Foucault, Michel. *Power/Knowledge:s Selected Interviews and Other Writings*. Brighton: Harvest, 1980.

Fowler, Gene. *The Ministry of Lament: Caring for the Bereaved*. St. Louis: Chalice, 2010.

Freud, Sigmund. "Mourning and Melancholia." *Standard Edition* 14 (1917) 1957–61.

Geertz, Clifford. *Local Knowledge: Further Essays in Interpretive Anthropology*. New York: Basic, 1983.

Giles, Richard. *Times and Seasons: Creating Transformative Worship Throughout the Year*. Norwich: Church, 2008.

Hedtke, Lorraine. "Creating Stories of Hope: A Narrative Approach to Illness, Death and Grief." *International Journal of Narrative Therapy and Community Work* 1 (2014) 1–10.

Hedtke, Lorraine, and John Winslade. *The Crafting of Grief: Constructing Aesthetic Responses to Loss*. New York: Routledge, 2016.

Kübler-Ross, Elizabeth. *On Death and Dying*. New York: Macmillan, 1969.

Lyotard, Jean-François. *The Postmodern Condition: A Report on Knowledge*. Manchester: Manchester University Press, 1984.

Malloy, Patrick. *Celebrating the Eucharist: A Practical Ceremonial Guide for Clergy and Other Liturgical Ministers*. New York: Church, 2007.

McCabe, Marilyn. *The Paradox of Loss: Toward a Relational Theory of Grief*. Wesport: Praeger, 2003.

Meadowcroft, Tim. "Finding Hope and Yearning for Love." In *Spirituality and Cancer: Christian Encounters*, edited by Tim Meadowcroft and Caroline Blyth, 219–23. Auckland: Accent, 2015.

Neimeyer, Robert, ed. *Meaning Reconstruction and the Experience of Loss*. Washington, DC: American Psychological Association, 2001.

Neimeyer, Robert, Dennis Klass, and Michael R. Dennis. "A Social Constructionist Account of Grief: Loss and the Narration of Meaning." *Death Studies* 38 (2014) 485–98.

Neimeyer, Robert, and Holly Prigerson. "Mourning and Meaning." *American Behavioral Scientist* 46 (2002) 235–51.

Neimeyer, Robert, and Louis Gamino. "The Experience of Grief and Bereavement." In *Handbook of Death and Dying*, edited by Clifton D. Bryant, 847–54. Thousand Oaks: SAGE, 2003.

Ord, Robyn. "'It's Like a Tattoo': Rethinking Dominant Discourses on Grief." *Canadian Social Work Review* 26 (2009) 195–211.

Penwarden, Sarah. "Conversations About Absence and Presence: Re-Membering a Loved Partner in Poetic Form." PhD diss., University of Waikato, 2018.

Rambo, Shelley. "Saturday in New Orleans." *Review and Expositor* 105 (2008) 229–44.

Rothaupt, Jeanne, and Kent Becker. "A Literature Review of Western Bereavement Theory: From Decathecting to Continuing Bonds." *Family Journal* 15 (2007) 6–15.

Sampson, Edward. *Celebrating the Other: A Dialogic Account of Human Nature*. Chagrin Falls: Taos Institute, 2008.

Sheppy, Paul. *Death, Liturgy and Ritual*. Vol. 1, *A Pastoral and Liturgical Theology*. Aldershot: Ashgate, 2003.

Speedy, Jane. "Failing to Come to Terms with Things: A Multi-Storied Conversation About Poststructuralist Ideas and Narrative Practices in Response to Some of Life's Failures." *Counselling and Psychotherapy Research* 5 (2005) 65–73.

———. "Using Poetic Documents: An Exploration of Poststructuralist Ideas and Poetic Practices in Narrative Therapy." *British Journal of Guidance and Counselling* 33 (2005) 283–98.

Spriggens, Lisa. "Christian Hope: Ethical Responses to Trauma." In *Stories of Therapy, Stories of Faith*, edited by Lex McMillan, Sarah Penwarden, and Siobhan Hunt, 114–28. Eugene, OR: Wipf & Stock, 2017.

Stroebe, Margaret, and Henk Schut. "Meaning Making in the Dual Process Model of Coping with Bereavement." In *Meaning Reconstruction and the Experience of Loss*, edited by Robert Neimeyer, 55–76. Washington, DC: American Psychological Association, 2001.

Vaughn, Bruce. "Recovering Grief in the Age of Grief Recovery." *Journal of Pastoral Theology* 3 (2003) 36–45.

White, Michael. "Narrative Practice and Community Assignments." *International Journal of Narrative Therapy and Community Work* 2 (2003) 17–56.

White, Michael, and David Epston. *Literate Means to Therapeutic Ends*. Adelaide: Dulwich Centre, 1989.

Worden, William. *Grief Counseling and Grief Therapy: A Handbook for the Mental Health Practitioner*. New York: Springer, 1982.

Chapter 10

Person-Centered Care and the Love of Neighbor

Mark G. Brett

Submissions to the Royal Commission into Aged Care Quality and Safety in Australia provide a number of pressing questions for a system of care that is conceived in terms of markets and consumers, especially when it comes to clients living with dementia. As Elizabeth Beattie puts it, there are numerous "threats to their personhood."[1] Indeed, some have put the view that there is no personhood in advanced dementia. One line of philosophical argument even suggests that people with late stage dementia could justifiably be euthanized.[2] In this paper, we will take up the question of personhood as a conceptual problem in aged care. I will show how some of the most difficult questions in the studies of dementia can shed light on the broader frameworks that should underpin the practice of spiritual care.

In his essay "The Value Given and Presupposed in Person-Centred Dementia Care," Stephen Ames diagnoses a problem that he finds in

---

1. Elizabeth Beattie is Professor of Aged and Dementia Care in the School of Nursing at the Queensland University of Technology. See Commonwealth of Australia, *Royal Commission into Aged Care Quality and Safety Interim Report, Vol. 2*. I am grateful to Ilsa Hampton, CEO of Meaningful Ageing Australia, for drawing my attention to this and other references relevant to the present discussion.

2. See, e.g., the views of Mary Warnock and Peter Singer, discussed by Swinton, "What's in a Name?," 236–41; cf. Singer, *Practical Ethics*, 175–217.

one of the most influential accounts of person-centered care.[3] Tom Kitwood's work, it is argued, claims that "each person has absolute value" but then provides no coherent explanation of how that absolute value is established; Kitwood simply invokes an influential strand of "Western philosophy," which needs no theological grounding.[4] Ames argues that personhood *does* require a "transcendent" or even theological grounding, and by implication, so does the practice of person-centered care. Reflecting on this debate with Kitwood in the context of a secular nation like Australia, however, there are particular difficulties with theological defenses of personhood. Insisting on a theological grounding seems to yield an account of care that would be relevant only within particular sectors of the population. Yet there are also problems with Kitwood's assumption that a functional consensus within "Western philosophy" might avoid recourse to theology, since this may also be too narrow a base in the context of multicultural societies. Especially in non-Western philosophical traditions and cultures, the idea of personhood is a fundamentally contested concept.[5]

In some respects, however, Ames has provided an argument that can potentially account for multiple definitions of personhood. Given his appeal to transcendence, the multicultural potential of the argument might seem difficult to grasp, but the potential is there, and it cannot be dismissed as a merely sectarian theology. He draws a distinction between, on the one hand, giving value to a person as a kind of gift, and on the other hand, recognizing this value as inherent, regardless of whether it is actually recognized in practice. Ames argues that recognizing a person's inherent value is crucial if we are to resolve the philosophical difficulties in Kitwood's account of person-centered care. These difficulties disappear once personhood is understood to be inherent, that is, to possess an ontological status or value quite apart from any practice of care that might endow it, or any philosophical variation in how the concept of personhood might be framed.

3. Ames "Person-Centred Dementia Care."

4. Kitwood, *Dementia Reconsidered*, 8. On the philosophical problems of personhood, see Higgs and Gilleard, "Interrogating Personhood and Dementia."

5. Western cultural assumptions are particularly evident in the Interim Report on the *Royal Commission into Aged Care Quality* when it translates personhood as "individuality": "The need to respect the individuality of those receiving care, no matter their cognitive function and no matter how challenging it is to care for them, emerged clearly" (*Royal Commission into Aged Care Quality*, 62).

The philosophical point is well taken, but we may nevertheless continue to doubt whether this ontology will yield any significant differences in the practice of care. Ames implicitly acknowledges this doubt when he lists a number of historic examples of the neglect of personhood: failing to care for asylum seekers, survivors of abuse, Indigenous peoples, or enslaved persons.[6] In this respect, the Royal Commission into Aged Care Quality has uncovered only the most recent examples in a long history of institutionalized abuse. However, in all these cases we find conspicuous examples of Christian leaders who have failed to recognize personhood, while at the same time affirming the existence of a God who underwrites the ontological value of human beings. This observation does not greatly affect the philosophical point that Ames is making, but it does illustrate the point that convictions about ontology may yield no great differences in actual practice. The affirmation of a transcendent source of value may not yield any improved quality of care.

There may, of course, be dramatically different practical outcomes if an overly narrow definition of personhood is accepted. Thus, as already noted, the philosophers Mary Warnock and Peter Singer have reached the notorious conclusion that people with dementia could justifiably be euthanized on the grounds that they are no longer persons. Their arguments require definitions of personhood that focus on an individual's capacities: self-control, a sense of the past and future, the ability to communicate, and so on. Thus, instead of accepting such an individualistic conception of personhood, John Swinton has drawn attention to the alternatives proposed by Robert Spaemann, among others. In Spaemann's account of personhood, the very fact of kinship within the whole human family can generate the kinds of responsibilities that flow from family obligations.[7] The capacities of a particular individual are on this account a secondary matter, and the primary category of personhood flows instead from being a member of the human species, and more specifically, from the experience of care that is owed within the context of genealogical connections.[8]

This argument addresses Warnock and Singer in some respects, particularly by de-linking personhood from individual performances

---

6. Ames, "Person-Centred Dementia Care," 8.

7. Spaemann, *Persons*.

8. See the discussion in Swinton, "What's in a Name?," 241–43.

of identity.[9] But arguments from a generic human kinship do not deal adequately with the fact that human care is most strongly focused within families or kinship networks who embody some unified sense of meaning and purpose. Hence, humans have readily killed other persons who were regarded as some kind of threat to a common good. Obligations to care for kin are generally strongest among close family, and extend outwards from that family focus by means of kinship analogies.

In the context of state-sponsored care, particular institutions take on some of the responsibilities that would otherwise belong to families, especially on matters that relate to the professionalized practices of health care. In institutionalized contexts, however, the health sciences are framed by management systems that are themselves accountable to funding derived from governments with resource constraints. The complex levels of accountability within the aged care "market"[10] often leave carers with very little space to exercise their convictions about the absolute value of persons, should they possess such convictions. In a secular society, the scope for shared norms within institutions has to be carefully negotiated. Any acknowledgement of personhood will, in practice, flow from an institutional culture as much as it does from carers whose underlying convictions or "ontologies" will vary considerably. Nevertheless, a large portion of state-sponsored care is still undertaken by faith-based agencies, so religious values are still very much woven into the fabric of aged care institutions, even if these values have been translated into a public discourse in various ways.

The Transcendent Value of Human Persons

This leads us to consider one other element in Ames's argument: that the worth of each human being is grounded in a transcendent reality that is "typically *incognito*, the hidden ground of the unconditional worth of each person." This claim about hidden grounds may in certain respects fit

---

9. This point does not detract from practices of care that do indeed recognize wider conceptions of selfhood, as for example in Batra et al., "Qualitative Assessment of Self-Identity in People with Advanced Dementia."

10. The Aged Care Sector Committee's *Aged Care Roadmap* (2016) signaled the intention of the sector to deliver a system that is "sustainable, consumer driven and market based." See online: https://www.health.gov.au/resources/publications/aged-care-roadmap. The 2019 Quality Standards refers to people in receipt of care as "consumers." Online: https://www.agedcarequality.gov.au/providers/standards.

neatly into a liberal political order that requires any religious specificities to be toned down.¹¹ This idea of a transcendence *incognito* provides the multicultural potential in the argument, since it insists on no particular religious construal, even if the underlying convictions of particular caring agencies may well include the belief that all human beings are "created in the image of God," as Ames notes.¹² When translated into secular norms, the image of God has been greatly influential in the formation of theories of human rights, as the philosopher Jürgen Habermas has noted.¹³ In this respect, an appeal to the *imago dei* is not inevitably sectarian. Nevertheless, it would be necessary to reflect for a moment on the ways in which this translation from "image of God" into "personhood" might still reflect its biblical origins.

In non-Western religious traditions, for example, human selfhood is often considered a distraction from larger, more-than-human realities.¹⁴ Especially in the Australian context, it would also be necessary to acknowledge that within Aboriginal and Torres Strait Islander cultures, a clear distinction between human persons and the wider relational networks of the natural world would not make sense.¹⁵ As a consequence, even if Kitwood's appeal to "Western philosophy" were enriched to include an invocation of the "image of God" shared by all human persons, as suggested by Ames, many non-Western religious traditions may still, by implication, be left out of account. This exclusivist consequence would, however, be quite at odds with the biblical roots of the *imago dei* language, and this biblical background is still relevant.

Specifically in Gen 1:27 it is important to notice a nuance in the original Hebrew version: the wording in relation to God is "image of Elohim" rather than "image of YHWH." According to the theology expounded in Genesis 1, humanity is not created in the image of the national deity, YHWH (the Lord in English translations) but in relation to a generically named divinity, Elohim. Within this same theology of transcendence (which biblical scholars attribute to a "Priestly" school of thought), even

---

11. See especially the influential argument from Rawls, "Idea of Public Reason Revisited."

12. Ames, "Person-Centred Dementia Care," 9.

13. E.g., Habermas, "On the Relation Between the Secular Liberal State and Religion."

14. Specifically in relation to aged care, see, e.g., Brijnath, *Unforgotten*.

15. McMillan et al., "Person-Centred Care as Caring for Country." Cf. Gee et al., "Aboriginal and Torres Strait Islander Social and Emotional Wellbeing."

the ancestors of Israel in Genesis did not know the national name of God (Exod 6:2–4). In other words, the Creator is *incognito*, and the very same transcendent reality might come to be known by a variety of different names, including but not restricted to the divine name that was later revealed to Israel.[16]

The deliberate non-naming of God in Genesis 1 presents an inclusive transcendence, in principle shared with all humankind.[17] In addition, there is another related version of inclusive theology that is expressed particularly in the book of Job,[18] and a combination of Genesis and Job points to a sociality that could be summarized very well by Luke Bretherton's recent account of political theology:

> As creatures, situated in various covenantal relations . . . we are always already in relationship with others. Our personhood is the fruit of a social and wider ecological womb as much as a single physical one; that is, we come to be in and through others not like us, including non-human others. This means we cannot exist without some kind of common life with a plurality of human and non-human ways of being alive.[19]

This broad vision of meaning, purpose and connectedness, with explicit reference to the context of nature, corresponds very well with what has been termed holistic or "ecological" models of spiritual care.[20] Even within the biblical traditions, a wide variety of solidarities and spiritual connections are affirmed.

Within the Priestly literature in the Hebrew Bible, there is a common understanding that social life is layered—stretching from the inner life of the family, through to the tribe, to the family of nations descended from Abraham, to all humans (friend and stranger), and then to other creatures who share blood or breath. This layered vision is articulated in Leviticus 19, for example, where one requirement speaks to loving "the

---

16. Here I have deliberately taken a different biblical route to the idea of an "impenetrable incognito" that Karl Barth tied only to Christology in his groundbreaking *Epistle to the Romans* (279). Nevertheless, there is something of a common cause with Barth in resisting "direct communication" about the divine, which wrongly domesticates God within conventional religion and ideology (cf. Lloyd, "Negative Political Theology of James Baldwin").

17. See especially de Pury, "Gottesname, Gottesbezeichnung und Gottesbegriff."

18. Brett, *Locations of God*, 121–31.

19. Bretherton, *Christ and the Common Life*, 22.

20. Rumbold, "Models of Spiritual Care," 180.

neighbor as yourself" (v. 18) while another requires loving "the stranger as yourself" (v. 34).[21] The neighbor normally belongs within an Israelite kinship group, and as is indicated by the laws governing strangers, it is assumed that loving strangers would require a greater moral energy beyond the natural energy devoted to one's partner, family, or friends.[22] This moral scenario is not greatly different in the New Testament, where the parable of the Good Samaritan urges people to go beyond their natural affections and obligations.[23] Even more dramatically, Jesus elsewhere calls for the love of enemies (e.g., in Luke 6:27–36). But the underlying assumption in all these New Testament texts is that the normal categories will need to be stretched in order to love the neighbor or enemy.

On Luke Bretherton's account of neighbor love, the conventional or institutional arrangements should always be seen as contingent, or open to revision. Letting go of these "contingent" social arrangements is a lot easier said than done, since they are often constructed and maintained over generations, if not centuries (as in the case of the conflict between Jews and Samaritans). But suspending our own expectations is a necessary condition for the love of neighbor. A neighbor does not arrive with a pre-assigned social category (like an ethnicity, religion, or gender), or a legal status (like citizen or refugee), or a role (like client or customer), all of which can conveniently structure our social expectations. The neighbor arrives in one's world simply as a person, or more broadly, as a creature of God, and loving them might well call us across great social distances—whether economic, cultural, or even geographical distances.[24] Ironically, this suspension of conventional identity formations is precisely what allows a carer to love a person in all their particularity, whatever the person's personal capabilities.

While at first glance this account of neighbor love might indeed appear utopian, Bretherton describes it as a vocation. It requires a particular mode of paying attention that suspends identity-based

---

21. Brett, "Natives and Immigrants in the Social Imagination of the Holiness School."

22. According to this layered social logic, there would be no inconsistency in Peter Singer's decision to pay for dementia care for his own mother, contra Ames, "Person-Centred Dementia Care," 10–11.

23. Cf. Manne's application of the Samaritan principle to refugee policy (Manne, "Australia's Shipwrecked Refugee Policy").

24. Cf. King, *Strength to Love*, 19.

interactions.²⁵ The love of neighbor cuts across established patterns of meaning.²⁶ One might need to acknowledge that this is not an everyday vocation, but one which entails liminal experiences of some kind. This kind of liminality, which suspends conventional categories, is reflected for example in the parable of the sheep and the goats in Matthew 25, where the love of the poor and the stranger is performed in a kind of cloud of unknowing. Matthew 25:37–38 makes clear that "the righteous" have no special spiritual powers that allow them to identify true members of the Christian community. Quite the contrary, it is clear that the righteous do not have such powers of discrimination, and this itself reveals the authenticity of a non-discriminating care. This parable points to a Christ who is hidden, or *incognito*.

In short, although the love of neighbor might be driven by a very particular set of religious commitments or motivations, a biblical theology that reflects on these models drawn from both the Hebrew Bible and the New Testament can help to shape the practice of spiritual care in a "cloud of unknowing." Not only is it unnecessary to spell out the religious convictions of the carers who work under secular constraints (whether they are designated spiritual care practitioners or any other members of a care team), it is unnecessary for good theological reasons.

Caring for Religious Persons with Dementia

The practice of person-centered care encounters some special problems when it comes to caring for religious persons with dementia. As already noted, the most common accounts of personhood assume a set of capabilities that may no longer be evident. But as John Swinton points out, some Christian convictions are just as likely to exacerbate the problems at issue, rather than ameliorate them (so, in this respect, nothing much is to be gained by Christian theologians blaming Enlightenment conceptions of rationality and autonomy as the root of the problem). Theologies of sin and salvation often assume a cognitively able self, competently shaping choices and memories. But what if a Christian is no longer able to remember the name of Jesus? Or as the psalmist puts it, when addressing the God of Israel: "Is your saving help known in the land of

---

25. Bretherton, *Christ and the Common Life*, 41.
26. This point is made in dialogue with the philosophy of Emmanuel Levinas in Eskenazi, "Love Your Neighbor as an Other."

forgetfulness?" (Ps 88:12).[27] Swinton argues that even when an individual has difficulties with memory recall, "these people remain tightly held within the memories of God."[28]

In the story of Israel, perhaps the most dramatic crisis in the continuity of identity comes with the destruction of Jerusalem, the dispersal of Judah's population and a forced migration to Babylon.[29] Addressing this context, the prophet Isaiah is ambivalent about the continuity of Israel's story, exhorting the people both to remember (44:21) and not to remember (43:18). But there is no ambiguity about the divine memory: "O Israel, you will not be forgotten by me" (44:21). Whatever the struggles of particular individuals, the continuity of the people's identity is carried by the communal and intergenerational self.[30] In most of the prophetic visions of salvation, for example, we find the redemption of future generations, rather than the resurrection of an individual. In the earlier traditions, there is a strong sense in which the individual does not need saving, as the Jewish scholar Jon Levenson has emphasized, because a person's identity is always linked to the next generations of their family.[31]

It might be assumed that such corporate theology gives way to a more individualistic emphasis in the New Testament, but this is not really the case.[32] Consider, for example, what the apostle Paul says in his letter to the Galatians: "I have been crucified with Christ; and it is no longer I who live, but it is Christ who lives in me. And the life I now live in the flesh I live by faith *in/of* the Son of God, who loved me and gave himself for me. I do not nullify the grace of God; for if justification comes through the law, then Christ died for nothing" (Gal 2:19–21). This text belongs to an early Christian tradition that emphasizes the faithfulness *of* Christ, rather than a cognitive faith *in* Christ. The cognitive conception of faith in Christ,

---

27. Swinton discusses this psalm in his book *Dementia* (262–64), in dialogue with Barclay, "Psalm 88: Living with Dementia."

28. Swinton, *Dementia*, 214–17, takes up the work of Childs, *Memory and Tradition in Israel*.

29. See further Frechette, "Old Testament as Controlled Substance."

30. In individualist cultures, there seems to be a more pronounced ambivalence about a person's legacy. See, e.g., the discussion of legacy documents in Martinez et al., "Dignity Therapy."

31. Levenson, *Resurrection and the Restoration of Israel*, esp. 166–80.

32. For a comprehensive overview of the relevant biblical texts, see especially Rosner, *Known by God*.

so distinctive of Protestant convictions, is only one aspect of the larger corporate reality of faithfulness within the body of Christ. Even when people may no longer be in control of their memory, "the church knows who they are."[33] Hence, it makes good sense for someone with dementia to ask of fellow Christians, "I need you to minister to me, to sing with me, to pray with me, to be my memory for me."[34] But Paul's argument does not point to any simple continuity of personhood. He puts a choice before his readers: does their identity and network of relationships flow from the self-giving love of Christ? If so, then this implies that the old self has already died; the old "I" no longer lives. The most basic theological claim is that a new self is constituted in the body of Christ.

If the person with dementia has difficulty constructing their own personal identity, some religious responses of this kind can helpfully affirm the wider social networks that are constituted by particular religious communities and traditions—whether Christian, Jewish, Islamic, and so on.[35] But there is no way of avoiding the diversity of religious and spiritual traditions that may be relevant in particular contexts of care. The shape of person-centered care would need to vary according to the particularity of a person's life story and relationships. This point is well established in the current guidelines for the practice of spiritual care.[36] But its implications have not been worked through in some of the Christian theological reflections on dementia.

Elizabeth MacKinlay, for example, begins one of her essays by acknowledging the problem of "continuity over time" for persons living with dementia. Her solution emphasizes the relationality of the self, and therefore the possibility that a person's identity may be carried by ongoing relationships, much as our previous discussion has affirmed. But when she says that all relationality is constituted by "Trinitarian love,"[37] this claim would need further clarification. Certainly, it would be better to

---

33. Goldingay, "Being Human."

34. See MacKinlay, "Theology of Dementia," 198, quoting from Bryden, *Dancing with Dementia*.

35. See, e.g., Ahmad and Khan, "Model of Spirituality for Ageing Muslims"; cf. Saeed, "Nature and Purpose of the Community (Ummah) in the Qur'an."

36. See, e.g., Meaningful Ageing Australia, *National Guidelines for Spiritual Care in Aged Care*; Spiritual Care Australia, "Standard 6: Respect for Diversity," in *Standards of Practice*.

37. MacKinlay, "Theology of Dementia," 188–92.

emphasize networks of relationship rather than individual personhood,[38] and perhaps the motivations of some spiritual care practitioners may be shaped by Trinitarian convictions, but how would these particular convictions translate into care for Jewish, Muslim, or Buddhist persons?[39] The argument seems unintentionally to have become exclusivist in its implications.

When it comes to the formation of spiritual care practitioners, it would seem that the love of neighbor moves away from conceptual formations of identity, whether the identity of a transcendent reality or the identity of creatures made in the "image of Elohim." God *incognito* undoes conceptual definitions even of personhood. Nevertheless, a practitioner would need to be ready for both kinds of creation narrative—one that affirms a particular name of God and one that refuses a name for transcendent reality.[40]

Conclusion

When it comes to the care of Christian persons, there is certainly value in Elizabeth MacKinlay's approach that says "We, in the body of Christ, become the memory for the person who can no longer remember."[41] But spiritual care practitioners who are working within state-sponsored agencies with non-Christian persons need a more comprehensive theological imagination in order to address the current diversity.[42] Instead of an indifferent secularism that efficiently manages an aged care "market," quality care will need to reflect the diversity of religious traditions as well as the most secular understandings of spirituality. Each formation of religion or spirituality can be seen as "contingent" from the point of view of neighbor love. The spiritual care practitioner might themselves come

---

38. See, e.g., Nolan et al., "Beyond 'Person-Centred' Care."

39. MacKinlay briefly acknowledges that "personhood can be upheld and affirmed within caring communities outside of faith communities" ("Theology of Dementia," 200), but provides no theological rationale in this particular essay. See further Ahmad and Khan, "Model of Spirituality for Ageing Muslims"; Saeed, "Nature and Purpose of the Community (Ummah) in the Qur'an."

40. This point seems to be overlooked by Swinton, *Dementia*, 166, when he invokes the Creator's name YHWH from the second creation narrative in Genesis and thereby neglects the Elohim of the first creation narrative.

41. MacKinlay, "Theology of Dementia," 196.

42. Baker et al., *Re-imagining Religion and Belief*.

from any one of these traditions but must be open to the actual lived experience of the particular persons whom they accompany. And beyond the specific capabilities of spiritual care practitioners, a holistic care will normally involve a variety of staff roles, and in this respect, "Spiritual care is everyone's business."[43] A person-centered care cannot assume a single concept of personhood or a single set or role definitions, but rather, it will embody a love of neighbor that reaches beyond any particular framework of identity.

Bibliography

Ahmad, Mahjabeen, and Shamsul Khan. "A Model of Spirituality for Ageing Muslims." *Journal of Religion and Health* 55 (2016) 830–43.
Ames, Stephen. "The Value Given and Presupposed in Person-Centred Dementia Care." *OBM Geriatrics* 3, no. 3 (2019) 1–17.
Baker, Chris, Beth R. Crisp, and Adam Dinham, eds. *Re-imagining Religion and Belief for 21st Century Policy and Practice*. Bristol: Policy, 2018.
Barclay, Aileen. "Psalm 88: Living with Dementia." *Journal of Religion, Disability, and Health* 16 (2012) 88–101.
Barth, Karl. *Epistle to the Romans*. Translated by Edwyn C. Hoskyns. 2nd ed. Oxford: Oxford University Press, 1933.
Batra, Sadhvi, Jacqueline Sullivan, Beverly R. Williams, and David S. Geldmacher. "Qualitative Assessment of Self-Identity in People with Advanced Dementia." *Dementia* 15 (2016) 1260–78.
Bretherton, Luke. *Christ and the Common Life: A Guide to Political Theology*. Grand Rapids: Eerdmans, 2019.
Brett, Mark G. *Locations of God: Political Theology in the Hebrew Bible*. New York: Oxford University Press, 2019.
———. "Natives and Immigrants in the Social Imagination of the Holiness School." In *Imagining the Other and Constructing Israelite Identity in the Early Second Temple Period*, edited by Ehud Ben Zvi and Diana Edelman, 89–104. New York: T&T Clark, 2014.
Brijnath, Bianca. *Unforgotten: Love and the Culture of Dementia Care in India*. New York: Berghahn, 2014.
Bryden, Christine. *Dancing with Dementia: My Story of Living Positively with Dementia*. London: Jessica Kingsley, 2005.
Childs, Brevard. *Memory and Tradition in Israel*. Naperville: Allenson, 1962.
Commonwealth of Australia. *Royal Commission into Aged Care Quality and Safety Interim Report*. Vol. 2, *Hearing Overviews and Case Studies*. Canberra: Commonwealth of Australia, 2019.
Eskenazi, Tamara Cohn. "Love your Neighbor as an Other: Reflections on Levinas's Ethics and the Hebrew Bible." In *Levinas and Biblical Studies*, edited by Tamara

---

43. See "Principle 3," in Meaningful Ageing Australia, *National Guidelines for Spiritual Care in Aged Care*.

Cohn Eskenazi, Gary A. Phillips, and David Jobling, 145–58. Atlanta: Society of Biblical Literature, 2003.

Frechette, Christopher. "The Old Testament as Controlled Substance: How Insights from Trauma Studies Reveal Healing Capacities in Potentially Harmful Texts." *Interpretation* 69 (2015) 21–34.

Gee, Graham, Pat Dudgeon, Clinton Schultz, Amanda Hart, and Kerrie Kelly. "Aboriginal and Torres Strait Islander Social and Emotional Wellbeing." In *Working Together: Aboriginal and Torres Strait Islander Mental Health and Wellbeing Principles and Practice*, edited by P. Dudgeon, H. Milroy, and R. Walker, 55–68. 2nd ed. Canberra: Australian Government, 2014.

Goldingay, John. "Being Human." In *Encounter with Mystery: Reflections on L'Arche and Living with Disability*, edited by Frances Young, 133–51. London: Darton, Longman and Todd, 1997.

Habermas, Jürgen. "On the Relation Between the Secular Liberal State and Religion." In *The Frankfurt School on Religion*, edited by E. Mendieta, 337–46. New York: Routledge, 2004.

Higgs, Paul, and Chris Gilleard. "Interrogating Personhood and Dementia." *Aging and Mental Health* 20 (2016) 773–80.

King, Martin Luther, Jr. *Strength to Love*. New York: Harper & Row, 1963.

Kitwood, Tom. *Dementia Reconsidered: The Person Comes First*. Buckingham: Open University Press, 1997.

Levenson, Jon D. *Resurrection and the Restoration of Israel: The Ultimate Victory of the God of Life*. New Haven: Yale University Press, 2006.

Lloyd, Vincent. "The Negative Political Theology of James Baldwin." In *A Poltical Companion to James Baldwin*, edited by Susan J. McWilliams, 171–94. Lexington: University Press of Kentucky, 2017.

MacKinlay, Elizabeth. "A Theology of Dementia." In *Finding Meaning in the Experience of Dementia*, by Elizabeth MacKinlay and Corinne Trevitt, 186–200. London: Jessica Kingsley, 2012.

Manne, Robert. "Australia's Shipwrecked Refugee Policy: Tragedy of Errors." *Monthly*, March 2013. www.themonthly.com.au/australia-s-shipwrecked-refugee-policy-tragedy-errors-guest-7637.

Martinez, Marina, Maria Arantzamendi, Alazne Belar, José Miguel Carrasco, Ana Carvajal, Maria Rullán, and Calos Centeno. "'Dignity Therapy': A Promising Intervention in Palliative Care: A Comprehensive Systematic Literature Review." *Palliative Medicine* 31 (2017) 492–509.

McMillan, Faye B., David R. Kampers, Victoria Traynor, and Jan Dewing. "Person-centred Care as Caring for Country: An Indigenous Australian Experience." *Dementia: The International Journal of Social Research and Practice* 9 (2010) 163–67.

Meaningful Ageing Australia. *National Guidelines for Spiritual Care in Aged Care*. Parkville: Meaningful Ageing Australia, 2016.

Nolan, Mike R., Sue Davies, Jayne Brown, John Keady, and Janet Nolan. "Beyond 'Person-centered' Care: A New Vision for Gerontological Nursing." *International Journal of Older People Nursing* 13 (2004) 45–53.

Pury, Albert de. "Gottesname, Gottesbezeichnung und Gottesbegriff: 'Elohim' als Indiz zur Entstehungsgeschichte des Pentateuch." In *Abschied vom Jahwisten: Die*

Komposition des Hexateuch in der jüngsten Diskussion, edited by Jan C. Gertz, Konrad Schmid, and Markus Witte, 25–47. Berlin: de Gruyter, 2002.

Rawls, John. "The Idea of Public Reason Revisited." *University of Chicago Law Review* 64 (1997) 765–807.

Rosner, Brian. *Known by God: A Biblical Theology of Personal Identity*. Grand Rapids: Zondervan, 2017.

Rumbold, Bruce. "Models of Spiritual Care." In *Oxford Textbook of Spirituality in Health Care*, edited by Mark R. Cobb, Christina M. Puchalski, and Bruce Rumbold, 175–83. Oxford: Oxford University Press, 2012.

Saeed, Abdullah. "The Nature and Purpose of the Community (Ummah) in the Qur'an." In *The Community of Believers: Christian and Muslim Perspectives*, edited by Lucinda Mosher and David Marshall, 15–27. Washington, DC: Georgetown University Press, 2015.

Singer, Peter. *Practical Ethics*. 2nd ed. Cambridge: Cambridge University Press, 1993.

Spaemann, Robert. *Persons: The Difference between "Someone" and "Something."* Translated by Oliver O'Donovan. Oxford: Oxford University Press, 2006.

Spiritual Care Australia. *Standards of Practice*. Collingwood: Spiritual Care Australia, 2013.

Swinton, John. *Dementia: Living in the Memories of God*. London: SCM, 2012.

———. "What's in a Name? Why People with Dementia Might Be Better Off without the Language of Personhood." *International Journal of Practical Theology* 18 (2014) 234–47.

Response 4: Therapy

Interdisciplinary Conversations as Expressions of Neighbor Love

Anne-Marie Ellithorpe

I RESPOND TO THESE therapeutic chapters as a practical theologian. While the term *practical theology* has been used interchangeably with *pastoral theology*, practical theology has a broader focus, including practices not only within but also beyond the church. Facilitating grieving, considering issues of personhood in relation to aged care, and supporting recovery from trauma all fit within the scope of practical theology. After all, practical theology in its broadest sense refers to the work of God's people as they seek to live reflectively and faithfully in everyday life.[1] Practical theology also refers to methodology for understanding or analysing theology in practice, as well as to a curricular area in theological education, and an academic discipline pursued by scholars to sustain and support the first three understandings.[2] Thus, while Sarah Penwarden, Mark Brett, and Art Wouters work within other disciplines, each one of them implicitly engages in the work of practical theology, broadly construed, as they engage with diverse disciplines in the pursuit of more faithful practice, and a more faithful theological imagination.

The intention of this book, as with the conference from which this volume emerged, is to foster interdisciplinary dialogue. Implicitly or explicitly, each scholar explores expressions of neighbor love within

1. See Miller-McLemore, "Introduction," 5.
2. Miller-McLemore, "Introduction," 5.

specific contexts, and emphasizes or depicts a need for dialogue, whether between disciplines, traditions, or cultures. Penwarden's exploration of grief emphasizes the need to respect the integrity and separateness of both counseling and theology, along with the need to acknowledge lived experience. Brett brings philosophers and practical, political, and biblical theologians into conversation, as he considers the concept of personhood in relation to person-centered aged care. As Wouters seeks to record an inner dialogue between "faith, theory, and profession," he depicts a commitment to the laying down of power in order to promote both dialogue and a power-with dynamic, challenging as this may be.

I consider these chapters in light of the interdisciplinary nature of practical theology, giving particular attention to the relationship between the disciplines inherent within these chapters. While practical theology, with its emphasis on practice, is inherently interdisciplinary, the relative status of the conversation partners may be construed in various ways. The relationship may be depicted as a one-way street, where the questions of the culture, or of the other discipline, are correlated with the answers of theology.³ Or the relationship between disciplines may be reciprocal, with a mutual dynamic of question and answer contributing towards a two-way bridge.⁴ A two-way exchange may be further characterized by a *mutually* critical and corrective process, with each discipline having the potential to be a source of new insight for the other, and to contribute towards alleviating blind spots of the other.⁵ Another analogy for the relationship between disciplines may be that of the reciprocity that characterizes communication amongst a community of friends.⁶ What then is the relationship between disciplines evident within each of these chapters?

Penwarden is most explicit in advocating for a three-way conversation between counseling, theology, and lived experience (in her case, of those who are grieving). Yet the conversation within "Grief as the Sounding of Multiple Notes" is perhaps best described as being between liturgical practice, counseling practice, and experience. The Easter Triduum, as three days interwoven into one, is perceptively recognized

---

3. See Tillich, *History of Christian Thought*, 391.

4. Hiltner, "Meaning and Importance of Pastoral Theology," 45, n. 10.

5. Tracy, *Blessed Rage for Order*, 46.

6. See Ellithorpe, "Towards a Practical Theology of Friendship," 15. This conversational analogy may be particularly helpful when more than two disciplines or subdisciplines are involved.

as representing the coexistent experiences of hope and despair, new life and struggle, in the face of bereavement and grief. The practice of double-listening is presented as listening for and acknowledging the coexistent experiences of death and recreation. These threads are brought alongside each other, but do not explicitly interrogate or challenge the other. Rather, a more complex relationship is evident, with all three threads (liturgical practice, therapeutic practice, and experience) challenging a linear theory of grieving, and encouraging attuned listening (by co-listeners and co-crafters of stories) for the sound of multiple notes.

Within "Person-Centered Care and the Love of Neighbor," Brett explores the question of personhood as a conceptual problem in aged care.[7] While a variety of perspectives are acknowledged, including philosophy and non-Western religious traditions, key conversation partners are within theological sub-disciplines.[8] Yet this does not lead to narrow conclusions but rather to advocacy for a more comprehensive theological imagination that addresses diversity within secular contexts. Brett identifies inclusive theology, inclusive transcendence, and the affirmation of a wide variety of solidarities and spiritual connections within the biblical traditions. He brings this inclusivity into conversation with political theologian Luke Bretherton's account of neighbor love, and considers implications for spiritual care practitioners working within state-sponsored agencies with non-Christian persons. Practitioners are encouraged to ground their care in inclusive, transcendent realities, and to be prepared for creation narratives that affirm a particular name of God, as well as for those that refuse a name for transcendent reality. Thus, person-centered care is able to adapt to a further implied dialogue partner, that is, the particularity of a person's life story and relationships.

The focus within "Sailing with the Wind" is on the author's inner dialogue between "faith, theory, and profession." This dialogue leads to advocacy for collaboration, dialogue, intersubjective consciousness, and "witness" practices, in the journey towards a peaceable psychology and power-with manner of relating that refuses to collude with empire. The

---

7. Brett acknowledges that the idea of personhood is not universal, and that personal convictions about ontology may not necessarily translate into practice.

8. While practical theology has tended to consider interdisciplinarity primarily in terms of conversation with non-theological disciplines, attention is now also being given to the need for dialogue between theological sub-disciplines in the pursuit of constructive proposals. See Osmer, "Toward a New Story of Practical Theology," 72; Tracy, "Correlational Model of Practical Theology Revisited," 50; also Ellithorpe, "Towards a Practical Theology of Friendship," 15.

key theological theme that emerges is God's laying down of God's power. Yet while power-with is a key emphasis throughout his writing, Wouters does not dwell at any length on theological insights regarding this theme. Clearly, modelling the laying down of power is integral to his own practice, as he seeks to empower rather than to invite recolonization. But he does not explore the implication of this theme for those who have been trapped in power-under relations, nor explore theological insights regarding power relevant to those trapped in power-under relations. Wouters acknowledges that while psychology is culture bound, it generally fails to appreciate its cultural particularity. Yet while recognizing the cultural embeddedness of his profession, the cultural embeddedness of his faith remains underexplored. Potential clearly remains for issues of power to be more thoroughly interrogated theologically.[9]

Significant variety is evident in the relationship between disciplines and sub-disciplines within these three chapters. Clearly interdisciplinary dialogue need not conform to a specific pattern. Nevertheless, there is certainly scope for more robust theological reflection and greater depth of engagement in the dialogue between theology and therapy. It is appropriate that such engagement begin with reflexivity, that is, with acknowledging one's own situatedness and pre-commitments.

While prevailing academic convention within many contexts tends to discount personal experience, the contextual, situated, and embedded nature of scholarship is now increasingly recognized within practical theology, as well as within the social sciences.[10] Reflexivity, that is, reflection on how one's position might influence one's practice and research, is increasingly evident within practical theology scholarship. While not overtly discussed within "Sailing with the Wind," reflexivity is nevertheless evident through Wouters' awareness of power issues, commitment to seeking power-with rather than power-over relationships, and acknowledgement of the challenge of maintaining an authentic not-knowing stance in the Solomon Islands with authenticity, in the pursuit of a power-with dynamic. Wouters does not discount personal experience, nor does he leave himself off the page.

In the pursuit of greater depth of engagement in the dialogue between theology and therapy, I propose several further analogies for

---

9. As David Tracy acknowledges, even so-called *orthodox* theologies involved interpretations of Christian sources and cultural understandings of their time (Tracy, *Blessed Rage for Order*, 35 n. 10; see also 23).

10. Graham, "State of the Art," 175; "On Becoming a Practical Theologian," 5.

interdisciplinary relationships that emerge from these chapters. From within "Sailing with the Wind," the emphasis on power-with relationships provides an apt analogy for a relationship of mutuality and disciplinary humility between theology and therapeutic disciplines. Drawing on the work of Harlene Anderson, Wouters speaks of the reciprocity of host-guest roles as a metaphor for the client-therapist relationship. Taking this imagery a step further, I suggest that the reciprocity of this host-guest role provides yet another intriguing metaphor for interdisciplinary conversations. As guest, each discipline assumes a posture of humility in learning from the other; as host, each discipline exhibits a willingness to make space for the other, and to communicate something of itself to the other. Drawing on analogies for the client-therapist within "Grief as the Sounding of Multiple Notes," it may also be that the interdisciplinary relationship ideally fostered is one of co-listeners and co-crafters of stories.

Interdisciplinary engagement may further be seen as an expression of neighbor love that requires a degree of liminality. Brett identifies the vocation of neighbor love as entailing "liminal experiences of some kind," within which conventional categories are suspended, and love and care are performed within "a kind of cloud of unknowing." Loving others well may call us across great distances economically and culturally. For scholars, dialogue across disciplinary divides is yet another expression of loving others well.

As I write, communities worldwide are grappling with crisis, grief, tensions, and trauma. Many are faced with the intertwined challenges of overcoming a pandemic and confronting various forms of prejudice and injustice. The interdisciplinary conversations that take place within each of these chapters are relevant not only to the contexts for which they were originally written, but also to contexts where we find loving our neighbors as ourselves needing to be expressed through unexpected practices. While a variety of analogies may be used to depict interdisciplinary relationships, and the relative status of the conversation partners construed in various ways, God's people clearly benefit from various forms of interdisciplinary dialogue, including those expressed within these chapters, as they seek to live reflectively and faithfully in everyday life, including in times of crisis.

Bibliography

Ellithorpe, Anne-Marie. "Towards a Practical Theology of Friendship." PhD diss., University of Queensland, 2018.

Graham, Elaine. "On Becoming a Practical Theologian: Past, Present and Future Tenses." *HTS Theological Studies* 73 (2017) 1–9.

———. "The State of the Art: Practical Theology Yesterday, Today and Tomorrow: New Directions in Practical Theology." *Theology* 120 (2017) 172–80.

Hiltner, Seward. "The Meaning and Importance of Pastoral Theology." In *The Blackwell Reader in Pastoral and Practical Theology*, edited by James Woodward and Stephen Pattison, 27–48. Malden: Blackwell, 2000.

Miller-McLemore, Bonnie J. "Introduction: The Contributions of Practical Theology." In *The Wiley Blackwell Companion to Practical Theology*, edited by Bonnie J. Miller-McLemore, 1–20. Malden: Wiley-Blackwell, 2012.

Osmer, Richard R. "Toward a New Story of Practical Theology." *Inernational Journal of Practical Theology* 16 (2012) 66–78.

Tillich, Paul. *A History of Christian Thought, from Its Judaic and Hellenistic Origins to Existentialism*. New York: Simon and Schuster, 1972.

Tracy, David. *Blessed Rage for Order: The New Pluralism in Theology*. Reprint, Chicago: University of Chicago Press, 1975.

———. "A Correlational Model of Practical Theology Revisited." In *Religion, Diversity and Conflict*, edited by Edward Foley, 49–61. Munster: LIT Verlag, 2011.

Part V

THEOLOGY

Chapter 11

Social Trinitarianism and Christian Counseling: A Critical Discussion

Cameron Coombe

Various figures in contemporary theology have sought to formulate new insights in theological anthropology on the basis of social Trinitarianism, and, more specifically, to apply these to counseling and ministry.[1] One example of this is provided by the book, *The Reciprocating Self* (*RS*), in which Jack Balswick, Pamela King, and Kevin Reimer draw on social Trinitarianism in order to establish a theologically informed, Christian approach to developmental theory that will guide Christian counselors in their practice.[2] Significantly, however, the authors do not enter into any critical discussion on the suitability of this connection, at least beyond some minor comments that I will note in the body of my argument. But while this is likely due to the limitations set by the nature of their project, it also raises a key methodological question: what justifies such an undertaking in the first place?

In this chapter I discuss *RS* as a test case for the advantages and limits of forming such a relationship between social Trinitarianism and the theory informing Christian counseling. First I offer a definition for

---

1. Some book-length examples of the latter include Buxton, *Trinity, Creation and Pastoral Ministry*; Seamands, *Ministry in the Image of God*; and Pembroke, *Renewing Pastoral Practice*. An interesting exception to this trend, likely by virtue of penning his work prior to the widespread popularization of social Trinitarianism, is Howe, *Image of God*.

2. Balswick et al., *Reciprocating Self*.

social Trinitarianism. I then provide an account of its role in the two editions of *RS*. Next I identify some of the advantages of drawing on social Trinitarianism in this manner, particularly in connection to formulating a distinctly Christian perspective in developmental theory. I proceed to discuss some of the major criticisms levelled against social Trinitarianism and the relevance of these to the work in *RS*. In my conclusion I consider diminishing interest in social Trinitarianism today and what this might mean for *RS* and similar projects.

Defining Social Trinitarianism

Social Trinitarianism has become increasingly popular in modern Roman Catholic and Protestant theology, especially since the 1980s. Eastern Orthodox theology has also seen developments in this regard, though these are typically understood to be in keeping with traditional accounts of the Trinity in Eastern Orthodox theology. In this chapter, the term social Trinitarianism encapsulates a wide variety of voices in the theology of the last four decades, loosely connected by shared concerns in the doctrine of the Trinity.

Gijsbert van den Brink helpfully identifies four main concerns shared by theologians who have been identified with this movement.[3] First, social Trinitarians tend to define the three persons of the Trinity as "distinct and fully equal centers of consciousness who together constitute the one God."[4] Second, just as important as claims of uniqueness and distinctness are those of interdependence and relationality. Each person is defined by their relationship to the other persons and never exists independently of them. Third, this theological construction is accompanied by a reorientation to the biblical sources that gave rise to the doctrine of the Trinity in the first place. Attendant criticism of the conclusions of key Western figures such as Augustine and Thomas Aquinas is often forwarded as well, contrasting these with contributions from Eastern Orthodoxy, for example, or alternative proposals in the patristic and medieval periods. Here, too, the social Trinitarian affirmation of three distinct centers of action and consciousness conflicts with established voices in the West, who advance a single center of action and consciousness—the one God—and ground unity in the one divine substance rather than the

---

3. Van den Brink, "Social Trinitarianism," 336.
4. Van den Brink, "Social Trinitarianism," 336.

sociality or interrelationality of the three persons. Fourth, social Trinitarians often seek to uncover the practical relevance of the doctrine of the Trinity, whether that be in the sphere of politics, ecclesiology, or human relationships in general.

While not all who call themselves social Trinitarians will exhibit all of these concerns in the same way, and while those who exhibit these or similar concerns may have some reservations about the label of social Trinitarian, I find van den Brink's schema to be helpful in identifying the rough outlines of this movement in modern theology. The first, second, and fourth concerns especially can be seen in RS.

Social Trinitarianism and *The Reciprocating Self*

The first edition of RS appeared in 2005 and the second in 2016.[5] In what follows I start with the aims and content of the first edition in order to provide some context for the adoption of social Trinitarian claims. I then proceed to explore the relevant changes made in the second edition.

The authors of RS begin by identifying the need for a distinctly theological approach to developmental theory, beyond that which is already provided in secular accounts. This theory is concerned primarily with the psychological and social development of the human self from infancy into late adulthood. It is of particular interest to those working in counseling and related areas, though Christian practitioners, among others, may be interested in additional aspects not typically covered in secular treatments, such as spiritual development. In this connection a problem in regard to the available literature on developmental theory immediately arises for practitioners. All contributions "share a common commitment to a naturalistic worldview."[6] This means that developmental theory in general differs fundamentally in its presuppositions from that of the Christian faith. Its vision is one that has no goal beyond that which is already actual and possible within a world without God. The authors thus seek to answer this with the formulation of a "developmental teleology."[7]

Other problems with existing developmental theory are also identified in RS. The piecemeal nature of the different contributions, for

---

5. Balswick et al., *Reciprocating Self*, 2nd ed.
6. Balswick et al., *Reciprocating Self*, 17; 2nd ed., 19.
7. Balswick et al., *Reciprocating Self*, 17; 2nd ed., 19.

example, focussing on isolated aspects of the developmental process, indicates the need for a more holistic approach, or an organizing principle in which to anchor ostensibly related contributions to the literature. And the widely held assumption of an "empty self" in developmental theory and forms of psychological therapy too closely approximates the consumer self of everyday North American life.[8] Such a self is one whose primary needs consist in self-care and individual realization and fulfilment. In this sense, it is a self that needs to be filled. But, for the authors of *RS*, this self derives from a lack of imagination regarding the goals and purposes of counseling. Another problem also arises here: the empty self of psychology corresponds to the introspective orientation of modern philosophy, bound up with its disinterest in a transcendent God and the relocation of the divine into the sphere of human subjectivity. Drawing upon insights from the social sciences, a discipline which has resisted this trend to individualization, and the reclamation of divine and human sociality in recent theology, *RS* thus proceeds to cultivate an alternative perspective in developmental theory.

The authors of *RS* cite the theological anthropologies of F. LeRon Shults and Stanley Grenz as key influences regarding the theological assumptions that guide their project.[9] To lesser extents, Jürgen Moltmann, Colin Gunton, Miroslav Volf, Ray Anderson, and Gary Deddo also play a role.[10] Each in their own way, these theologians have applied social Trinitarian insights in the sphere of anthropology, reflecting on what it means to be human persons in light of the divine persons. As such, the authors of *RS*, too, can claim, "We believe a correspondence exists between relationality in the holy Trinity and relationality in human beings."[11] Indeed, they continue, this connection is integral to the purpose of the book. Like the persons of the Trinity, the human self is "reciprocating." It is both distinct as an individual self and its identity consists necessarily in relationship to other human persons.

8. Balswick et al., *Reciprocating Self*, 18; 2nd ed., 20.

9. Shults, *Reforming Theological Anthropology*; and Grenz, *Social God*. See, e.g., Balswick et al., *Reciprocating Self*, 19–20; 2nd ed., 22–23.

10. Balswick et al., *Reciprocating Self*, 20; 2nd ed., 23. It should be noted that Moltmann's *Coming of God* is the only work of his that appears in the bibliography of *RS*. His earlier *Trinity and the Kingdom* and *God and Creation*, however, treats this subject in much greater depth. Also absent is Volf, "Social Program." Nonetheless, the literature on the relationship between the Trinity and human persons and community is extensive and the authors cannot be expected to offer an exhaustive account of it.

11. Balswick et al., *Reciprocating Self*, 21; 2nd ed., 24.

As the basis for such a connection between human and divine persons, the authors of *RS* point to the biblical concept of the image of God, presented in Genesis 1: "We draw upon a theological analogy, warranted by the doctrine of the imago Dei, that makes a comparison from the unique Trinitarian persons in relationship to human persons being and becoming in relationship."[12] But the Christian tradition has not always understood the image of God in this manner: "Since the time of the early church fathers, reason and will have been most often identified as what comprises the divine image within humans."[13] Nonetheless, contemporary developments in the doctrine of the Trinity, corresponding with a general turn towards relationality in theological anthropology, problematize this individualistic notion of the image of God. The authors of *RS* thus draw upon an alternative notion, one in which a connection can be established between the "particularity and relatedness" of divine persons, and that of human persons.[14]

The first implication of this analogy is that of particularity. There are three particular and distinct persons of the Trinity. "One is never compromised by another."[15] Analogously, the particularity of human persons is not to be dissolved in human relationship. Rather, the unity of these relationships is compatible with the distinct gifts and identities of the respective human persons. Paul discusses a similar notion in 1 Corinthians 12 with the image of the body that has different parts but is nonetheless one body. Closely related, the second implication of the analogy to the Trinity is that of relationality. "Just as God exists in relationship, humans are to exist in relationship."[16] As such, throughout the NT the church is an essential part of the life of the believer. Following on from this, the final implication of the analogy is that of reciprocity, "the glue that holds the relational polarities of uniqueness and unity together."[17] Each divine person loves the other and this love is reciprocated by the loved person. There is unity in shared love but also distinctness that belongs to each person in loving and being loved. Analogously, for human beings, "in the reciprocating relationship there is give and take, and take and give.

12. Balswick et al., *Reciprocating Self*, 30; 2nd ed., 35.
13. Balswick et al., *Reciprocating Self*, 30-31; adapted in 2nd ed., 36: "Reason, will and love have always been contenders for the attribute indicative of the image of God."
14. Balswick et al., *Reciprocating Self*, 31; 2nd ed., 36.
15. Balswick et al., *Reciprocating Self*, 33; 2nd ed., 38.
16. Balswick et al., *Reciprocating Self*, 35; 2nd ed., 40.
17. Balswick et al., *Reciprocating Self*, 35; 2nd ed., 40.

A high view of both the self and other is required to value the giving and the receiving."[18]

The development of an analogy between divine and human persons is central to the main thesis of *RS*. At the end of their chapter on the human self, having begun with the analogy of the Trinity suggested by the notion of the image of God, the authors can present their concept of the reciprocating self: "The reciprocating self does not treat the other as a mere utilitarian object from which it only takes. It does not seek fusion, where it takes to the extent that it demands the loss and sacrifice of the other. It is not dissociated—where there is no give or take. Rather the reciprocating self lives in a mutual relationship of sharing and receiving with another."[19]

Just over a decade later, the authors of *RS* published a second edition of their work. Alongside drawing upon new research and paradigms in the context of developmental theory, they write, "in addition to our trinitarian perspective of human nature, we also wanted to emphasize a christological perspective."[20] In the associated chapter then, "we point to Jesus Christ as the perfect image of God and recognize that becoming like Christ is God's intention for all of humanity."[21] A new reference to the theologian Kathryn Tanner suggests some influence on her part.[22] Nonetheless, the additions are relatively minor, and the christological orientation is intended to complement rather than replace the original Trinitarian one. Nor do the authors see any conflict in the two commitments: "Imaging God is on a trajectory and headed toward becoming more like Christ as we live out the relatedness modeled by the Trinity."[23] The second edition of *RS*, then, provides some extra content concerning Christology, but it does not depart in any significant way from the theological underpinnings of the first edition. In view of this, the application

---

18. Balswick et al., *Reciprocating Self*, 36; 2nd ed., 42.

19. Balswick et al., *Reciprocating Self*, 49; 2nd ed., 54.

20. Balswick et al., *Reciprocating Self*, 2nd ed., 9. The content I address in this paragraph, alongside that of the rest of this section, has been adapted into an article by Pamela King, the primary author of the corresponding material in Balswick et al., *Reciprocating Self*. See King, "Reciprocating Self."

21. Balswick et al., *Reciprocating Self*, 2nd ed., 31.

22. Balswick et al., *Reciprocating Self*, 2nd ed., 36; compare with 1st ed., 31. Two works of Tanner's appear in the bibliography of the second edition, though the authors do not otherwise interact with her in the text. But see King, "Reciprocating Self." Interestingly, Tanner is critical of social Trinitarianism. I explore some of this below.

23. Balswick et al., *Reciprocating Self*, 2nd ed., 45.

of various features of social Trinitarianism to a Christian theory of human development calls for further reflection.

Advantages of a Social Trinitarian Groundwork

There are certainly advantages in resourcing social Trinitarian theology for developmental theory. Perhaps most importantly, the central and determining subject of theology, God, is here also made the central theme of developmental theory. The very identity of a Christian approach to developmental theory as Christian is established through continual reference to its foundation in the triune God. This allows for the unique contribution that faith might make to developmental theory to stand out more clearly, especially in light of other approaches that might fundamentally diverge in their presuppositions. Similarly, Christian counseling and other areas informed by this approach to developmental theory can more self-consciously align themselves with the reality of the reign of God, serving as ministries, callings, and gift of God to the church.

Interestingly, RS provides a potential advantage not only for Christian developmental theory and other practical theologies, but, conversely, for the doctrine of the Trinity itself. It has become something of a modern tradition for new contributions or introductions to Trinitarian theology to open with a comment decrying the gradual irrelevance for Christian practice that the doctrine of the Trinity has acquired in the Christian tradition.[24] This, of course, typically opens the way for the author's own contribution, which is intended to restore or consolidate the relevance of the doctrine. From this point of view, then, Christian counseling and ministry will not only do well to continue reflecting on the triune God for their own enrichment. Surely this enrichment will also extend from them to Trinitarian theology, where the latter finds its rightful place not only in orthodox doctrine and liturgy, for example, but in its relationship to the practice of church communities and the individual Christian.

In addition to these methodological advantages, more specific gains are also visible. For example, the authors of RS present a particularly fruitful reflection on the implications of the concept of perichoresis for human relationships: "Such relationships are characterized by mutuality,

---

24. E.g., Rahner, *Trinity*, 10–15; Moltmann, *Crucified God*, 235–41; LaCugna, *God for Us*, ix, 1–8; Peters, *God as Trinity*, 14–20. As noted earlier, van den Brink views this quest for the practical relevance of the doctrine of the Trinity as a central feature of social Trinitarianism. See van den Brink, "Social Trinitarianism," 336.

give and take, and they enable the self to be known most fully in the process of knowing another... There is room to encounter the other and to encounter the self through the other. The self is never lost in the face of the other. The other does not impinge on the self, but the other promotes the presence of the self."[25] The authors avoid the narcissistic and functionally solipsistic nature of an introspective psychology, as well as the inverse danger of eclipsing the self in the other, a problem that feminist theology has been especially successful in identifying.[26] Perichoresis here appears not only to be of theological value but also a fertile and serviceable image for human relationships.

The Limits of Social Trinitarianism

It would be one-sided to attend just to the advantages of this adoption of social Trinitarian insights without also attending to the potential problems it gives rise to.[27] Indeed, the authors of *RS* already acknowledge some of the limitations of this connection. They draw upon social Trinitarianism without presuming to answer every question, and *RS* is written for theorists and practitioners interested in developmental theory, not primarily for theologians. The authors also demonstrate awareness of a potential problem when reflecting on the relationship between divine and human sociality. They write, "We recognize that God is triune and human beings are not, . . . Humans are not identical with the imago but bear the imago."[28] Thus some distinction between divine and human sociality must be maintained. Nonetheless, potential problems remain.

While the following will somewhat outweigh the preceding in terms of length, it is not my intention to define the use of social Trinitarianism in *RS* as especially problematic. The chief reason for this imbalance in my approach is to draw attention to that which seems to have been overlooked by the authors. Other treatments may find these disadvantages to be largely surmountable.

A first difficulty arises in regard to the practical value of social Trinitarianism. The authors of *RS* rightly recognize that Jesus "paradoxically claims a degree of equality with the Father and that 'the Father is

---

25. Balswick et al., *Reciprocating Self*, 36; 2nd ed., 41–42.
26. See, e.g., Selak, "Orthodoxy, Orthopraxis, and Orthopathy."
27. For a more comprehensive treatment, see van den Brink, "Social Trinitarianism."
28. Balswick et al., *Reciprocating Self*, 38; 2nd ed., 45.

greater than I."²⁹ Thankfully, however, no such claim is transferred into the anthropological sphere! But this is not the case with others who have drawn on a particular reading of the Trinity to inform their theological anthropology. Wayne Grudem, for example, among others, has drawn a connection between the Trinity and gender roles in marriage, pointing to 1 Cor 11:3: "Just as God the Father has authority over the Son, though the two are equal in deity, so in marriage, the husband has authority over the wife, though they are equal in personhood."³⁰ Thus, "they are equal in importance but have different roles."³¹ Criticisms of Grudem's theology of gender abound, problematizing his claims on biblical, theological, and sociological levels. So, too, his analogy between intratrinitarian subordination and marital subordination has also been rejected by various readers, who argue that ancient theologians did not understand the Trinity in the same way.³²

Grudem is not typically associated with social Trinitarianism. Another figure, however, the Orthodox John Zizioulas, has influenced the movement significantly. Notably, his theology has been criticized for a similar reason. Zizioulas's ecclesiology and Trinitarianism mutually inform each other, resulting in a theology that affirms the hierarchical ministry of the bishop: "Just as, in the Trinity, the very being of God is a movement from the Father to the Son and to the Spirit, which is returned finally to the person of the Father, so in the Church, too, everything moves from a ministry reflecting and imaging the Father"—namely the ministry of the bishop—"to the rest of the members, in order that it may finally be returned to 'the Father who is in heaven.'"³³ The Father's constitution as cause of the Trinity finds an earthly correspondence in the office of bishop. Although Zizioulas is often associated with other social Trinitarians, as Stephen Holmes observes, "The hierarchical and authoritarian nature of his social vision, however, is distinctly at odds with the mainstream of the movement."³⁴

29. Balswick et al., *Reciprocating Self*, 33; 2nd ed., 37.
30. Grudem, *Systematic Theology*, 459.
31. Grudem, *Systematic Theology*, 460.
32. Giles, "Evangelical Theological Society." Giles has published widely on the topic and his contributions are too many to be listed here. See also the range of viewpoints represented in Jowers and House, *New Evangelical Subordinationism*.
33. Zizioulas, *Communion and Otherness*, 147–48.
34. Holmes, "Three versus One?," 80. Holmes continues, "The ecclesiology is strongly hierarchical, reinforcing sacerdotalism, structure, and authority. For

Of course, there are also many who find Grudem's or Zizioulas's models instructive. I cannot offer any detailed criticism here. But their claims reveal a basic problem in regard to the possibility of drawing such connections between the doctrine of the Trinity and being human, namely, the potential for abuse—moulding the doctrine to suit the needs of the theologian. This has led theologians like Kathryn Tanner to take a minimalist approach to the relationship between divine and human sociality, finding Christology as opposed to Trinitarian theology—rather than in addition to it—to be more suitable in this regard. Because of the very nature of theological approaches to the differentiation of the divine persons, which almost always and inevitably rely on some sense of ordering, when transferred to the anthropological sphere they are "therefore ripe for the justification of human hierarchy."[35] Recall the reference in *RS* to Jesus' statement: "The Father is greater than I."

Conversely, social Trinitarians in general are well-known for their more democratic anthropologies, grounded in the free and mutual fellowship of the divine persons. Yet this, too, is problematic. As Stephen R. Holmes notes, Miroslav Volf resources Zizioulas's social doctrine of the Trinity to inform his own ecclesiology, but, while they share the same view of God, Volf sharply departs from Zizioulas in finding there a decisively non-hierarchical model for church life.[36] Social Trinitarianism thus leaves itself open to the charge of projection. So, Karen Kilby writes, "We first project our best ideas about human community onto the Trinity, and then claim to have discovered in the Trinity a new map for structuring human communities."[37]

While all areas of theology are subject to different kinds of ideological appropriation, a point that van den Brink has made in response to this criticism,[38] there is yet a more basic matter at stake here. As Tanner notes, "What is difficult to understand—the proper character of human society—is explicated with reference to what is surely only more

---

Zizioulas, as a Greek Orthodox bishop, the priesthood remains solely male, and so his ecclesiology leads to gender inequalities that would be found troubling by most Western societies" (82). For an exposition and criticism of this aspect of Zizioulas's theology, see Koutloumousianos, *One and the Three*.

35. Tanner, "Social Trinitarianism," 372.
36. Holmes, "Three versus One?," 82–84.
37. Kilby, "Trinity, Tradition, and Politics," 75.
38. Van den Brink, "Social Trinitarianism," 338–39.

obscure—the character of divine community."[39] This is not to say that *RS* is simply guilty by association with the likes of Grudem and Zizioulas.[40] Indeed, the authors appear to favor an anthropology that is minimally hierarchical. This is to say, however, that this is a weakness of *RS*, insofar as the connection between the personal or relational differences within the Trinity and power in human relationships remains ambiguous and open for potentially harmful interpretation. Certainly, the authors should not be held responsible for harmful interpretations of their work. But whether such interpretations have been adequately precluded is another matter. To avoid this, future contributions to Christian developmental theory should devote more critical attention to conflicting applications of Trinitarian difference to theological anthropology and ecclesiology.[41]

Another criticism of social Trinitarianism concerns the problem of divine unity. Key voices in the Christian tradition, following the biblical text, worked hard to uphold the oneness of God in the context of a doctrine of the Trinity that might otherwise be seen as a threat in this connection. But critics of social Trinitarianism have argued that the movement compromises this ancient endeavor. So, Norman Metzler contends, "That the mutual self-differentiation in the Godhead, which the fathers did assert, implies three independent, personal centers of action in eternal relationship with one another as in some sense plural entities, would seem to extend decisively beyond the bounds of the intent of the Trinitarian doctrine, and invite us to embrace some type of personalistic tritheism."[42] Tritheism is the belief, considered heresy by orthodox Christianity, that there are three gods.

Versions of this criticism are well attested. Take, for example, that which has been levelled against the archetypal work of social Trinitarianism, *The Trinity and the Kingdom*, by Jürgen Moltmann: Moltmann's social doctrine of the Trinity "verges on tritheism";[43] "Moltmann's thinking

---

39. Tanner, "Social Trinitarianism," 378.

40. Major proponents of evangelical subordinationism such as Grudem do not appear in Balswick et al., *Reciprocating Self*. Zizioulas does, but this is to be expected in any serious work engaging social Trinitarianism today.

41. An instructive reflection on power in human relationships in light of a social doctrine of the Trinity is provided by Jayme Koerselman in "Uniqueness and Belonging."

42. Metzler, "Trinity in Contemporary Theology," 285–86.

43. O'Collins, *Tripersonal God*, 158.

tends towards tritheism";[44] "Moltmann's doctrine of God begs the question as to whether it is so one-sided in its rejection of monarchy that it falls into the opposite error of tritheism";[45] and, most strikingly, "despite the evident scorn with which he anticipates the charge, The Trinity and the Kingdom is about the closest thing to tritheism that any of us are ever likely to see"![46] The reception of Moltmann's doctrine of the Trinity is just one instance of a broader trend to reject social Trinitarian insights with the charge of tritheism. In a lengthy treatment of social Trinitarianism in analytical theology, for example, Brian Leftow advances the thesis that such a theology "cannot be both orthodox and a version of monotheism."[47] He proceeds to defend this claim in detail.

Of course, detractors of social Trinitarianism do not hold a monopoly over the truth. The criticisms just noted have their corresponding counter-criticisms.[48] For *RS*, the problem is not so much taking a position in a debate that has not yet been settled; this is often necessary in any debate. The problem is rather that readers unaware that this is even a point of contention are led to believe they are setting out from effectively non-controversial claims about the nature of God, contested not just by a minority but a diverse range of experienced and intelligent theologians. And if this is to become a cornerstone in someone's ministry or practice, that person remains unprepared for engaging co-workers, clients, or those in clients' support networks, such as pastors, who might take exception to such a framework.

The Anthropological Problem

In addition to potential difficulties concerning the doctrine of the Trinity, the resultant anthropology of *RS* is also subject to criticism. For the authors of *RS*, the transferral of unity, particularity, and relationality into the human sphere functions to uphold the integrity of the human individual as an individual in relationship, while nonetheless maintaining

44. Molnar, *Divine Freedom*, 386, n. 26.
45. Grenz and Olson, *20th-Century Theology*, 185.
46. Hunsinger, "Review," 131.
47. Leftow, "Anti Social Trinitarianism," 204.
48. Moltmann, anticipating this criticism on the basis of the response to his earlier work, defends against the charge of tritheism already in *Trinity and Kingdom*, 243, n. 43. See, more recently, Neal, *Theology as Hope*, 106–9. On Leftow's essay, see, e.g., Davis, *Christian Philosophical Theology*, 74–78.

the discrete selfhood of that individual. That is, the self is not dissolved in the relationships it forms with others. This is all well and good insofar as such a framework is grounded in the eternal perichoresis of the divine persons, in which one person gives their self fully to another without dissolution. Insofar as Christology is concerned, however, problems soon arise. For example, how do the authors affirm Jesus' call to self-denial in following him to the cross? "If any want to become my followers, let them deny themselves and take up their cross and follow me" (Mark 8:34).[49] Jesus himself "emptied himself, taking the form of a slave, being born in human likeness. And being found in human form, he humbled himself and became obedient to the point of death—even death on a cross" (Phil 2:7–8). And this christological center finds powerful expression in the exclamations of Moses, "But now, if you will only forgive their sin—but if not, blot me out of the book that you have written" (Exod 32:32), and of Paul, "I could wish that I myself were accursed and cut off from Christ for the sake of my own people, my kindred according to the flesh" (Rom 9:3). Clients of Christian counselors might express genuine interest in this kind of cruciform self-denial, and such an interest may indeed be a divine call! While this is a more extreme example, it does reveal one limit of drawing analogies between divine and human sociality.

An Obsolescent Paradigm?

In early twentieth century NT studies, the notion of the "Gnostic redeemer myth" began to be promulgated. The theory pointed to a redeemer figure in pre-Christian Gnosticism who served as an archetype for later Christian beliefs. It continued to increase in popularity with scholarly celebrities such as Rudolf Bultmann and Ernst Käsemann applying the paradigm enthusiastically and apparently fruitfully in their own exegesis. But this all came to a sudden halt in 1961 with a monograph revealing the paucity of evidence for the theory.[50]

The scholarly world is a world of ever-new hypotheses, revision of current hypotheses, and often rejection of hypotheses fundamental to the work of those in previous generations. Such a generational shift has been suggested concerning the social Trinitarian movement:

---

49. All citations of Scripture are taken from the NRSV.
50. See Hurtado, "Fashions, Fallacies and Future Prospects," 303–05. The monograph mentioned is Carsten Colpe's *Die religionsgeschichtliche Schule*.

The tide of social trinitarianism in academic theology seems to have turned during the past couple of years. Some of its most outstanding representatives (Catherine LaCugna, Stanley Grenz, Colin Gunton) died at a relatively young age. Others have moved towards other theological concerns (Plantinga), or even started to downplay the (social) doctrine of the Trinity for the sake of these (Volf). Most interestingly, however, theologians of a newer generation who have addressed the topic have turned out to be much more sceptical of social trinitarianism.[51]

I have engaged some of the latter group throughout this chapter.

There is no telling what the state of the conversation in Trinitarian theology will be in the next forty years. Will social Trinitarianism become obsolete like the gnostic redeemer myth? I doubt it. But surely a clearer assessment of its various advantages and limits will be able to be given. And what of those who apply social Trinitarian insights that are later found to be problematic—here perhaps the authors of *RS*? Conclusions based on the theory of a gnostic redeemer myth will rarely be serviceable in future biblical scholarship, except maybe as examples of dead ends. But this is different to the application of social Trinitarianism in *RS*. If such a paradigm is indeed later found to be untenable, it can then be said that it was not the purpose of *RS* to provide a contribution to the doctrine of the Trinity. The aim of the authors was to allow the doctrine to speak to being human, rather than vice versa. That is, the claims of human distinctiveness, relationality, and reciprocity, though here grounded in a particular understanding of the Trinity, do not need social Trinitarianism to legitimate them. And, notably, a significant amount of theoretical groundwork following the material on the Trinity in *RS* is influenced by the personalistic philosophy of the Jewish thinker, Martin Buber.[52] Of course, for the Christian practitioner, the question of the relationship between developmental theory and theology should not be neglected, but neither does it need to proceed along the same lines. There are other avenues promising fruitful engagement, such as Christology or the doctrine of creation.

In this chapter I have not attempted to provide any conclusive rebuttal of the application of social Trinitarianism to developmental theory.

---

51. Van den Brink, "Social Trinitarianism," 337. Van den Brink explains that Volf downplays his interest in the Trinity because he seeks to find common ground in the dialogue with Islam.

52. Balswick et al., *Reciprocating Self,* 40–48; 2nd ed., 48–54.

Rather, I have reflected critically on the relationship in order to suggest a way forward. First, I think it would be helpful for future contributions in related areas, whether they be developmental theory, counseling practice, or ministry, to comment, however briefly, on the still open nature of this debate in Trinitarian theology. This would benefit readers by promoting critical reflection on the theological paradigms employed, and, if a social Trinitarian paradigm is to be nonetheless taken up, allow them to see it as one paradigm rather than the paradigm that underpins the respective project. Second, similarly, I encourage the authors of *RS*, among others, to consider additional paradigms. These might not supersede the role that social Trinitarianism plays, but they could be presented as alternative paradigms with their own strengths and weaknesses. I have already noted Christology and the doctrine of creation as possibilities above. Indeed, the second edition of *RS* takes up Christology in this connection, though, in my judgement, this is somewhat underdeveloped. More attention to this area of theology as an alternative paradigm alongside social Trinitarianism will be of benefit to future readers.[53]

Bibliography

Balswick, Jack O., Pamela Ebstyne King, and Kevin S. Reimer. *The Reciprocating Self: Human Development in Theological Perspective*. Downers Grove: InterVarsity, 2005.

———. *The Reciprocating Self: Human Development in Theological Perspective*. 2nd ed. Downers Grove: InterVarsity, 2016.

Buxton, Graham. *The Trinity, Creation and Pastoral Ministry: Imaging the Perichoretic God*. Eugene, OR: Wipf & Stock, 2005.

Davis, Stephen T. *Christian Philosophical Theology*. Oxford: Oxford University Press, 2006.

Giles, Kevin. "The Evangelical Theological Society and the Doctrine of the Trinity." *Evangelical Quarterly* 80 (2008) 323–38.

Grenz, Stanley. *The Social God and the Relational Self: A Trinitarian Theology of the Imago Dei*. Louisville: Westminster John Knox, 2001.

Grenz, Stanley J., and Roger E. Olson. *20th-Century Theology: God and the World in a Transitional Age*. Downers Grove: InterVarsity, 1992.

Grudem, Wayne. *Systematic Theology: An Introduction to Biblical Doctrine*. Grand Rapids: Zondervan, 1994.

---

53. See, e.g., Tanner, "Social Trinitarianism," 371: "It would be better to steer one's immediate attention away from the Trinity when trying to determine the proper character of human relations in Christian terms. Christology, I suggest, is the far more direct and less misleading avenue to take when making socio-political judgments on Christian grounds."

Holmes, Stephen R. "Three versus One? Some Problems of Social Trinitarianism." *Journal of Reformed Theology* 3 (2009) 77–89.

Howe, Leroy T. *The Image of God: A Theology for Pastoral Care and Counseling*. Nashville: Abingdon, 1985.

Hunsinger, George. "Review of *The Trinity and the Kingdom: The Doctrine of God*, by Jürgen Moltmann." *Thomist* 47 (1983) 129–39.

Hurtado, Larry W. "Fashions, Fallacies and Future Prospects in New Testament Studies." *Journal for the Study of the New Testament* 36 (2014) 299–324.

Jowers, Dennis W., and H. Wayne House. *The New Evangelical Subordinationism?: Perspectives on the Equality of God the Father and God the Son*. Eugene, OR: Wipf & Stock, 2012.

Kilby, Karen. "Trinity, Tradition, and Politics." In *Recent Developments in Trinitarian Theology: An International Symposium*, edited by Chalamet Christophe and Vial Marc, 73–86. Minneapolis: Augsburg Fortress, 2014.

King, Pamela Ebstyne. "The Reciprocating Self: Trinitarian and Christological Anthropologies of Being and Becoming." *Journal of Psychology and Christianity* 35 (2016) 215–32.

Koerselman Jayme. "Uniqueness and Belonging: Healing through Relationship." In *Stories of Therapy, Stories of Faith*, edited by Lex McMillan, Sarah Penwarden, and Siobhan Hunt, 61–76. Eugene, OR: Wipf & Stock, 2017.

Koutloumousianos, Chrysostom. *The One and the Three: Nature, Person and Triadic Monarchy in the Greek and Irish Patristic Tradition*. Cambridge: James Clarke & Co., 2015.

LaCugna, Catherine Mowry. *God for Us: The Trinity and the Christian Life*. San Francisco: Harper San Francisco, 1991.

Leftow, Brian. "Anti Social Trinitarianism." In *The Trinity: An Interdisciplinary Symposium on the Trinity*, edited by Stephen T. Davis, Daniel Kendall, and Gerald O'Collins, 204–50. Oxford: Oxford University Press, 1999.

Metzler, Norman. "The Trinity in Contemporary Theology: Questioning the Social Trinity." *Concordia Theological Quarterly* 67 (2003) 270–87.

Molnar, Paul D. *Divine Freedom and the Doctrine of the Immanent Trinity: In Dialogue with Karl Barth and Contemporary Theology*. 2nd ed. London: Bloomsbury T&T Clark, 2017.

Moltmann, Jürgen. *The Coming of God*. Translated by Margaret Kohl. Minneapolis: Fortress, 1996.

———. *The Crucified God: The Cross of Christ as the Foundation and Criticism of Christian Theology*. Translated by R. A. Wilson and John Bowden. Minneapolis: Fortress, 1993.

———. *God and Creation*. Translated by Margaret Kohl. Minneapolis: Fortress, 1993.

———. *The Trinity and the Kingdom*. Translated by Margaret Kohl. Minneapolis: Fortress, 1993.

Neal, Ryan A. *Theology as Hope: On the Ground and Implications of Jürgen Moltmann's Doctrine of Hope*. Eugene, OR: Pickwick, 2008.

O'Collins, Gerald. *The Tripersonal God: Understanding and Interpreting the Trinity*. New York: Paulist, 1999.

Pembroke, Neil. *Renewing Pastoral Practice: Trinitarian Perspectives on Pastoral Care and Counselling*. Aldershot: Ashgate, 2006.

Peters, Ted. *God as Trinity: Relationality and the Temporality in Divine Life*. Louisville: Westminster John Knox, 1993.

Rahner, Karl. *The Trinity*. Translated by Joseph Donceel. New York: Crossroad Herder, 1997.

Seamands, Stephen. *Ministry in the Image of God: The Trinitarian Shape of Christian Service*. Downers Grove: InterVarsity, 2005.

Selak, Annie. "Orthodoxy, Orthopraxis, and Orthopathy: Evaluating the Feminist Kenosis Debate." *Modern Theology* 33 (2017) 529–48.

Shults, F. LeRon. *Reforming Theological Anthropology: After the Philosophical Turn to Relationality*. Grand Rapids: Eerdmans, 2003.

Tanner, Kathryn. "Social Trinitarianism and Its Critics." In *Rethinking Trinitarian Theology: Disputed Questions and Contemporary Issues in Trinitarian Theology*, edited by Robert J. Wozniak and Giulio Maspero, 368–86. London: Continuum, 2012.

Van den Brink, Gijsbert. "Social Trinitarianism: A Discussion of Some Recent Theological Criticisms." *International Journal of Systematic Theology* 16 (2014) 331–50.

Volf, Miroslav. "'The Trinity Is Our Social Program': The Doctrine of the Trinity and the Shape of Social Engagement." *Modern Theology* 14 (1998) 403–23.

Zizioulas, John D. *Communion and Otherness: Further Studies in Personhood and the Church*. Edited by Paul McPartlan. London: T&T Clark, 2006.

Chapter 12

Verbalizing Hate in the Psalms

Richard Neville

This study investigates *verbalizing* hate in the Psalms. It seeks to understand better those instances where the psalmist says he hates someone or something.[1] To do so I will be drawing on the field of biblical studies as well as research into emotion carried out by moral psychologists and philosophers.

Verbalizing Hate in the Psalms as the Product of a Vindictive Culture

One approach to this question is to simply acknowledge that such expressions of hate are of a piece with the violent and vindictive cultures of the ancient Near East, of which Israel was one. In support of this we might point to the violent taking of the land of Canaan (Joshua 1–12), the law requiring an eye for an eye and a tooth for a tooth (Exod 21:23–25), as well as stories of revenge such as Samson and the Philistines (Judg 15:3, 7; 16:28). There is a popular impression that the Old Testament portrays ancient Israelites as violent and vengeful, and this view is sometimes endorsed by Old Testament specialists.[2] On this view of

---

1. The use of masculine pronouns here when referring to the psalmist reflects the reality that whenever a psalm is attributed to someone by name, that person is male.

2. Blenkinsopp, "Reconciliation in the Middle East," 346.

things, expressions of hate in the Psalms are an unsurprising feature of ancient Israelite culture.

Nevertheless, this explanation of the use of hate language in the Psalms cannot stand. Israelite law prohibited hate and revenge, and encouraged a non-violent response to injury. Leviticus 19:17 is explicit on the question of hate, "Do not hate a fellow Israelite in your heart" (NIV).[3] Instead, the law requires that the injured party respond to injury by speaking with the person who caused the injury. That is, they are instructed to *reprove* them (Lev 19:17). The law also prohibits acts of vengeance, "You shall not take vengeance or bear a grudge against any of your people" (Lev 19:18). The required response is to "love your neighbor as yourself" (Lev 19:18). This love is extended to include neighbors who are not native born Israelites, a group referred to as resident aliens (Lev 19:34; Deut 10:18–19).

There are also laws governing the treatment of one's enemies. Two of these appear in a paragraph dealing with impartiality and justice (Exod 23:1–8).[4] When an enemy's ox or donkey goes astray an Israelite is to restore it (Exod 23:4), and when an enemy's donkey falls under its burden, an Israelite must help his enemy (Exod 23:5).

These are not the laws of a culture that condones an individual hating or taking revenge when someone has injured them. On the contrary, the law prohibits that kind of behavior, encourages love for one's neighbor even when that neighbor is of foreign origin, and requires the just treatment of one's enemy. So expressions of hatred in the Psalms cannot be explained simply as the consequence of a vindictive culture.

Verbalizing Hate in the Psalms as a Failure to Conform to the Law

Another possible solution is to argue for a contradiction between the law and the expressions of hate in the Psalms. On this view of things the Psalms contain honest expressions of hate in spite of what the law presents as a better way. It might be that while the law sets the official standard, Psalms reflects the reality that Israelites failed to live up to that standard.

---

3. Unless otherwise indicated, English translations are from the NRSV.
4. For a discussion of this text see Gane, *Old Testament Law for Christians*, 222–28.

It is unlikely, however, that Israel's songbook would contain expressions of hate so discordant with the nation's laws. More telling is the fact that the psalmists express their hatred for the wicked in prayers addressed to God in which the psalmists seek the Lord's help. In Psalm 26, for example, the psalmist's claim, "I hate the company of evildoers" (26:5) is accompanied by an invitation for God to probe his heart and mind (26:2), and the psalmist's request for deliverance is based on his innocence (26:6) and blameless life (26:11). It is highly unlikely that someone who is seeking divine help based on his blameless life would at the same time express sentiments so contradictory to the divine will.

The strong words of Psalm 139, "Do I not hate those who hate you, O Lord? And do I not loathe those who rise up against you? I hate them with perfect hatred . . ." (139:21–22a), are likewise followed by the invitation, "Search me, O God, and know my heart" (139:23), as though this would confirm the psalmist's hatred for the wicked, and receive divine approval. And the psalmist's words in Psalm 31, "I hate those who cling to worthless idols" (31:6 NIV), are immediately followed by an expression of trust in the Lord.[5] It is hardly possible that these expressions of hate can be explained as deviations from Israelite piety, or sentiments offered in defiance of the law. They have every appearance of being offered to God in anticipation of his approval. Indeed, the psalmist will sometimes express hatred of the wicked and love of God's law in the same breath, "I hate the double-minded, but I love your law" (Ps 119:113).

There is also an instance in which contempt (an emotion akin to hate[6]) is encouraged. Psalm 15 opens with the question, "Lord, who may abide in your tent? Who may dwell on your holy hill?" There follows a description of the person who deserves such a privilege, and one of their characteristics is that they *despise* or have *contempt* for the wicked.[7]

> [2] Those who walk blamelessly, and do what is right,
>   and speak the truth from their heart;
> [3] who do not slander with their tongue,
>   and do no evil to their friends,
>   nor take up a reproach against their neighbors;

---

5. The NRSV follows an alternative reading and translates this, "You [Lord] hate those who pay regard to worthless idols."

6. Mason, *Moral Psychology of Contempt*, xvi.

7. This is not the commonly used term for the *wicked*. Other translations render it *vile* (NIV) and *contemptible* (Tanakh).

> ⁴ in whose eyes the wicked are *despised*,
>> but who honor those who fear the LORD;
>> who stand by their oath even to their hurt. (Ps 15:2–4)

There is no escaping the fact that ancient Israelite faith viewed some expressions of hate (and contempt) in positive terms. But if this is the case, then ancient Israelite faith contained a remarkable contradiction, prohibiting hatred (Lev 19:17), encouraging love of neighbors (Lev 19:18) and resident aliens (Lev 19:34), mandating the just treatment of enemies (Exod 23:4–5), and instructing its people to feed their enemies (Prov 25:21), but at the same time viewing some expressions of hate as virtuous.[8]

Some Insights Taken from Research into Emotion

Before looking more closely at expressions of hate in the Psalms, it will be helpful to introduce some insights from research into emotion.[9] Space will only allow a brief description of these insights with little in the way of supporting argument. Footnotes will identify works that provide more detailed discussions of the points presented here.

First, emotions are shaped to a significant degree by culture. Anthropologists in particular, have shown that emotions vary from culture to culture.[10] This includes differences in what gives rise to a particular emotion, the ways in which an emotion is manifest in a particular culture, and the repertoire of emotions present in any particular culture.[11] This confirms the impression that some biblical texts use the language of emotion in ways quite foreign to speakers of English.

---

8. "Hatred is an important spiritual and moral virtue (see 139:19–22)" (Goldingay, *Psalms*, 3:143).

9. The study of emotion has been carried out around two poles. One pole maintains emotion has a neurological basis and, as such, emotion is universal and unchanging through human history and across cultures. The other pole argues that emotion is socially constructed, exhibiting change over time and variation between cultures. This essay focuses on the constructed nature of emotion, without denying the importance of biology. For a discussion of these polarities see Plamper, *History of Emotions*, 1–9, and chs. 2 (social constructivism) and 3 (universalism).

10. Lutz, *Unnatural Emotions*; and the relevant chapters in Harré and Parrott, *Emotions*.

11. See Solomon, *True to Our Feelings*, 252–62.

How is it, for example, that Jesus can teach his followers to hate their parents (Luke 14:26)?

Second, the popular equation of emotion with *feeling* is mistaken.[12] Emotions are more than feelings, and while emotions include feeling, they can exist without experiencing a feeling. Robert Roberts observes, "Novelists describe, and psychotherapists regularly confront, people who are angry, resentful, envious, and anxious, yet do not feel these emotions ... Emotions are paradigmatically felt, but emotions may occur independently of the corresponding feeling."[13]

Third, emotions are not inherently irrational.[14] Robert Solomon, for example, writes, "It is a myth that emotions are dumb feelings, or necessarily stupid and unthinking responses, or irrational as such."[15] On the contrary they are intelligent, and as such they play a vital part in the moral life.[16]

Roberts defines emotions as *concern-based construals*. The term *construal* is his preferred term for the way a person perceives or interprets a situation. For example, Roberts describes a situation in which a parent is watching his toddler totter toward the edge of a wall with a three-foot drop to the ground. The parent's construal of the situation involves the identification of the child as their own and the recognition of the threat to the child's well-being. This construal does not itself constitute an emotion. There also needs to be a *concern*, which in this case is the parent's care for their child's well-being. It is the perceived danger to their child in conjunction with the parent's concern for the child's well-being that produces the emotion fear. Roberts illustrates the role of the concern here by replacing the parent in the story with an adolescent.

> We can easily imagine an adolescent watching the child treading dangerously close to the edge of the wall, seeing that the child is in danger of falling off and thus in need of protection, without

---

12. Solomon, *True to Our Feelings*, 2, 137–41. The error is particularly acute when emotions are reduced to physiological perturbations or bodily states (Roberts, *Emotions*, 151–55).

13. Roberts, *Emotions*, 60.

14. The quality of an emotion is dependent on a number of factors (Roberts, *Emotions in the Moral Life*, 60–61).

15. Solomon, *True to Our Feelings*, 126.

16. Solomon, *True to Our Feelings*, 3. For a lengthy argument advocating the intelligence of emotions from the perspective of moral philosophy, see Nussbaum, *Upheavals of Thought*.

experiencing any anxiety or fear. Perhaps the adolescent is just watching idly, with the most minimal interest, or perhaps he is curious to see whether the child will fall. In the latter case, he will have some emotion, but it will not be fear (it might even be hope).[17]

This illustration is sufficient to suggest how emotions might function in a person's moral life. Given that a person's concerns are shaped by "concepts and narratives,"[18] it is clear that people's emotional responses will vary according to the concepts and narratives that shape their concerns. For example, Roberts observes,

> The person who gets inordinately excited about finding five dollars on the street is seeing himself as the object of extraordinarily good fortune, based on a concern for good fortune and a certain conception of good fortune. Compare him with the person who rejoiced intensely at the election of Nelson Mandela to the presidency of South Africa, out of a concern for justice and the well-being of that country. That rejoicing traded on a very different and more mature understanding of good fortune.[19]

Similarly, Roberts points out that Christians will respond to situations in an emotionally distinctive manner because their *concerns* and how they *construe* situations are also distinctive.

> Consider the joy that the apostles felt after being arrested, imprisoned, and beaten for telling the good news about Jesus (Acts 5:41). Arrest, imprisonment, and beating are not typical occasions for joy among human beings. Most people, when such things happen to them, perceive the situation as unfortunate and are likely to feel distressed, angry, fearful, or sad; but the apostles respond with joy because they see themselves as having been "counted worthy of suffering disgrace for the Name" of Jesus. Given that they were persecuted for their forthright

---

17. Roberts, *Emotions in the Moral Life*, 47–48.
18. "The very same behaviour of binding wounds, dispensing medicine, providing a comfortable place to lie, might be practiced by anyone. The distinctiveness of Christian compassion lies in how the Christian *conceives* himself, the sufferer, the suffering, and the larger universe in which he acts ... And this will be true of all emotions ... So a Christian psychology of ethics of emotions will have to conceive of them in such a way that they can be shaped by concepts and narratives" (Roberts, *Spiritual Emotions*, 29–30).
19. Roberts, *Spiritual Emotions*, 15–16.

witness to Jesus, the persecution seems to them to be a very good thing. This is because they love Jesus, want to imitate him and to associate themselves with his ministry. Thus a situation that would be repugnant to people with a different interpretive scheme and/or different concerns is for them an occasion for rejoicing. The apostles' concern-based perception [construal] is an important spiritual state because it is a manifestation of their concern for the kingdom of God, their affection for the Lord, and their understanding of themselves and their situation in terms of the gospel.[20]

Finally, hate reflects a moral stance.[21] When a person hates lying, this reflects the view that lying is evil and deserves to be hated. This kind of moral stance is evident in the psalmist's (and God's) hatred of evildoers (Ps 26:5), those who hate the Lord (Ps 139:21), wrongdoers (Ps 5:5), those who pay regard to worthless idols (Ps 31:6), evil (Ps 97:10), those who love violence (Ps 11:5), and the work of those who fall away (Ps 101:3).

Verbalizing Emotions in the Book of Psalms

Emotion features a great deal in the book of Psalms. This includes anger, delight, disgust, contempt, hate, jealousy, envy, joy, longing, love, awe, and hope.[22] There are also references to behaviors (rejoicing, laughter, crying) and physiological processes (tears, trembling) associated with certain emotions. Of particular interest here are the references to emotions and

20. Roberts, *Spiritual Emotions*, 13.

21. "Hatred is not simply a reflex of revulsion, but a considered antagonism or animosity based on ethical judgment" (Konstan, *Emotions of the Ancient Greeks*, 187). Elsewhere he calls hate a "moral emotion" (200). Roberts' understanding of emotions can explain a more spontaneous form of hate in moral terms without appealing to judgment or reflection. Like the visual perception of a basketball referee, or a bird-watcher, a person's moral perception or construal of a situation reflects that person's moral heritage, "virtues like compassion, justice, and generosity will equip their possessor with emotional sensitivities that allow her to discern the moral features of situations; and these powers of perception, like visual ones, will have resulted from nurture and experience within a moral tradition" (Roberts, *Emotions in the Moral Life*, 93). He would prefer to see emotions as "the perceptual *basis* of our moral judgments" (112, emphasis added).

22. There is no definitive list of emotions for English, much less for ancient Hebrew. Ancient Israelites would not have identified a category equivalent to the English term *emotion* made up of what English speakers think of as emotions. The category *emotion* is a relatively recent development in English, arising in the seventeenth century. For an account of the rise of emotion as a category, see Dixon, *From Passions to Emotions*.

their associated behaviors and physiological expressions that occur in the psalmist's *report* of his own emotional states. Psalm 119 is a striking example of this practice:

> [14] I *rejoice* in following your statutes as one rejoices in great riches.
> [16] I *delight* in your decrees; I will not neglect your word.
> [20] My soul is *consumed with longing* for your laws at all times.
> [24] Your statutes are my *delight*; they are my counsellors.
> [35] Direct me in the path of your commands, for there I find *delight*.
> [47] for I *delight* in your commands because I *love* them.
> [48] I reach out for your commands, which I *love*, that I may meditate on your decrees.
> [53] *Indignation* grips me because of the wicked, who have forsaken your law.
> [70] Their hearts are callous and unfeeling, but I *delight* in your law.
> [74] May those who fear you rejoice when they see me,
>   for I have put my *hope* in your word.
> [92] If your law had not been my *delight*, I would have perished in my affliction.
> [97] Oh, how I *love* your law! I meditate on it all day long.
> [104] I gain understanding from your precepts; therefore I *hate* every wrong path.
> [111] Your statutes are my heritage forever; they are the *joy* of my heart.
> [113] I *hate* double-minded people, but I *love* your law.
> [119] All the wicked of the earth you discard like dross; therefore I *love* your statutes.
> [120] My flesh *trembles* in *fear* of you; I stand in *awe* of your laws.
> [127] Because I *love* your commands more than gold, more than pure gold,
> [128] and because I consider all your precepts right, I *hate* every wrong path.
> [136] *Streams of tears* flow from my eyes, for your law is not obeyed.
> [140] Your promises have been thoroughly tested, and your servant *loves* them.
> [143] Trouble and distress have come upon me, but your commands give me *delight*.
> [159] See how I *love* your precepts;
>   preserve my life, LORD, in accordance with your love.
> [161] Rulers persecute me without cause, but *my heart trembles* at your word.
> [162] I *rejoice* in your promise like one who finds great spoil.
> [163] I *hate* and *detest* falsehood but I *love* your law.
> [167] I obey your statutes, for I *love* them greatly.
> [174] I *long for* your salvation, LORD, and your law gives me *delight*. (NIV)

The psalmist's deployment here of so many emotional terms invites explanation. Some of the observations in the previous section will serve us well here. We noted, for example, that the emotional life of a morally mature person will differ from that of a morally immature person. Similarly, the emotional life of a faithful Israelite will have distinctive contours. This is because each of these groups construe or interpret situations differently, and the concerns that inform their emotional lives also vary. As Roberts observes, "In a person's emotions (admittedly in some more than others) we have indicators of her character that are as potent as her actions."[23] Roberts' concept of a *passion* will help to clarify why this is the case. He defines a passion as a kind of *on-going master concern*: "I use [passion] to refer neither to emotions nor to a general spiritedness of personality, but to a person's long-term, *characteristic* interests, concerns, and preoccupations . . . A passion in this sense is a concern that defines one's psychological identity."[24] Passions are stable and long term *concerns* that enter into a person's character to become character traits: "Emotions are based on concerns, some concerns are passions, and passions are character traits, on-going master concerns that deeply characterize a person."[25]

Drawing on Roberts' definition of passions as on-going master concerns, the list of emotions in Psalm 119 can be explained as emotions of someone with a passion to be a loyal devotee of the Lord, especially as this is manifest in his devotion to God's law.[26] That is, he fears the Lord and trembles at his word; he loves the law, and longs for it; the statutes of the Lord are the joy of his heart and the object of his delight; he loves the Lord's commands and his promises, he hopes in his word, and longs for his salvation; he weeps when the law is disobeyed, and is indignant when the wicked forsake the law; and he hates falsehood, double-minded people, and every wrong path. These are the emotions (physiological expressions, etc.) of a life governed by a passion for faithfulness and obedience to the Lord.

How Expressions of Hate Function in the Book of Psalms

What is true of the psalmist's vocalization of his emotions in Psalm 119 is also true of how the psalmists vocalize their hate elsewhere in the book

---

23. Roberts, *Emotions*, 324.
24. Roberts, *Spiritual Emotions*, 17.
25. Roberts, *Spiritual Emotions*, 20.
26. The psalmist is explicit on this point: "I have chosen the way of faithfulness [*derek 'emunah*]; I set your ordinances before me" (Ps 119:30).

of Psalms. In each instance it is apparent the psalmist is seeking to present himself as loyal to the Lord. Furthermore, these claims to faithfulness typically feature in contexts where the psalmists are seeking divine help. This is the case in Psalm 119. It has been characterized as a wisdom psalm,[27] and a Torah psalm.[28] However, Gordon Wenham gives good reason for identifying it as an individual lament.[29] And in the context of a lament the psalmist's claim to faithfulness is an important part of his appeal for divine help: "The central message of the poem is clear: the psalmist is waiting for divine intervention to free him. He counts on Yahweh for his hope of salvation. *Fidelity to God ensures the hope of final victory.* The word that God reveals allows the one who learns it and practices it to overcome all the crises of life while awaiting divine vindication."[30]

All of this can be framed in terms of Roberts' understanding of emotion. The psalmist is working from a *concern* over his safety. This, combined with the psalmist's *construal* of his circumstances as threatening, results in anxiety or fear, which generates the *consequent concern* to escape the crisis by appealing to the Lord for help.[31] And to improve the likelihood of a successful petition for help the psalmist presents himself as having the emotional profile of someone loyal to the Lord.

The psalmist's verbalization of his emotions in Psalm 26 has a similar function. The psalmist asks God to deliver him, and not take his life along with sinners, the bloodthirsty, those who plot, and those who take bribes (26:9–10). He supports his request for help by declaring his innocence (26:6), and his blamelessness (26:11). And among the particulars the psalmist declares what he loves and hates, "I do not sit with the worthless, nor do I consort with hypocrites; I *hate* the company of evildoers, and will not sit with the wicked" (26:4–5). By contrast he *loves* the house where God lives (26:8), which is also where he worships God (26:6–7). His verbalization of what he loves and hates presents him as blameless in his emotion, and this complements his blameless behaviour (refusing to sit with evildoers, and telling of the Lord's wondrous deeds). Once again,

---

27. DeClaissé-Walford et al., *Psalms*, 870.
28. Goldingay, *Psalms*, 3:381.
29. Wenham, *Psalms as Torah*, 83.
30. Wenham, *Psalms as Torah*, 84; emphasis added.

31. Emotions can have consequent concerns. Anger, for example, has the consequent concern "to punish, to get rectificatory justice" (Roberts, *Emotions*, 157; and for fear and its consequent concern, see 160–61).

the psalmist describes what he loves and hates as part of his claim to loyalty, and as a means of supporting his request for divine aid.

Psalm 139 includes some of the strongest declarations of hate found in the Psalter. The closing section of the psalm reads,

> ¹⁹ O that you would kill the wicked, O God,
>   and that the bloodthirsty would depart from me—
> ²⁰ those who speak of you maliciously,
>   and lift themselves up against you for evil!
> ²¹ Do I not hate those who hate you, O LORD?
>   And do I not loathe those who rise up against you?
> ²² I hate them with perfect hatred;
>   I count them my enemies.
> ²³ Search me, O God, and know my heart;
>   test me and know my thoughts.
> ²⁴ See if there is any wicked way in me,
>   and lead me in the way everlasting.

Psalm 139 falls into four sections of six verses each. The first three sections describe the Lord's intimate knowledge of the psalmist, and his constant presence with him from the time the Lord formed him in the womb. Following on from this, in the fourth section (above) there is a shift in tone as the psalmist declares that he hates the wicked, and there is mention of both the destruction of, and distancing from, the wicked. And then the psalmist invites the Lord to examine his heart (139:23–24). The word translated *wicked* in v. 24 is better translated *idolatrous*, in which case the psalmist invites God to see if there is any idolatrous way in him.³² All of these features of the last section suggest that once again the psalmist uses the language of hate as part of his presentation of himself as someone loyal to the Lord.

How then does the final section fit with the descriptions of the Lord's intimate knowledge and constant presence with the psalmist as it is described in the first three sections? When the psalmist invites God to examine him and determine whether or not he is loyal as he claims, he does so aware that God has known him intimately from the time he was formed in the womb, and that the Lord is all too capable of discovering whether or not his claim to faithfulness is true. The psalmist would hardly invite the God of vv. 1–18 to examine him (in vv. 23–24) unless he was confident of his own loyalty. "One could imagine [Psalm 139] being used by someone who has been accused of wrongdoing. The logic of the

---

32. So too Allen, *Psalms 101–150*, 260; Goldingay, *Psalms*, 3:639.

psalm is then that the seriousness of the acknowledgment in vv. 1–18 makes it unlikely that someone would be willing to say the psalm before God and not mean it."[33]

The king's expression of hate in Ps 101:5 (for this text see below "How Hate Can Be a Virtue") bolsters his request for the Lord's intervention. However, the need for divine intervention in that psalm is obscured by translating v. 2 "When shall I attain it?" in the NRSV. As Goldingay observes, it is better translated as a question directed at the Lord, "When will you come to me?" (NIV), suggesting the psalmist is seeking divine help.[34] There is a consistent pattern of use for expressions of hate. They appear in contexts where the psalmist is at pains to establish his faithfulness or innocence, typically to facilitate God's help.

How Hate Can Be a Virtue

The psalmists' expression of their hate for the wicked as part of their presentation of their loyalty, suggests that hating the wicked is considered a virtue.[35] How can this be so? It is relevant that loyalty is foundational to the biblical faith. Loyalty and exclusivity are at the heart of the nation's covenant relationship with the Lord. In Deuteronomy this is expressed in a call to love the Lord: "Hear, O Israel: YHWH our God, YHWH is the one and only. So you should love YHWH your God with all your thinking, with all your longing, and with all your striving."[36]

YHWH is Israel's *one and only*, and as such "the people of Israel must be exclusive in their faithfulness and allegiance to him...whatever 'other gods' there may be, such 'other gods' should be of no existential interest to Israel, but rather are to be displaced, rejected and discarded, since Israel's focus is to be on YHWH alone."[37] Loyalty to the Lord meant the rejection not only of other gods, but of the wicked who set themselves in opposition to the Lord. And just as loyalty was expressed as love, so rejection could be expressed as hate. This logic is apparent in a treaty from

---

33. Goldingay, *Psalms*, 3:628; similarly, Allen, *Psalms 101–150*, 260.

34. "'When?' is the plea of a suppliant under pressure (42:2[3]; 119:82, 84; compare the 'until when?' of, e.g., 74:10; 80:4[5]; 94:3)" (Goldingay, *Psalms*, 3:142; see also 3:138).

35. Virtue here is used in the non-technical sense of a "commendable trait."

36. Deut 6:4–5, translation by Moberly, *Old Testament Theology*, 24.

37. Moberly, *Old Testament Theology*, 20.

the early thirteenth century BCE between the Hittite king Muršili and his Amurru vassal Duppi-Tešub.[38] Referring to himself as "My Majesty," Muršili tells Duppi-Tešub, "Whoever is My Majesty's enemy shall be your enemy, and whoever is My Majesty's friend shall be your friend."[39]

It is also evident that when the psalmists express hate for the wicked and their deeds, they are adopting the Lord's perspective on the wicked: "The Lord tests the righteous and the wicked, and his soul hates the lover of violence" (Ps 11:5); "You hate all evildoers" (Ps 5:5b; cf. Isa 6:8). The Lord's disposition towards wickedness is expected of the faithful: "Let those who love the Lord hate evil" (Ps 97:10 NIV); "To fear the Lord is hatred of evil" (Prov 8:13). This solidarity with the Lord's view of things explains why the psalmists can express their hate in anticipation of divine approval.

More particularly, divine hatred of the wicked has two associated behaviors. First, the Lord does not admit the wicked into his presence. And second, the Lord will destroy the wicked. Both of these behaviors are evident in Psalm 5.

> [4] For you are not a God who delights in wickedness;
>   evil will not sojourn with you.
> [5] The boastful will not stand before your eyes;
>   you hate all evildoers.
> [6] You destroy those who speak lies;
>   the LORD abhors the bloodthirsty and deceitful. (Ps 5:4–6)

A faithful king followed the divine model. He too hated the wicked, and this was accompanied by the same two responses of distancing and destruction.

> [3] I will not set before my eyes anything that is base.
>   I hate the work of those who fall away; it shall not cling to me.
> [4] Perverseness of heart shall be far from me;
>   I will know nothing of evil.
> [5] One who secretly slanders I will destroy.
>   A haughty look and an arrogant heart I will not tolerate.
> [6] I will look with favour on the faithful in the land,
>   so that they may live with me;
>   whoever walks in the way that is blameless shall minister to me.

---

38. Israel's covenant documents (Exodus 20–24 and Deuteronomy) share a number of features with ancient Near Eastern suzerain-vassal treaties.

39. "Treaty between Muršili and Duppi—Tešub," translated by Itamar Singer (*COS* 2.2.17b:96–98); cf. "I am a companion of all who fear you" (Ps 119:63).

> ⁷ No one who practices deceit shall remain in my house;
>   no one who utters lies shall continue in my presence.
> ⁸ Morning by morning I will destroy all the wicked in the land,
>   cutting off all evildoers from the city of the LORD. (Ps 101:3–8)

Coming now to the faithful Israelite, once again expressions of hate can be accompanied by either or both distancing and destruction.

> ⁴ I do not sit with the worthless,
>   nor do I consort with hypocrites;
> ⁵ I hate the company of evildoers,
>   and will not sit with the wicked. (Ps 26:4–5)

In the lead up to his declaration of hate for the wicked, the psalmist asks God to destroy them, and instructs the wicked to keep their distance.

> O God, if You would only slay the wicked—
>   you murderers away from me. (Ps 139:19 Tanakh)

A crucial difference here is that, unlike the Lord and the king, the faithful Israelite does not attempt to destroy the wicked himself. This is because justice, including the punishment of the wicked, was viewed as a divine prerogative, and the delegated duty of the divinely appointed king. Instead, the individual Israelite could show solidarity with the Lord's purposes by *praying* that the Lord carry out his judgment of the wicked, and by expressing his desire to distance himself from them. The psalmist's direct address to the wicked in Ps 139:19 ("you murderers away from me") is rhetorical for the Lord's benefit, and not for the wicked.[40] The psalmist enacts telling the wicked to depart from him, knowing that the Lord looks on with approval.

What Does the Psalmist Experience When He Hates the Wicked and Their Deeds?

One of the most challenging aspects of studying emotions in ancient texts is discovering what, if anything, a person experienced or felt when they were ascribed a particular emotion. It is difficult, and often impossible, to know what someone felt when they experienced an

---

40. The figure is *apostrophe* and involves the psalmist turning away from the person he is addressing (in this case the Lord), and speaking to an imaginary audience (Bullinger, *Figures of Speech*, 901–3).

emotion.⁴¹ Nevertheless, it is possible to give some definition to what the psalmists felt when they hated by comparing hate with what the psalmist says about anger in Psalm 37. In the face of mistreatment at the hands of the wicked, the psalmist advises his audience to *refrain* from anger and *let go of* wrath. The righteous must not get themselves riled up because it only leads to doing evil (Ps 37:8).⁴² Instead, the righteous are to leave the wicked in the Lord's hands (Ps 37:5). And at several points in Psalm 37 the psalmist assures his audience that the Lord will deal with the wicked by, for example, removing them from the land (Ps 37:9, 22).

The point of interest here is the fact that the Israelite is encouraged to hate, but told to let go of anger. The reason given for the latter is that anger only leads to evil (Ps 37:8). This is because anger carries a desire to pay back the person who has caused injury. The desire for revenge is widely reckoned to be an integral part of anger, and this view is ancient.⁴³ The desire to punish, which can be very strong, made anger a dangerous emotion that needed to be controlled. The fact that the psalmist shows no comparable concern in the case of hate suggests that it did not carry the same affective component. On the contrary, as we noted earlier, the movement associated with hate tends to be *away from* rather than *towards* its object.⁴⁴ And when the psalmist hates, he expresses a desire for the destruction of the wicked but shows no compulsion to carry out the task himself, "O that you would kill the wicked, O God" (Ps 139:19).

Where hate's natural expression is a call for divine judgment on the wicked, anger has to be relinquished *first* in order to give opportunity for divine intervention. In other words, whereas hate invites divine justice, anger preempts it. Using Roberts' language, whereas anger has

---

41. "In the end there is a gap between what people felt and what historians can know about those feelings, yet there is nevertheless a value to be found in discovering these faint traces of past generations' sensibilities" (Matt, "Recovering the Invisible," 44).

42. The translation "do not get yourself riled up" is an alternative translation to "do not fret" (NRSV Ps 37:1, 7, 8). Something of this nature seems preferable. The verb is a common one for anger, but in this case it has a distinct form that has a meaning something like "do not cause yourself to be angry."

43. Fisher, *Vehement Passions*, 171–98 (esp. 178); Griswold, *Forgiveness*, 39; Harris, *Restraining Rage*, 57–63, 95, 134; Konstan, *Emotions of the Greeks*, 41, 43, 65–67; Nussbaum, *Anger and Forgiveness*, 15; Schlimm, *From Fratricide to Forgiveness*, 68; Roberts, *Emotions*, 157.

44. "Although it does not necessarily indicate that wicked intentions accompany such hate, it does imply a distancing from the hated person, that person's removal from the surroundings of the person who hates" (Lipiński, "שָׂנֵא *śānēʾ*," 164).

a consequent concern in the form of a desire to punish its object, hate's consequent concern is for divine judgment on its object. This is why hate is a virtue, but anger must be re-directed to seek divine intervention.

The prohibition against hate in Lev 19:17 is an exception that proves the rule,

> Do not hate your fellow in your heart.
> Instead you must reprove them,
> so that you do not incur guilt.[45]

In this instance hate does result in some kind of pay back, and that pay back is the sin for which the person will *incur guilt*. The next verse is explicit, "Do not seek revenge" (Lev 19:18). Hate here is prohibited because, like anger, it leads to vengeful action. Why does hate here differ from hate in the psalmists' vocalization of hate? Hate in Lev 19:17 is called "hate in the heart." Unlike English, the heart in Hebrew was commonly considered the locus of cognition, and so *hate in the heart* refers to the vindictive thinking that takes place in the mind in response to injury, and which leads to revenge. Notice also that this hate is in response to personal injury, whereas the psalmist is responding to the wicked, who are the Lord's enemy. This is why he can say, "I count them my enemies" (Ps 139:22). They are the Lord's enemies, and only *become* the psalmist's enemies because the psalmist aligns himself with the Lord. The language of hate is used to express this alignment. It has more the character of a chosen disposition than a reactive feeling (to injury).

The point of interest here is that hate in the psalmists' vocalizations can be a virtue because its consequent concerns are entirely different from anger's consequent concern, and whatever affective element is present is expressed in terms of those concerns (e.g., distancing, divine justice), and not in seeking to punish the object of hate.

A number of studies involving ancient Hebrew emotional terms have concluded that in some instances terms referring to an emotion focus on behaviour[46] or volition,[47] with little if any reference to affect.[48]

---

45. This and subsequent translations of clauses from Lev 19:17 and 18 are mine.

46. This leads Anderson to observe, "In every text in which a term like love, hate, or honor occurs, the interpreter should be sensitive to a possible behavioral referent" (Anderson, *Time to Mourn, a Time to Dance*, 14; Wells, "Hated Wife," 135–36).

47. Muffs, *Love and Joy*, 44–45; Peels, "I Hate Them with a Perfect Hatred," 46.

48. This is how scholars have understood love in Deuteronomy: "Characteristic of Deuteronomy is love which can be commanded, i.e., loyalty" (Weinfeld, *Deuteronomy and the Deuteronomic School*, 333). Similarly, Moran argues that love in Deuteronomy

It is at least possible, then, that the psalmists' confessions of hate which occur as part of their claims to faithfulness, are more about volition and disposition than feeling.[49] Vocalizations of hate are the psalmist's deliberate presentation of himself as one who rejects the Lord's enemies (the wicked, violent, etc.) and their wicked ways. A similar distinction also appears in Aristotle's discussion of hatred. He observes, "Anger is accompanied by pain, but hatred is not; for he who is angry suffers pain, but he who hates does not."[50] Konstan explains, "But hatred of a class of people, such as thieves, no doubt lacks the acute sense of injury that results from an intentional slight, and this, I imagine, is why Aristotle describes it—by contrast with anger—as a painless emotion."[51]

Conclusions

The psalmists' hate is a consequent concern, arising from their loyal and exclusive love for the Lord. The psalmists *verbalize* hate as a means of presenting themselves to the Lord as loyal. This verbalization expresses their rejection of anyone and anything that is opposed to God. To the extent that this hate has an affective component, it might be described as a moral aversion or repugnance for wickedness. The consequent concerns of the psalmists' hate are a desire to distance themselves from wickedness and the wicked, and a desire for the Lord to carry out his judgment on the wicked.

Aversion for the wicked and for wickedness does not carry the emotional *affect* that would move the psalmist to violence. This renders hate a "safe" psychological state. Hate is treated as a virtue because it is an aversion to wickedness and a desire for just judgment that lacks a compulsion to revenge.

The association of verbalized hate with a moral stance suggests it might fruitfully be compared with recent studies of contempt.[52] These

---

is a covenantal love, and is comparable to the love found in ancient Near Eastern treaties, which "may be defined in terms of loyalty, service and obedience" (Moran, "Love of God in Deuteronomy," 81–82). There have been recent attempts to modify this view, for example, by Arnold, "Love-Fear Antinomy in Deuteronomy," 551–69.

49. Roberts' distinction between love as an attachment or disposition, and love as an emotion may be relevant here (*Emotions*, 285–89).

50. Aristotle, *Rhetoric* 2.4.31, cited in Konstan, *Emotions of the Greeks*, 186.

51. Konstan, *Emotions of the Greeks*, 192.

52. In at least one instance the psalmist views contempt as a virtue in much the

studies seek to determine whether or not contempt has a role to play in the moral life along with other reactive attitudes, as was the view of some ancient philosophers, including Aristotle.[53] Macalaster Bell, for example, makes the case that, "The best response to racists, be they living or dead, is active contempt."[54]

The call to absolute loyalty carries through to the New Testament (Matt 22:37; Mark 12:30; Luke 10:27). The language of loving and hating is used to express undivided loyalty (Matt 6:24), and the priority of allegiance to Jesus over allegiance to one's parents (Luke 14:26). Furthermore, there is the expectation of rejecting (refusing to love or befriend) all that is opposed to God.

> You adulterous people, don't you know that love of the world is hatred of God? Therefore, anyone who chooses to be a friend of the world becomes an enemy of God. (Jas 4:4 NIV)

> Do not love the world or the things in the world. The love of the Father is not in those who love the world. (1 John 2:15)

This refusal to love the world can be compared with the Psalmist's refusal to consort with the wicked (Ps 26:4–5). It must be held in tension with the expectation of caring for one's enemies that runs across both Testaments (Matt 5:44, cf. Exod 23:4–5; Prov 25:21–22). It is essential to the integrity of biblical faith that the *yes* that is loving one's enemy should stand alongside the *no* that is opposed to evil, and those who champion it. The psalmists' vocalization of hate needs to be understood in terms of this tension. Similarly, by asking "your kingdom come" Christians not only anticipate universal righteousness and peace, but also the final distancing from (Rev 21:27; 22:14) and destruction of (Rev 20:15) all that is irremediably opposed to God. Seen in this context, the psalmists' commitment to distancing themselves from wickedness, and their

---

same way that hate is. The person who can live in God's presence is one, "in whose eyes the wicked are *despised*" (Ps 15:4). The verb "despised" (*bāzâ*) is used of treating or viewing something with contempt. Mason reports that psychologists suggest contempt is among the "exclusion" family of emotions, which seek to socially exclude the person who is their object. By contrast, anger is among the "attack" emotions (Mason, *Moral Psychology of Contempt*, xvi). This difference is not unlike the distinction drawn here between anger (revenge) and verbalized hate (aversion/distancing). In their study of hate Sternberg and Sternberg identify seven types of hate of which "cool hate" is described in terms of disgust and aversion (Sternberg and Sternberg, *Nature of Hate*, 74).

53. Mason, *Moral Psychology of Contempt*, xvi.
54. Bell, "Contempt, Honor, and Addressing Racism," 3–15.

prayers for God's judgment on the wicked are an attempt to live in loyal obedience to God and his purposes.

Bibliography

Allen, Leslie C. *Psalms 101–150*. Waco: Word, 1983.
Anderson, Gary. *A Time to Mourn, a Time to Dance: The Expression of Grief and Joy in Israelite Religion*. University Park: Pennsylvania State University Press, 1991.
Arnold, B. T. "The Love-Fear Antinomy in Deuteronomy 5–11." *Vetus Testamentum* 61 (2011) 551–69.
Bell, Macalaster. "Contempt, Honor, and Addressing Racism." In *The Moral Psychology of Contempt*, edited by Michelle Mason, 3–15. London: Rowman & Littlefield, 2018.
Blenkinsopp, Joseph. "Reconciliation in the Middle East. A Biblical Perspective." *Theology Today* 65 (2008) 344–55.
Bullinger, E. W. 1898. *Figures of Speech Used in the Bible*. Reprint, Grand Rapids: Baker, 1968.
deClaissé-Walford, Nancy, Rolf A. Jacobson, and Beth LaNeel Tanner. *The Book of Psalms*. Grand Rapids: Eerdmans, 2014.
Dixon, Thomas. *From Passions to Emotions: The Creation of a Secular Category*. Cambridge: Cambridge University Press, 2003.
Fisher, Philip. *The Vehement Passions*. Princeton: Princeton University Press, 2002.
Gane, Roy E. *Old Testament Law for Christians: Original Context and Enduring Application*. Grand Rapids: Baker Academic, 2017.
Goldingay, John. *Psalms*. 3 vols. Grand Rapids: Baker, 2008.
Griswold, Charles L. *Forgiveness: A Philosophical Exploration*. Cambridge: Cambridge University Press, 2007.
Harré, Rom, and W. Gerrod Parrott, eds. *The Emotions: Social, Cultural and Biological Dimensions*. London: SAGE, 1996.
Harris, William V. *Restraining Rage: The Ideology of Anger Control in Classical Antiquity*. Cambridge: Harvard University Press, 2004.
Konstan, David. *The Emotions of the Ancient Greeks: Studies in Aristotle and Classical Literature*. Toronto: University of Toronto Press, 2006.
Lipiński, E. "שׂנא *śānēʾ*." In vol. 14, *Theological Dictionary of the Old Testament*, edited by G. Johannes Botterweck, Helmwer Ringgren, and Heinz-Josef Fabry, 164–74. Translated by Douglas W. Stott. Grand Rapids: Eerdmans, 2004.
Lutz, Catherine A. *Unnatural Emotions: Everyday Sentiments on a Melanesian Atoll and Their Challenge to Western Theory*. Chicago: University of Chicago Press, 1998.
Mason, Michelle, ed. *The Moral Psychology of Contempt*. London: Rowman & Littlefield, 2018.
Matt, Susan J. "Recovering the Invisible. Methods for the Historical Study of the Emotions." In *Doing Emotions History*, edited by Susan J. Matt and Peter N. Stearns, 41–53. Springfield: University of Illinois Press, 2014.
Moberly, R. W. L. *Old Testament Theology: Reading the Hebrew Bible as Christian Scripture*. Grand Rapids: Baker, 2013.
Moran, William L. "The Ancient near Eastern Background of the Love of God in Deuteronomy." *Catholic Biblical Quarterly* 25 (1963) 77–87.

Muffs, Yochanan. *Love and Joy: Law, Language and Religion in Ancient Israel*. New York: Jewish Theological Seminary of America, 1992.

Nussbaum, Martha C. *Anger and Forgiveness: Resentment, Generosity, Justice*. Oxford: Oxford University Press, 2016.

———. *Upheavals of Thought: The Intelligence of Emotions*. Cambridge: Cambridge University Press, 2001.

Peels, Eric. "I Hate Them with a Perfect Hatred (Psalm 139:21–22)." *Tyndale Bulletin* 59 (2008) 35–51.

Plamper, Jan. *The History of Emotions: An Introduction*. Translated by Keith Tribe. Oxford: Oxford University Press, 2015.

Roberts, Robert C. *Emotions in the Moral Life*. Cambridge: Cambridge University Press, 2013.

———. *Emotions: An Essay in Aid of Moral Psychology*. Cambridge: Cambridge University Press, 2003.

———. *Spiritual Emotions: A Psychology of Christian Virtues*. Grand Rapids: Eerdmans, 2007.

Schlimm, Matthew R. *From Fratricide to Forgiveness: The Language and Ethics of Anger in Genesis*. Winona Lake: Eisenbrauns, 2011.

Singer, Itamar. "Treaty between Muršili and Duppi—Tešub." In vol. 2, *The Context of Scripture*, edited by William W. Hallo and K. Lawson Younger Jr., 96–98. Leiden: Brill, 2002.

Solomon, Robert C. *True to Our Feelings: What Our Emotions Are Really Telling Us*. Oxford: Oxford University Press, 2007.

Sternberg, Robert J., and Karin Sternberg. *The Nature of Hate*. Cambridge: Cambridge University Press, 2008.

Weinfeld, Moshe. *Deuteronomy and the Deuteronomic School*. Oxford: Clarendon, 1972.

Wells, Bruce. "The Hated Wife in Deuteronomic Law." *Vetus Testamentum* 60 (2010) 131–46.

Wenham, Gordon J. *Psalms as Torah: Reading Biblical Psalms Ethically*. Grand Rapids: Baker, 2012.

Chapter 13

Creation and Social Practice: The Wisdom of Psalm 104 as Prequel to Theology and Social Practice

Tim Meadowcroft

Much that has been written about the integration of theology and social practice has concerned itself with Trinitarian or christological insights.[1] In this paper I propose a prequel to all of that, namely, a consideration of God as creator—including as creator of human beings. It is a prequel in that a prequel is both prior and not prior. A prequel fills out a story that has already been told and enriches it.[2] At the same time, there is nothing wrong with the fact that the story that was previously told started chronologically in the middle. There is even a richness about such a beginning point in that it places on center stage the essence of the story, implying what has been and pointing towards what may become. This is perhaps the strength of christological and Trinitarian approaches to social practice. In that sense, theological accounts of social practice based on the doctrine of creation are not innately prior.[3] At the same time, though, christological and Trinitarian approaches may be enriched

---

1. See, e.g., a number of essays in McMillan et al., *Stories of Therapy, Stories of Faith*.

2. Ideally if not in actual achievement, going by the contribution of some recent film prequels.

3. It will be recognized that I am flirting with various understandings of Christ at this point. A Barthian view, for example, would not locate a doctrine of creation in the way that I am, and might describe the priority of Christ differently.

by an account of a broader theological framework. Accordingly, I offer this essay as a kind of prior consideration of the subject in hand, while also accepting that it may also function as a backdrop to christological and Trinitarian approaches.

My aim in doing so is not so much to prescribe how and what social practice ought to be in the light of God's creating, as to suggest a field within which social practice is drawn to play. I do so by the old-fashioned method of reading through and reflecting on a passage of Scripture in the light of the question at hand. The passage is Psalm 104, a marvellous wisdom hymn to creation and its creator. In the light of that reading, I suggest some key features of the field which God has given to us in which to play that I believe are relevant to a Christian theory of social practice.

Psalm 104

Psalm 104 has long been recognized as a piece of wisdom poetry, and is a masterly reflection on the created order in a series of psalms of thanksgiving that end Book 4 of the psalter (Psalms 103–106).

Creation as the Garment of God (vv. 1–4)

The first two verses deploy a clothing metaphor. I offer a fairly literal translation of the Hebrew text: "*Adonai*, my God, you are exceedingly great. You put on a garment of majesty and splendour, clothed in light as a cloak, spreading out the heavens as a tent." There is a sense here of God donning that which he has created as a garment. At the risk of eisegesis, I think of it like God putting on a priestly garment of some sort.[4] There is intimacy and beauty and even wonder in the image. This is the interpretive key to the picture of creation. Everything that may be observed, all the processes that are described, flow on from God putting on the cloak of "honor and majesty," like the flowing skirts of Taranaki, in the North Island of New Zealand. It is not a surprise then to find some scholars of biblical wisdom more generally deploying the category of wonder in their descriptions.[5]

---

4. A member of a liturgical tradition might even say that creation is the chasuble of God.

5. E.g., Brown, *Wisdom's Wonder*.

This expresses itself in the verb forms deployed in vv. 1–4 by the psalmist. Excluding the opening "Bless the Lord, O my soul," the first two verbs are indicative in form, followed by a series of participial actions, which thus modify or derive from the opening actions of God. Thus, in the matter of creation, the organizing action taken by God is first, to be great (*gdl*, a stative form), and then to put on "honor and majesty." The verb translated as "are clothed" by the NRSV is in fact an active form. Making allowance for ancient cosmological notions, the act of putting on this garment is seen in the stretching out of the heavens, the setting in place of the waters, the establishment of the clouds and the wind. In this picture, the creation of various aspects of the "heavens" are particular manifestations of the greatness and splendor of God. That human beings remain especially moved by the majesty of the heavens is perhaps an instinctive response to that fact.

There are two very interesting turns of phrase in v. 4, by which aspects of creation are assigned as agents of God within creation. The winds are God's *mal'akim*, "messengers" or prophets or heavenly beings—all of those come within the semantic field of this term. There is a hint that this garment of creation worn by God bears in some way the voice of God; it speaks to us, and acts as God's agent on us. And "fire and flame" are *meshareith*, those who serve or minister or engage in ritual activity—all those come within the semantic field. There is thus a hint here of creation engaging in worship on behalf of God and/or working on behalf of God. There is a dual possibility here, of creation as God's agent, and creation as responsive to God. Both are important understandings, and in fact each—agency and response—should be allowed to inhere in the other.

The Terror of the Deep (vv. 5–9)

Then follows a series of actions on the part of God around the arrangement of water in the created order (vv. 5–9). From vast cosmic wonder, the psalmist now zooms in onto that which is most essential to life on earth: water. The creative process entails first of all the creation of water per se. Again, making allowance for ancient cosmology, the creation of the waters and the "deep" somehow are necessary for the stability of the earth (vv. 5–6). But it is not enough that there be vast amounts of water, such that "the deep" (*tehom*) covers the entire earth and even the mountains (v. 6). Water is also destructive of life when it is out of place. The term *tehom* is a multi-layered one, embracing simply ocean as well as ancient mythic deluge.[6] As the descriptor of those waters which covered the mountains in the ancient flood (Gen 7:20), it is as much evocative of terror as of life. Yet this object of terror is a garment for the earth, just as light is a garment enwrapping God (v. 2). Even the terror of water is the wonder of God and God's creation. Such a notion is counter-intuitive to the ancients who felt deeply afraid of the watery chaos.[7] And it is counter-intuitive to moderns, also, for whom individual health and happiness have become the final goals.

That which is terrifying needs further action from the creator. So vv. 7–9 show God gradually shaping the water around mountains and valleys, as the waters obey his voice (v. 8). They are set within boundaries so that they can achieve the purpose of their existence. Just as God created the terrible deep, so now God brings order to the waters. Note that God creates the terror and God creates the order. As we will see towards the end of the Psalm, despite God's limiting of the objects of terror within creation, they still retain the power to cause the earth to "tremble" (v. 31).

Purpose in Creation (vv. 10–13)

It emerges in the next section (vv. 10–13) that this ordering is characterized by purpose. To that end, the arranging of water continues as God moves beyond the major work of making oceans and vast rivers and lakes—those bodies of water that form land masses—and continues to create the means for water to be accessible on those land masses for those who depend on it: springs and streams and precipitation that "waters the mountains" (v. 13). As a result, the birds and wild asses may flourish, and, in a summary statement, we read literally that "the earth is sated" (v. 13), and God's work in creation produces fruit. There is a purpose of fruitfulness in all this creative activity.

---

6. Kraus, *Psalms 60–150*, 300: Kraus evokes the first verse of this Psalm with his observation that ". . . the primeval flood covered all lands like a garment (Gen. 1:2)."

7. "The sea [is] no more" in the vision of the new heaven and the new earth (Rev 21:1), although waters are not banished; there is a "river of the water of life" (Rev 22:1).

Instrumentality in Creation (vv. 14–23)

And then comes a profound reflection on what I am calling the instrumentality that is built into the natural world (vv. 14–23). By this I mean that something bigger is going on than merely that God has a purpose in creation, although that is profound enough on its own. What is implicit in the previous section is now stated in explicit detail, namely, that the created world itself exists on behalf of other parts of the created order. Creation at every turn reflects the purposeful nature of its creator. Thus, grass grows for cattle and plants for the use of people, both to feed them and for their pleasure. And there is joy in the human experience of this instrumentality; it is more than merely getting fed. Wine makes the heart glad (v. 15), an easy enough point with which to identify, but even the experience of being fed by bread has to do with the human spirit, with the broader experience of wellbeing: "bread to strengthen the human heart" (v. 15).[8] From the perspective of humanity, the created order does more than simply keep the machine going; it results in flourishing and wellbeing, and even beauty—"oil to make the face shine" (v. 15).[9]

But wait, there's more (vv. 16–23). The trees of Lebanon provide nests for the birds; the fir trees house the stork; the mountains exist for the wild goats and the rocks for the coney; the moon marks the seasons so that the animal world can rest and plant and reap and make love and order its life; darkness gives shelter for the nocturnal animals to go about their life and work; and the sun draws people out for the work to which God has called them.

Incidentally, lest we allow our thinking to reduce to the assumption that creation exists entirely for human beings as the crown of creation, it is intriguing how interwoven humanity is with other elements in creation. There does not appear here to be a special status given to human beings.[10] They/we participate with the rest of creation in joyful worship of God and cooperation with God in the instrumentality or purposed nature of creation.

---

8. Brown, *Sacred Sense*, 64, references the reformer John Calvin's love of v. 15. He writes: "Calvin found a kindred spirit in the ancient psalmist. Both the reformer and the sage were intoxicated with creation's wonder."

9. Kraus, *Psalms 60–150*, 300, writes of "the cheering and refreshing gift of the Creator."

10. Brown, *Seven Pillars of Creation*, 150, notes: "Absent . . . is any hint of human dominion."

In Wisdom (vv. 24–26)

Verses 24–26 add two important dimensions to this vision. The first is that both wild animals and the mythic creatures, inhabitants of chaos, are included in this description of creation. The wild goats are there, as is "Leviathan" (v. 26), a mythic creature of the chaotic "deep" (*tehom*).[11] This is in addition to the earlier inclusion of domesticated creatures, such as cattle, deployed specifically for the needs of humanity (v. 14). There is no part of creation that is not included as the majestic garment of God. That includes those parts that also are experienced as harbingers of terror. There is an instrumentality and purpose, and even potential responsiveness, throughout the created order. The psalmist, as Hans-Joachim Kraus so eloquently puts it, "inserts into a picture full of friendliness and playful beauty the dark colors of that which is chaotic."[12]

The second comment from this section is that all of this has been made "in wisdom" (v. 24). This is not the place to examine the sprawling wisdom tradition permeating the Hebrew Scriptures, covering everything from the basic how to's of everyday life to the moral choices that face us to the deepest conundrums confronting humanity as we seek to live out our calling as creatures *imago Dei* in the setting of our *imago mundi*. Suffice to say that, as the majestic garment of God, creation is in some sense a moral entity, a place that has to do with good and evil. Creation can never finally be objectified—reduced to a "thing"—so pervasive is the wisdom of God within it. Even the Leviathan is made by God "to laugh" (from the root *schq*, v. 26), setting the reader in mind of wisdom as a child playing next to God and laughing with joy as God created this amazing cosmos (Prov 8:30–31). A sense of the joy and goodness of creation pervades the Psalm.

Wonder (vv. 27–30)

So far we have seen that creation is an outworking of the very essence of God, that it acts as God's agent, and that within creation itself is built a kind of mutual benefit and even joy. This takes us back to the category of "wonder." In that respect, to this point in the psalm the character of God has been seen, as has the agency of God which is woven into creation.

---

11. Kraus, *Psalms 60–150*, 303.
12. Kraus, *Psalms 60–150*, 303.

William Brown considers the significance of this agency of God in creation alongside the joy and wonder: "If, God-forbid, the creator were to *stop* enjoying creation, the world would collapse or wither away."[13] We know this because that is precisely what happened at the time of the great flood (Gen 6:6), when God's joy in what he had made, we are told, turned into grief, and we witnessed the unpicking of creation.

So we come to a section (vv. 27–30) that celebrates the direct engagement with God in the processes of ongoing creation—what could also be expressed as the sustaining of creation. It opens with the declaration that "all of them" (*kulam*)—the entire created order—look to Yahweh. First, note again that this is not confined to the human part of creation; the theme of "intrinsic worth" continues.[14] The attribution of emotion—"dismay" (v. 29)—echoes something seen back in v. 4, a responsiveness on the part of the entire created order to its creator. As such it echoes the early verses of Psalm 19, "the heavens are telling the glory of God" (Ps 19:1), and the vision of deutero-Isaiah that "the trees of the field shall clap their hands" (Isa 55:12) in joy and wonder.

Earlier we noted that both the terror and the order are God's creation; both in some sense reflect that God sees the world and it is good. And this "goodness" involves both joy and pain, flourishing and loss, death and renewal. The experience of both is uncompromisingly named as the action of God; God opens his hand toward and God also hides his face from creation (vv. 28 and 29). Where creation is experienced as death-dealing and puzzling, such does not imply the absence of God, nor does it imply the ascendancy of forces other than God.

A Human Response (vv. 31–35)

Finally, the psalmist comes to the human response to all of this (vv. 31–35), but still in the broader context of God's engagement with creation. The psalmist prays for the Lord to "rejoice in his works" (v. 31), in all that he has achieved in creation. Is there just a hint in that turn of phrase that there may be aspects of God's works that he may not be inclined to rejoice in? This is the mystery that remains at the end of the psalm: that all of

---

13. Brown, *Seven Pillars of Creation*, 148.

14. The Earth Bible project has formulated six "ecojustice principles," of which the first is that "the universe, Earth and all its components have intrinsic worth/value" (Earth Bible Team, "Guiding Ecojustice Principles").

God's works are good and joyful, both the order and the terror; that some of God's works may be experienced by God's creation, if not by God, as dismaying and death-dealing; and that, while all of creation is the work of God, there is just the hint that things happen within God's creation in which God may not wish to rejoice. Brown puts it more forcefully: "While the psalm includes even the monstrous Leviathan within the orbit of God's providential care, it has no room for the wicked."[15]

For if God is inherent in creation, God is also other and not able fully to be grasped by human beings.

Psalm 104 and Social Practice

What might this all have to say to a theology of social practice? I hope by now it is clear that it says much. But first, to reiterate my opening comment, it speaks not so much to prescribe as to offer us a field in which to play. There are a number of features of this field that can now be traced.

First, *there is the call to wonder*. God's creation is imbued with the wonder of God, and so calls forth wonder. This wonder is experienced by all of nature, in the psalmist's view, and expresses itself as a playful joy. It also expresses itself in a desire that the different elements of creation experience flourishing and fruitfulness. There is joy because creation makes God joyful, and there is flourishing because God creates. And our practice is called to be characterised by this joyful wonder at an extravagant creation and, within that, human flourishing. Our practice is also called to draw forth that wonder and joy and flourishing in others, wherever the human experience is joyless and incurious and poverty-stricken. I return to this particular theme below. Those behind the growth of the "forest school" movement are onto something.[16]

But this wonder is not banal, and it is not self-seeking. It brings with it *an awareness that human beings are special, but they are special in the context of the intrinsic worth of each part of the created order*. Our goal as human beings is not therefore flourishing for its own sake, or what we might call self-fulfilment. It is that we play our part within creation, that we capture a sense of our own instrumentality and purposed existence. That is the manner by which we flourish. To speak of it as "service" in the vulgar sense is too narrow a notion, with its connotations of duty and

---

15. Brown, *Seven Pillars of Creation*, 144.
16. See https://www.theforestschool.co.nz/.

even drudgery. It is only service to the extent that it is so expressed in v. 4 of Psalm 104, an outflowing of the worship of God. The better term in contemporary English with which to express that might be "ministry," as long as we free that term from a narrow church context. It is ministry in the sense that all we do and are is an inseparable intertwining of worship and work directed towards and on behalf of the creator. As practitioners, our call is to be expressions of just that: worship and work.

In reflecting more on what our practice might actually look like, we are drawn back to *the instrumental and purposed nature of the created order*, not just as a whole but within each part. Our task is to envisage all that we do in those terms. And it is from there that we enhance this vision and experience in others. That is a multi-faceted thing. It may mean teaching so that others discover their significance to others. It may be working for a world in which no person is devalued or reduced to insignificance. It may entail helping people to re-orientate their lives and re-narrate themselves in new outward facing directions. In the context of an appreciation of the intrinsic worth of the entire created order, it constitutes a call to re-appreciate the importance of self-conscious and deliberate care of creation—and in doing so to hear more clearly creation as the "messenger" of God. This too is ministry, a combination of worship and work. All that we do is fired by a sense of purpose and instrumentality.

Implicit in this sense of purpose and instrumentality is *an appreciation of agency*. God has built into creation risk and freedom, both physical and moral. Human beings flourish and exercise their calling in that context: in participation in risk, in exercising choice, in the discernment of good and evil and participation in the options offered by them. Practitioners walk with others also through their own exercise of agency and are themselves both terrified and inspired by the call to agency in the work of God.

We are terrified because God's good creation, the field in which we play, *includes the mysterious and the terrible* that is the result of this inherent risk and freedom. One simply cannot take pleasure in creation without incorporating the mystery and the terror. Psalm 104 reflects the biblical wisdom tradition, which itself indicates in numerous ways that the path of wisdom entails the ability to do so: to discern responses to shifting circumstances; to deal with the many ironies that life throws up; to stand in humility before the transcendent. This too is part of human flourishing, and this too is a concern in social practice in its various forms.

Finally, the mysterious and the terrible bring this prequel up to the point at which so much theological reflection on social practice begins: to an appreciation of the one of whom it is said:

> He is . . . the firstborn of all creation; for in him all things in heaven and on earth were created, things visible and invisible . . .—all things have been created through him and for him. He himself is before all things, and *in him all things hold together.* (Col 1:15–17)

And so . . .

And so we plant and sow, we tend, we teach, we counsel, we nurture, we rehabilitate, we engage, we advocate—out of a profound and joyful sense of wonder at God's world and our place in it. And out of an equally profound understanding of our own roles and responsibilities as members within this purposed creation, rejoicing and resisting in the face of both order and terror. Thus we reflect the image of God and draw forth that reflection in others. For "in [Christ] all the fullness of God was pleased to dwell" (Col 1:19).

Bibliography

Brown, William P. *Sacred Sense: Discovering the Wonder of God's Word and World.* Grand Rapids: Eerdmans, 2015.

———. *The Seven Pillars of Creation: The Bible, Science, and the Ecology of Wonder.* Oxford: Oxford University Press, 2010.

———. *Wisdom's Wonder: Character, Creation, and Crisis in the Bible's Wisdom Literature.* Grand Rapids: Eerdmans, 2014.

Earth Bible Team. "Guiding Ecojustice Principles." In *Readings from the Perspective of Earth*, edited by Norman C. Habel, 42–44. Sheffield: Sheffield Academic, 2000.

Kraus, Hans-Joachim. *Psalms 60–150: A Continental Commentary.* Translated by Hilton C. Oswald. Minneapolis: Fortress, 1993.

McMillan, Lex, Sarah Penwarden, and Siobhan Hunt, eds. *Stories of Therapy, Stories of Faith.* Eugene, OR: Wipf & Stock, 2017.

Response 5: Theology

Finding Middle Ground

Lex S. McMillan

My task here is to consider the three stimulating essays written by Cameron Coombe, Richard Neville, and Tim Meadowcroft from my perspective as a professional counselor who claims Christian identity. As I do so I am struck by the way they all engage at depth with the contours of human life. Furthermore, I am drawn to admire the apparent ease with which the authors engage Scripture and mine its life affirming themes.

I still remember the anticipation that arose in me when I heard that Laidlaw College was organising a conference as a forum for conversation between social science practitioners and Christian theologians. My experience of anticipation was in response to a hope I hold that practice might be grounded and developed in concert with sound theological anthropology. This has been a long-held interest of mine inspired in the beginning by works such as Roger Hurding's *Roots and Shoots* and Larry Crabb's *Inside Out*.[1] Now, after a career that has spanned three decades, I am still eager to be part of a deepening conversation about what it means to be human and well, a conversation in dialogue both with counseling psychologies and Christian theology.

The first aspect I want to highlight is that these authors meet us as social science practitioners on middle ground and offer us their insights in language that is accessible to our work and commitments. I have come to think that one lifetime is just too short a time for a counselor

---

1. Crabb, *Inside Out*; Hurding, *Roots and Shoots*.

or social worker to develop the professional requirements of theoretical mastery and practice maturity, *and* to achieve more than a general level of theological insight with which to engage practice. For this reason, it is valuable when biblical scholars and theologians meet us halfway and contribute their disciplinary expertise in a manner that can be utilised by practitioners. I illustrate this with three examples: first, how Meadowcroft presents creation theology in such a way that social practitioners can understand their work from this larger perspective; second, the manner in which Neville tackles and dismisses the commonly held notion that the Old Testament represents a God who legitimizes hate and violence is also critically important. I know of counselors who claim their identity as Christian for whom this misunderstanding has become a significant stumbling block to faith. And third, Coombe's questioning of whether the social Trinitarian view of God and people is well grounded is particularly timely for the Laidlaw group, with whom I am engaged, who teach the Bachelor of Counseling. I say this because key themes drawn from the social Trinitarian metaphor feature prominently with Laidlaw's counselor education programmes, and Coombe brings important theological nuance to the work. While the average Christian counselor may recognise the relevance of creation theology, sound exegesis, and critical reflection, engaging well in these kinds of enquiries is most often beyond us. This leads me to my first conclusion, that while practitioners of the social sciences need access to mature theological insight, it is not a requirement that counselors hold master's degrees in each branch of theology related to the complexity of people's lives *if* we have dialogue partners such as these three to meet us on conversational middle ground.

The second aspect I would like to comment on is the telos or goal of interdisciplinary dialogues between therapy and theology. Is it to merely provide practice with theological guidance, or might the focus be broader than this? I am in favour of it being broader in terms of aiming to have both dialogue partners contributing *and* being enriched by the other. This would seem to me to better represent the heart of dialogue, and the style of relating that sits at the core of our incarnational faith. By incarnational heart I mean the Son of God becoming fully human, and in doing so both changing the world and being changed by the vulnerable encounter. All this to say, I am grateful for the approach taken by these authors to both offer theological insight *and* utilize psychological insight on behalf of this. As I read Meadowcroft's and Neville's work I observe a two-way dialogue rather than a one-way flow of insight from theology to practice. Neville, for example, utilises psychological insight through people such as Roberts as one of his hermeneutics with which to interpret the ancient texts.[2] This method is similar—albeit in the reverse—to the way I seek to use theological insight to assist my interpretation of psychological observations.[3]

It seems to me that this more *practical* theological—or two-way—approach, as opposed to an *applied*—or one-way—theological approach is more honoring of us as social practitioners. I say this for two reasons. First it treats us with integrity, as people with something unique to contribute. And second, it hints that other disciplinary enquiries in addition to the theological one are potential sources of theological disclosure. Seward Hiltner has posited that "if we hold that theology is always an assimilation of the faith, not just the abstract idea of the faith apart from its reception, then it becomes necessary to say that culture may find answers to questions raised by faith as well as to assert that faith has answers to questions raised by culture."[4]

When the theologically disclosive potential of practice is acknowledged, a genuine two-way interdisciplinary dialogue is possible, and as a result the development of more fully formed understandings of human flourishing might emerge. As I read these three essays, I experience myself being honored as a social scientist and enriched by the unique contributions they offer me. This leads me to my third and final observation—the reason I referred to experiencing joyful anticipation at the prospect of engaging in this dialogue—that practitioners at the coal faces of people's lives need large stories through which to make sense of the fragmented nature of lives that we encounter on a daily basis.

My interest in this third theme relates to an observation that as therapeutic practitioners it is all too easy when involved in the minutiae of people's struggles to overlook the larger issues at stake. I hear the authors each in their own way imploring us to stand back and view our work on the large canvas of biblical faith. Neville's reminder to "say no to evil and those who champion it," as we "anticipate universal righteousness and peace" and "the final distancing from destruction," has me thinking about attempting to adopt a caring stance towards hurt and a staunch one towards injustice. Large story perspectives such as this

2. Roberts, *Emotions in the Moral Life*.
3. McMillan, "Persons, Divine and Human, and Therapy."
4. Hiltner, *Preface to Pastoral Theology*, 223.

also have me thinking about ways I might collaborate as a counselor with social workers to find concrete ways to stand against both personal and institutional wickedness. In a similar way Meadowcroft's engagement with the Psalms places before us a large canvas of creation through which we might conceive of our work as a participation in the ongoing creation project: "rejoicing and resisting in the face of both order and terror." While Coombe's approach is different in that his task is to critique a particular theological tradition, in doing so he also emphasizes the value in holding a "right" view of God. This too can be seen as being on behalf of formulating a large canvas view of people, problems, and wellbeing. Together these three examples offer us potent reminders to look beyond the detail of people's lives and relationships to larger questions about what we know *together*, how to respond to tragedy, and where life is to be found.

In conclusion, the three themes that I have drawn attention to—offering theological insight in accessible language, a willingness to vulnerably engage in two-way dialogue, and the call to view social practice from the perspective of the large canvas of biblical faith—are valuable contributions to the practice community. Furthermore, as a result of engaging with these papers I am different in two ways. First, I now want to read more practical theology in support of my work, as over recent years I have let this discipline slip. Second, I am inspired to approach sacred texts with reverence similar to that with which practitioners strive to approach the texts of people's lives.

Bibliography

Crabb, Larry. *Inside Out*. Colorado Springs: NavPress, 1988.
Hiltner, Seward. *Preface to Pastoral Theology*. Nashville: Abingdon, 1958.
Hurding, Roger. *Roots and Shoots: A Guide to Counselling and Psychotherapy*. London: Hodder & Stoughton, 1986.
McMillan, Lex. "Persons, Divine and Human, and Therapy: A Critical Correlation between a Trinitarian Analogy of Persons and Narrative Therapy." PhD diss., University of Queensland, 2016.
Roberts, Robert C. *Emotions in the Moral Life*. Cambridge: Cambridge University Press, 2013.

Afterword

Lisa Spriggens and Tim Meadowcroft

Despite our having promised not to arrive at firm conclusions or defined modes of action in this collection, we cannot resist making some concluding observations about what has emerged in the pages of this book. We do so by each providing some commentary in our own voice.

Lisa Spriggens

The doing of integration has always carried more interest for me than the outcome it hopes to produce and so my reflection on these essays concentrates on the way in which contributors have engaged in integrative thinking and writing, rather than any conclusion that might have emerged.

It has long been recognized that a significant challenge to the integration of theology and areas of social vocation is the limit to individual capacity to become expert in multiple fields of study. Dialogue requires equal representation. It is far more achievable to engage individual players, rather than one person who can speak expertly from multiple disciplines. In order to navigate complex disciplines our contributors locate themselves in their particular discipline. From these sites of expertise, the authors have then shown themselves to be tentatively drawing on knowledge from other disciplines. Theologians have dipped their toes into psychology or counseling theory; pastoral carers have engaged with the text of Scripture; counselors have consulted theology. It is important to identify the particular disciplines we work from, to locate ourselves, to drop a pin on the map. It is equally important to take a step towards those disciplines we wish to engage with, dipping our toes in other ponds (a somewhat clunky metaphorical shift), recognizing the limitations of our knowledge as we do.

The risk of dipping toes into areas we know less about is that the nuance and complexity of the integrative conversation can get lost. There is also a risk that the complexity of being human is not attended to. Social vocations are relational practices, practices designed to meet and address human suffering and need. Likewise, theology embraces its own complexity, one which grapples with language, meaning, and context. These essays recognize the nature of these disciplines, and tread lightly in an effort to preserve and honor complexity.

In many of these essays we are introduced to the author as person, as well as the professions from which they speak. Integration is represented as a deeply personal experience which is outworked in professional practice or thought. Commonly we can feel invited to separate our personal and professional selves, a practice which seldom sits comfortably for those engaged in theology or social vocations. The rigor of dialogue is safer within a professional context. Positioned as representatives of professions, or specialties, it is easier to speak and hear a response to an idea, rather than to more personally held beliefs or values. It is clear, however, in these essays that there is still room for the personal, that the rigor of the conversation must also be generous enough to hold the personhood of the participants and respond with care to the vulnerability this requires of those in conversation. The authors of these essays are grappling with the implications of integration at both deeply personal and professional levels.

Emerging from these essays are guideposts, directing our way as we continue in conversation, locating ourselves and reaching for new knowledge, holding complexity and honoring the vulnerability of those we are journeying with.

Tim Meadowcroft

Building on Lisa's reflection on the process of integration, I suggest some themes that have emerged from this process. If I could summarize what has emerged in one phrase, it would be: *the search for integrity*. I mean "integrity" not in the simplified popular sense of honesty or probity or adherence to principle, although it must include that; rather, I intend it in the sense of a state of being undivided or whole in some way. I think of a system which has many parts that in some way cohere together without compromise to the intrinsic worth of the various parts. The ultimate expression of such integrity, I suggest, is Christ, the undivided one, in whom, we are told, "all things hold together" and in whom also "the fullness of God was pleased to dwell" (Col 1:17, 19). Taking these two phrases together, we might say that in Christ all things cohere, not in a monochrome way but such that the amazing fullness of God in all its rich diversity is drawn forth. Each writer in this book has sought, in his or her own way, and however imperfectly, to reflect in their vocation this integrity, this cohesion around diversity characteristic of the God revealed in Jesus Christ. We understand, often inarticulately, that to live faithfully is to live in the light of and in the strength of the one in whom all the complex strands of the human experience begin to make sense. At a basic level, to live with integrity is to look like Jesus.

In the light of that a number of recurring tendencies in this set of essays could be noted. I would like to recognize two in particular. The first is the relationality that is foundational to all social vocation. Endemic to these essays is an anthropology that understands humanity as fundamentally relational in character. For some of our writers this is drawn partly from an understanding of God as essentially relational in God's Trinitarian expressions, while for others the incarnate nature of creator God's relating to God's creation speaks strongly. In any case, the result is a concern to understand better relational humanity in the light of a relational God. It is no accident, then, that the notion of hospitality recurs throughout this set of essays. This theme is used in several ways, it seems to me: to affirm the value of healthy relationships; to explore the delicate dance around power and friendship inherent in the exercise of hospitality; and to bring a challenge to make room for the Other in our midst. Given also that the sharing of food is a key component in the exercise of hospitality, meals crop up regularly.

A second tendency evident is one also alluded to by Lisa but in slightly different terms: a tension arising from a regularly felt sense of being limited by our own professional commitments and identities. The quest for integrity is compelled to acknowledge that all things may hold together in Christ but they do not do so in each individual; we are each only capable of glimpsing and exhibiting a small part of the fullness of God. In vocational terms, each practitioner works and lives in the context of a set of professional commitments and methodologies, and a limited number of them can only ever be grasped by a single human being. This has a double effect, I suggest. On the one hand, it draws us back to the importance of relationality; we can only begin to experience vocational integrity in Christ in the context of a web of relationships, each one bringing to the table a different aspect of this fulness of God that draws us on. On the other hand, and a little more particularly, each practitioner bears a responsibility to a guild of specialists and fellow practitioners as well as to our conversation partners in the quest for an integrated practice of vocation. It is not always clear where one of those commitments needs to give way to another. Where do our models and methodologies attract fundamental critique from this quest for the fullness of God, and where do they enable that quest? Once again, the answers are discovered in relationship and conversation. This dialogic process is driven by the limitations of our own humanity; in practical terms, we cannot discover vocational integrity on our own. At the same time, the felt need for vocational integrity is forged in a glimpse of the God who calls us into vocation as one in whom all things hold together. Human limitation and the nature of God are intertwined in the quest undertaken by this collection of essays.

That is why the search for vocational integrity is a never-ending conversation, for it is fundamentally dialogic in nature. This book is a mere snapshot of part of that conversation at a particular point in time; it cannot be definitive. But we hope that it has modelled something of what the conversation can look like, and provided a spur for further work in the quest for vocational integrity.

www.ingramcontent.com/pod-product-compliance
Lightning Source LLC
Chambersburg PA
CBHW071245230426
43668CB00011B/1600